Cities and Sustainability

Cities are the most likely actors to design and bring about lasting sustainability. An agreement among the world's larger cities is possible, and probably a necessary but insufficient condition to achieve sustainable development.

Cities and Sustainability explores the ways in which cities are both the biggest threat to sustainability and the most powerful tool to get us to sustainable development. Employing an innovative methodology to a complex issue, this book proposes new metrics and approaches that assume cities as fundamental in the search for sustainability. Providing population projections for the world's larger cities and a hierarchy of sustainable cities, the author develops two new tools: (i) a cities approach to physical and socio-economic boundaries and (ii) sustainability costs curves. These tools are designed to be implemented in a multi-stakeholder, integrated partnership that truly maximizes the benefits of cities in the quest for sustainability.

Applying the tools outlined in the book to case studies from Dakar, Mumbai, São Paulo, Shanghai and Toronto, this volume will be of great relevance to students, scholars and practitioners with an interest in urban and city management, climate change, and environment and sustainability more broadly.

Daniel Hoornweg is an Associate Professor and Richard Marceau Chair in the Faculty of Energy Systems and Nuclear Science at the University of Ontario Institute of Technology, Canada.

Routledge Studies in Sustainability

Cities and Sustainability

A new approach

Daniel Hoornweg

Routledge
Taylor & Francis Group

LONDON AND NEW YORK

earthscan
from Routledge

First published 2016
by Routledge
2 Park Square, Milton Park, Abingdon, Oxon OX14 4RN

and by Routledge
711 Third Avenue, New York, NY 10017

First issued in paperback 2018

Routledge is an imprint of the Taylor & Francis Group, an informa business

British Library Cataloguing-in-Publication Data
A catalogue record for this book is available from the British Library

Library of Congress Cataloging-in-Publication Data
Names: Hoornweg, Daniel A. (Daniel Arthur), 1961- author.
Title: Cities and sustainability : a new approach / Daniel Hoornweg.
Description: Abingdon, Oxon ; New York, NY : Routledge, 2016. |
Series: Routledge studies in sustainability
Identifiers: LCCN 2016010245 | ISBN 9781138678361 (hb) |
ISBN 9781315558998 (ebook)
Subjects: LCSH: Sustainable urban development. | Sustainable
development. | Regional planning--Environmental aspects. |
Urban economics--Environmental aspects. | Urban policy--
Environmental aspects.
Classification: LCC HT241 .H66 2016 | DDC 307.1/416--dc23
LC record available at https://lccn.loc.gov/2016010245

ISBN 13: 978-1-138-57953-8 (pbk)
ISBN 13: 978-1-138-67836-1 (hbk)

Typeset in Goudy
by Saxon Graphics Ltd, Derby

Dedication

This thesis is dedicated to a few of the women in my life.

First, my wonderful wife Jacquie, who makes me smile from the inside out, and our two lovely daughters, Kate and Shannon; my mother Maria, one continuous act of kindness; and my sisters, Tina, Mary Ann and Judy, who taught me early, and Rena, who tried a bit later.

The *pumulung* woman in Semarang and the small, hungry girl in Harare whose names (and lives) I will never know.

My female engineering students, who I so hope increase in numbers. My amazing bosses over the years, many dedicated teachers, and my impressive colleagues.

And, most importantly, tomorrow's girls, who – if we can house, clothe, educate and treat them with respect – will get us out of this mess.

Contents

Illustrations

Tables

Box

Annexes

Acknowledgements

This book summarises my PhD thesis, 'A Cities Approach to Sustainability'. A graduate student over 50 has even more people to thank than usual. At the top of the list is my advisor Chris Kennedy. I met Chris while working at the World Bank and saw how high-quality, understated research could have such a tremendous impact. Chris's enthusiasm and good nature convinced me to undertake the effort, and his support enabled me to finish. I am very thankful. I also want to thank the other members of my PhD committee: Eric Miller, Patricia McCarney, Kim Pressnail and Michael Sanio.

My colleagues at the University of Ontario Institute of Technology, former Deans Brent Lewis and George Bereznai, encouraged me to 'hurry up and get a PhD'. I appreciate their confidence, as well as the university's support, including that of President Tim McTiernan and former Provost Richard Marceau. Michelle Cholak helped with the preparation of my thesis and this book, always with a smile and good cheer. Kevin Pope, Ofelia Jianu, Azin Behdadi and Mehdi Hosseini assisted with research. The best part about working at a university is the students. I am thankful when they show up to class, but I am terrified at the task in front of them: building cities and providing energy to 2.5 billion more people during their careers.

The idea for the thesis and this book was seeded at Rio+20 (Rio de Janeiro, June 2012) in the back seats of taxis with Rachel Kyte and Andrew Steer of the World Bank. They probably were not aware of it at the time, but I hope I have done some justice to their wise council.

I am fortunate to be married to my best friend and confidante, who also happens to be a great editor. Jacquie encouraged me to stick to this work and helped with the effort.

Last, but never least, are the professionals and citizens who toil every day to design, build and manage our cities. The mayors, councillors, planners, engineers, receptionists, reporters, waste collectors, street sweepers, snow plow operators, accountants and the many people who run the world's cities help us all. Cities are humanity's greatest accomplishment, and there is no work more important than the work of cities.

Foreword

It is hard to imagine how we can build the inclusive and therefore more prosperous world that is on track for zero net emissions in order to combat the punishing impacts of climate change without conceiving of, building, refurbishing and living in cities differently from how we do today. The pursuit of sustainable development while embraced globally (both through the unanimous adoption of 17 Sustainable Development Goals and the Paris Agreement) is to be achieved through bottom-up, globally connected processes. Nowhere do communities and decision making at scale meet more immediately than at the city level, and over the recent past we have seen a dynamism and preparedness for action among city leaders, who themselves are networked, that has outstripped that of national leadership. As both crucibles of innovation and demonstration, cities deserve and desperately need our support to drive opportunity creation in zero-carbon economies for their burgeoning populations.

Rachel Kyte, Special Representative of the UN Secretary General for Sustainable Energy and CEO, Sustainable Energy for All

The Importance of a Cities Approach to Sustainability

With rapid urban growth, the dynamism of cities represents a major sustainable development opportunity. By getting urban development right, cities can offer better livelihoods, improve social inclusion and reduce pollution. The spatial concentration of urban areas is a unique characteristic that enables economies of scale and effective use of amenities. As urban land use is growing more rapidly than urban populations, we need to build mixed-use and compact cities that offer higher levels of well-being at lower levels of resource use and emissions.

A Cities Approach to Sustainability would need to rally all urban actors around practical problem solving to address the specific challenges of access to services, promote integrated and innovative infrastructure design and ensure resilience to climate change. This is why the Member States of the United Nations have adopted a dedicated goal to make cities and human settlements inclusive, safe, resilient and sustainable as part of the 2030 Agenda. The New Urban Agenda, to be adopted at the Habitat III Conference in October 2016, will provide further opportunities to embrace a new model of urban development that is fit for the twenty-first century.

Rafael Tuts, Coordinator, Urban Planning and Design Branch, UN-Habitat

Cities are playing a key role in designing local integrated solutions for a sustainable planet. Sustainable development requires sustainable territorial development, including metropolitan regions, intermediary cities and rural areas. Global sustainability challenges require as well holistic approaches integrating the economic, social, environmental and cultural dimensions of development rooted in the realities of the territory.

Josep Roig, Secretary General, United Cities and Local Government (UCLG)

Resource-efficient cities, engines to sustainability. Many of the problems that are attributed to 'cities', are consequences of the economic development of citizens who act as consumers of goods and services within their roles in government, the private sector, civil society, as well as individual households. It is particularly important to take into consideration the growing global middle class, who are not only expected to live longer due to improvements in healthcare, but are also characterized by their increased purchasing capacity.

In making the case for cities as positive agents for sustainability, it is important to make the distinction between the impacts of cities themselves *vis à vis* the economic development and wealth creation associated with urban development. With the expected additional middle class of about 3 billion in some 30 years, the cities can be characterized as the 'industries of the three-quarters' in the sense that, as an order of magnitude, cities will host three quarters of the population, produce three quarters of the GDP, consume three quarters of the resources, emit three quarters of the waste and CO_2 emissions. This is to say that there could be no sustainability if not at city level and with resource- efficient cities with the aim to deliver sustainable consumption and production.

However, this requires knowledge about and understanding of resource flows to and within cities. Considering the huge pressures cities will be facing from a resource supply and demand perspective, there is a need to support cities and their networks in better identifying and realising the economic, social and environmental benefits of resource efficiency and sustainable consumption and production. With improved knowledge of flows with relevant data on transport, processing, use and disposal, local leaders should be able to better plan their city and community needs, in relation to their income, consumption patterns and lifestyles.

Ultimately, resource-efficient cities combine greater productivity and innovation with lower costs and reduced environmental impacts, making them the engines to sustainability.

Arab Hoballah, Chief, Sustainable Lifestyles, Cities and Industry,
United Nations Environment Program

The world is facing arguably the largest challenge in the history of the humanity with growing population, increasing middle class and rapid urbanization. It is urgent that we find a sustainable way of producing, consuming and living. The role of cities in fighting climate change and achieving sustainable development is increasingly recognized in the international community. The single goal for cities under SDG adopted in September and the commitment by mayors at COP21 both in 2015 are cases in point.

If planned and managed well, compact, resilient, inclusive and resource-efficient cities can drive development, growth and the creation of jobs, while also contributing to a healthier, better quality of life for residents and the long-term protection of the global environment. In a rapidly urbanizing world, how we design and build the cities of the future will play a critical role in protecting the global commons, the planet's finite environmental resources that have provided for the sconditions enjoyed by humanity for thousands of years.

That is why the GEF (Global Environment Facility) Council approved the Sustainable Cities Program in 2015, which is expected to mobilize up to $1.5 billion over the next five years for urban sustainability programs for 24 cities in 11 developing countries: Brazil, Cote D'Ivoire, China, India, Malaysia, Mexico, Paraguay, Peru, Senegal, South Africa and Vietnam. Coordinated by the World Bank and supported by multilateral development banks, UN organizations, think tanks and various city networks, the knowledge-sharing programme will provide access to cutting-edge tools and promote an integrated approach to sustainable urban planning and financing.

Naoko Ishii, CEO and Chairperson, Global Environment Facility

The numbers are quite startling: already, half the global population resides in cities, and this is set to increase to 70 per cent by 2050. Decisions that national leaders, local officials, developers and planners in developing countries make today on what to build, where to build and how much to invest in job creation are 'locking in' how big or small the incremental GHG footprint will be over the next century. While applying past models of urban development could lock these cities into congestion, sprawl and inefficient resource use, more recent climate friendly approaches have the potentials of promoting compact, connected and sustainable resource use in these cities. Following the climate agreement at COP21 in Paris, we are witnessing an upsurge in the latter set of ideas aimed at ensuring that the cities of tomorrow provide a better quality of life for citizens, as well as safeguard the urban, regional and global environment.

Andrew Steer, President and CEO, World Resources Institute

The critical role of cities in sustainable development is being recognized globally. The developing world is urbanizing rapidly and by 2050 two thirds of the world population is expected to live in cities. Thus sustainable development has to be at the crux of urbanization and cities must follow this path intentionally and with much deliberation. Cities need to take a measured approach towards environmental, social and economic sustainability. It is estimated that cities are responsible for two thirds of global energy consumption, 70 per cent of GHG emissions and produce 80 per cent of the world's GDP and at the same time poverty and inequality are increasingly concentrating in cities. We already see many cities taking the lead in innovative financing mechanisms, policy and regulatory reforms, efficient use of land and transport, waste management and reduction, energy efficiency measures, use of renewable energy and reduction of GHG emissions and adopting policies to bring about social and economic inclusion through better delivery of services. And at the center of this is city leadership and engaged citizens.

Abha Joshi-Ghani Director, Leadership, Learning and Innovation, World Bank

With the recently UN-adopted '2030 Agenda for Sustainable Development' and its 17 Sustainable Development Goals, the importance of urban sustainable development is strongly recognized by nations who commit in Goal 11 'to make cities and human settlements inclusive, safe, resilient and sustainable'. Building upon the lessons of the voluntary Local Agenda 21 in 1992 at the first Rio Summit, local leaders now must and can excel as central transformers of change. Our cities are home to half of the world's people and three quarters of its economic output, and this will rise by 2030, the target year of the SDGs. Yet our cities are also places of deprivation as well as environmental degradation and many suffer from severe air and water pollution, congestion and unsolved waste problems. Mayors and subnational leaders must thus take a defining role in embracing, endorsing, implementing and monitoring transformative change. Simultaneously, the international community as well as our national governments must set the right frames to ensure synergy and integration between global and national goals and the ambitious local sustainability plans and programmes.

Gino Van Begin, Secretary General, ICLEI

The list of cities continuously inhabited for more than a thousand years is a very long one: ancient cities such as Luxor, Varanasi, Beirut and Beijing, as well as more recent ones such as Rome, Istanbul, London, Dublin, Cusco and Quito. These cities have grown, flourished, waxed and waned in their regional influence. They have catalyzed cultural and political change and upheaval, and served as hubs in the flow patterns of economic trade, human migration and socio-cultural dynamism. They have outlasted Troy, Chichen Itza, Memphis, Macchu Picchu and Paestum, all centres of political, military, cultural and economic potency in their time.

In their present iterations, the above cities fall along a wide spectrum of economic vibrancy, social inclusiveness, political stability, quality of life and global reach. Their longevity, however, gives them status as sustainable cities, each with its own intrinsic vitality. There are, perhaps, some common facets to this sustainability that, in turn, underpin the potency of cities as critical enablers of sustainable development.

Speculatively: the ability to absorb populations, cultures, trade goods, technologies and knowledge frameworks; a learned adaptability and resilience to natural and human-induced disruptive events; the practice of scaling technological solutions to the supply of energy, infrastructure and transportation; the extension of geographic reach to procure and replenish food stocks and domestic goods and trade in cultural and economic resources; and a sizable and diversely skilled population base with functioning governance structures, collectively enable innovation, complex problem solving, adaptive management systems, social cohesion and system reorganization to support sustainable development.

Linking city initiatives across digital global networks accelerates changes in the conditions essential for long-term sustainability – from 3,000 years ago to 3,000 years hence.

Tim McTiernan, President, University of Ontario Institute of Technology

1 Searching for sustainability – the urgency of an effective approach

This century's broad demographic and geopolitical trends are reasonably well known and set the landscape for the United States to likely remain the dominant military power. India will eclipse China as the world's most populous country around 2022; China, with an aging population, may see an economic decline, similar to Japan and much of Europe; Australia, Canada, New Zealand and most of Europe will decline slightly in terms of global influence; and Africa will experience the fastest and largest growth in cities, economies and relative global impact, especially in the second half of the century.

Access to resources, especially water, food and energy, will continue to be critical. Energy for cities and transportation will remain a key priority, particularly in light of the shift to low-carbon alternatives. Larger (primary) and mid-size (secondary) cities will be tasked with the shift to low-carbon energy sources while increasing resilience in light of a more changeable and extreme climate, and probably more concerns with security, including cyber-security and population migrations and declines. Sustainability and sustainable development will remain crucial objectives.

Introduction

Suppose a group of well-intentioned professionals were asked to advise a rich patron, a government, a powerful agency, or maybe a corporation, to 'suggest an effective way to help move humanity toward sustainable development.' Maybe the leaders of China, India or the USA called, or the United Nations Secretary General and World Bank President had friends over for dinner, turned to them and said 'We could use your help.' How should the group respond? How could such a 'big deal' be defined, negotiated and monitored?[1]

This book provides a response to the question of how we might achieve sustainability, and, from that, sustainable development. An applied science approach (bio-physical and social) integrated within a multi-stakeholder partnership is proposed. Only a partial or 'shadow agreement' is suggested, but hopefully this would serve as the start of a global process that leads to comprehensive sustainable development.

The process for a planetary 'deal' proposed in this book involves the world's largest cities. An argument is made why cities are the most likely actors to design and bring about such an agreement. An agreement among those metropolitan areas with five million or more residents by 2050 (about 120 'Future Five' cities) is possible, and is likely a necessary but not sufficient condition to achieve sustainable development. Each city is viewed as a unique system as well as collectively within a 'system-of-systems', and more broadly within local and global ecosystems and economies.

Countries will continue to negotiate international agreements, e.g. trade agreements, Rio+30 and COP25+. The city-centric effort described here would not supplant those efforts. Rather, cities with their unique characteristics of immobility, complexity, system dynamics, anchors of economic development and crucibles of culture, offer an alternative approach to negotiating global agreements. By focusing at the city-scale, issues become clearer, and a more pragmatic road map to sustainability emerges.

A practical methodology to define sustainable development and move the world's largest cities toward that goal is both possible and urgent. A systems approach is needed, where a significant part of the overall system (the world's largest cities) is analysed. In any possible future sustainable development agreement cities must be engaged in a meaningful and monitored way. By introducing sustainability into this limited system, the belief is that this could be sufficiently comprehensive to eventually bring about sustainability in global systems. The challenge facing humanity for the next 35 years is enormous. Everything we have done to this point pales in scale. However, when work is at hand, every carpenter, and engineer, knows that having the right tools is one of best indicators of success. This book proposes tools that might help build a more durable, equitable and sustainable society.

A key priority for sustainable development is to provide, and follow, a methodology to enhance the sustainability of long-lived urban infrastructure. This key infrastructure forms the 'bones' of sustainable cities. The methodology of a 'bones' focus when applied to the world's larger cities can underpin a global agreement on sustainable development.

The approach developed in this book is built on the following key components:

- Start with the world's largest cities (those expected to have populations of 5 million-plus by 2050);
- Include all of these cities (about 120);
- Define sustainability locally for each city, based on planetary boundaries, global development goals and local conditions;
- Estimate sustainability potential and cost for all new large-scale long-term urban infrastructure within, and mainly serving, these cities;
- Base the above initiatives on an urban systems approach following a hierarchy of sustainable cities with ongoing open-source publication of key information.

Defining cities	Boundaries and limits	Sustainability cost curves	Moving to sustainability
• Hierarchy of sustainable city • 'Future Fives' (population projections) • A systems approach • System boundaries (metro areas) • Institutions working with cities	• Rockstrom et al. and Steffen et al. biophysical boundaries – a city perspective • SDGs at the city level • e.g. Dakar, Mumbai, São Paulo, Shanghai and Toronto • 14 sustainability objectives (7 physical, 7 socio-economic)	• 'Vision 2050' • Discount rate assumptions • e.g. Dakar, Mumbai, São Paulo, Shanghai and Toronto • Project's impact on sustainability objectives • Facilitates 'green finance'	• Data scan for all 'Future Fives' cities • Institutional support • 'Open source' iterative • Role of professions • Applying the tools • Assists in prioritizing infrastructure finance (and better capture of benefits)

Figure 1.1   A cities approach to sustainability.

A cities perspective

From a cursory perspective, sustainable development is easy to define as development that meets the needs of today without limiting the ability of tomorrow's generations to meet their own needs. This implies a measure of equity to future generations. But sustainable development is more complicated than this, or certainly more difficult to achieve than such a short definition seems to imply.

Sustainable development is the nexus of wealth generation, economy, equity, environmental degradation, urbanization, well-being, culture, creativity, and local and global governance. To a large extent, sustainable development is driven by cities, the way they are built and managed, and the way people live in them.

Wealth and equity

Beginning around 1800, the world has undergone an unprecedented increase in wealth. In just 200 years wealth increased from about $200 per capita (with less than 1 billion people and an average life expectancy of around 40 years) to more than $6,500 per capita today (with more than 7 billion people and an average life expectancy of 78 years). This massive growth in wealth, however, has not been uniform, and not without cost.

Last year, people living in the Democratic Republic of Congo had an average income of $220. For the entire *year*. That's less than a dollar per day for more than 60 million people. Meanwhile, in Bermuda, residents made about $107,000. Bermuda may be an anomaly with just 60,000 residents; however, Norway, with 5 million citizens, had a per capita income of almost $100,000 in 2015.

In 2015 there were 1,826 billionaires with a combined wealth of $7.05 trillion (about $4 billion each). The 62 richest people alone have more wealth than the poorest half of the world's population combined. The wealth of the world's richest one per cent of population is about $110 trillion (or 65 times the world's poorest half of the population – more than 3.5 billion people).[2]

Environmental degradation

At the start of the Industrial Revolution the atmospheric concentration of CO_2 was about 280 ppm, roughly the same value for 11,000 years during the Holocene, and the end of the last glaciation. In 2014 atmospheric CO_2 concentrations surpassed 400 ppm for the first time in the last 600,000 years; they are increasing by more than 2 ppm per year and are not likely to plateau before reaching 500 ppm. Even though aspirational targets aim for a maximum 1.5°C increase, humanity should plan for a 4°C warming this century (see World Bank, 'Turn Down the Heat', 2014 – a lower value is still possible; however, prudence suggests preparing for at least 3°–4°C warming). Massive planetary changes will be associated with this climate perturbation.

Schoolchildren around the world can recount the extinction of passenger pigeons and the threat to buffalo, rhinos, tigers and whales. The loss of biodiversity is the greatest threat to the planet and humanity. Rockstrom et al. (2009) call for a biodiversity loss not to exceed an extinction rate of 10 per million species per year (the current rate of extinction exceeds 100 species; pre-industrial loss rates were 0.01–1 per million species per year). This planetary boundary was updated by Steffen et al. (2015) to maintain a biodiversity intactness index at or above 90 per cent.

Localized pollution, especially in cities, was a constant condition during the last two centuries. Cholera, smog, waste dumps, hazardous waste sites and destruction of local waterways as well as thalidomide, lead poisoning and vehicle emissions are by-products of industrialization and its associated increase in wealth. These wastes are often most concentrated in urban areas.

Urbanization and cities

Inextricably linked with industrialization and wealth is urbanization and the growth of cities. The pace of urbanization worldwide is still increasing (in concert with increased resource consumption and pollution such as greenhouse gas [GHG] emissions). In 1800, the world was about 5 per cent urban. By 1900, urbanization was increasing quickly in most industrialized countries, yet the world was still less than 15 per cent urbanized. In 2008 the world passed the 50 per cent urban mark and the pace of urbanization is still increasing.

In 1950 there was only one city with a population of more than 10 million (New York). Today, there are 27 'megacities', and by 2050, when most of Asia will have urbanized, there will likely be 50 or more cities that are home to least 10 million people. The last wave of urbanization will be in Africa. By the end of this century, 17 of the world's 25 largest cities may be in Africa, each with more than 25 million residents, and the world's 3 largest cities, Lagos, Kinshasa and Dar es Salaam, with more than 70 million.

Urbanization and cities present a paradox. On one hand, urbanization and its associated increase in wealth is the main driver of local and global environmental degradation. For example, if including Scopes 1 (local), 2 (directly imported) and

3 (embodied) emissions, cities, or, better stated, the people living in cities, are responsible for more than 80 per cent of global GHG emissions (Hoornweg, Sugar and Trejos Gomez, 2011). On the other hand, well-designed and managed cities provide the highest quality of life for least amount of resource consumption. Sustainability in the latter half of this century is much more likely if cities grow even larger and urbanization proceeds faster in the next few decades.

Cities are complex adaptive systems that often exhibit attributes more akin to natural ecosystems. Like animate entities – a mouse or a whale, for example – cities adhere to scaling laws. If the 'demons of density' can be overcome, such as traffic, pollution and crime, cities would naturally evolve to larger conurbations as greater economy can be delivered with fewer resources. Flow in cities also follows nature's evolved hierarchies. People flowing through a street, for example, have an uncanny resemblance to streams, fish and birds.

Cities and global governance

States and nations are mostly a political, cultural or ethnic construct. The rise of today's collection of states can be traced to the Treaty of Westphalia (1648). Less than a quarter of today's 200 or so countries existed with their current boundaries and governance structures a century ago. Yet every one of the world's largest cities has been continuously inhabited for more than 200 years. Cities being immobile are largely defined by geography, trade and the flow of resources.

Canada provides an interesting perspective on the relative roles of cities and countries in global and regional geopolitics. In 1867, when Canada was created through the British North America Act, more than 80 per cent of Canada's population of 3.6 million was rural. In distributing constitutional powers, provinces were seen as key, mainly for resource development and protection of territorial borders. With heavy losses in the First World War and growing industrialization, Canada surpassed the 50 per cent urban mark in 1921 (one of the earliest in Organization for Economic Co-operation and Development [OECD]-member countries to reach this milestone). Montreal was the largest city in Canada up until 1970, when it was surpassed by Toronto due to benefits of the Auto Pact and separatist frictions in Quebec.

Canadian cities played important roles in developing international associations. Metropolis was first headquartered in Montreal (1985); so too ICLEI in Toronto (1990). Vancouver hosted the first Habitat Conference (1976) and Greenpeace started in Vancouver (1971). Toronto also served as chair for the C40 from 2008 to 2010, and now hosts the Global City Indicators Facility and World Council on City Data. Canadian cities consistently score high on liveability compared to international peers.

Despite Canada's international reputation as a global resource supplier, Canadian cities contribute an unduly large share of the Country's GDP (about 80 per cent).[3] The relatively small constitutional role for Canadian cities and few local finance tools are a source of consternation for municipal representatives.

City representatives often feel short shrift in political power *vis à vis* their national (and regional) representatives. Many countries provide disproportionality large influence to rural voters and governments. Much of this has to do with the organic (apolitical) development of cities. Large cities are also almost always divided into many local jurisdictions. In countries like Australia, Brazil and Canada, this was purposeful. Cities were sub-divided to help ensure that their political power did not exceed their regional and national counterparts (moving the capitals away from Sydney, Rio de Janeiro and Montreal or Toronto highlights this well).

Cities leading sustainable development efforts

As early as the fourteenth century an autonomous grouping of cities in Northern Europe convened the Hanseatic League to promote and protect trade within the region. The Hanseatic League was largely replaced through the emergence of local nations, especially Sweden, Germany and Prussia. Today's nations negotiating for collective agreements can be traced back to the unsuccessful League of Nations. The League was replaced by the United Nations, yet systemic challenges remain.

The world's 197 participants in the UNFCCC (United Nations Framework Convention on Climate Change) are disparate. Side arrangements such as the China–US agreement on GHG emission reductions, or G20 proposals, will continue to emerge. Countries can also opt out of an agreement. Another approach may be possible. Cities, which can be more pragmatic (non-mobile) and less political (the projection of power generally extends only to certainty of resource availability), can enter into ongoing 'applied sustainability' negotiations.

By selecting a target date, say 2050, cities can work collectively toward maximum future sustainability. This agreement would not be sufficient for global sustainable development; however, it is arguably a pre-condition. The approach, based on applied science and open-source metrics, is sufficiently robust to warrant consideration (and support from the engineering community, among others). The tools and framework to move the world's largest cities toward sustainable development are presented in the following chapters.

The proposed city-based sustainable development 'deal' is less an agreement between participating cities than it is a suggested methodology for ongoing monitoring of urban behaviour (resource use, environmental impact, quality of life). Most of the cities discussed here will likely outlive their respective countries, transnational agencies and businesses. The sustainability of key local and planetary systems depends on cities collaborating and bringing along their citizens, agencies, countries and corporations.

All politics is local[4]

Elinor Ostrom echoed this sentiment when providing encouragement for Rio+20, suggesting the success of sustainable development would be delivered through sustainable cities and their ability to 'green from the grassroots'. Her blog supporting a grassroots, city-based approach to sustainable development was published just before Rio+20, on June 12, 2012, ironically the same day as her death. Similarly, Donella Meadows, the key author of *The Limits to Growth* and a preeminent systems engineer, wrote in 2008 on how to intervene in complex systems, reinforcing the importance of local nodes (cities) and their criticality within overall hierarchies (Meadows, 2008; Meadows, Randers, Meadows, 2004).

The city-system is likely the optimum unit of action for sustainable development with its confluence of personal and local passions and aspirations and criticality in global systems. Cities are the main drivers of material flows and energy consumption around the world.

Perhaps surprisingly, there is no consensus on the boundaries of most of the world's cities. As the key impetus for our economies and environmental degradation, a better understanding of cities is a critical prerequisite of sustainable development. Countries negotiate sustainability agreements on behalf of their cities (the key nexus of wealth, population, pollution). However, cities, especially the larger ones, are a patchwork of overlapping service and political boundaries not easily spoken for by their national governments. Cities are partitioned and aggregated along political imperatives and efficiency objectives.

The boundaries of 20 of the world's 27 megacities largely correspond to a metropolitan government boundary (Kennedy et al., 2015), and with satellite imagery urban agglomerations can be reasonably well defined (Angel et al., 2011). Populations of major urban agglomerations are probably best defined by the UN DESA, and projected here to 2050 and 2100 (Annex 1A and 1B).

Permanence of habitation is usually well defined for the world's larger cities (at least 200 years at the sites of all cities); however, the boundaries of cities, like countries, are largely ephemeral. So too is the number of people living in a city – this also ebbs and flows with changes in demographics, economy and local political pressures. Estimating future populations for larger cities is difficult, as many cities, for example, are coastal, and with sea-level rise and increased storm severity these cities may face inordinate pressures for migration out of them.

As cities are even more dynamic than their host nations, 'final' boundaries or population estimates are impossible. The approach outlined here recommends the emergence of annual (or biennial) publication of boundary and population estimates (and key materials flows and quality of life). Ideally, publication of this information will be authorized by cities; however, there are sufficient data sets to merge toward general consensus on these values.

The 'boundary issue'

All of the world's larger cities are challenged with the 'boundary issue' (except Singapore). City boundaries are as ephemeral and arbitrary as other political boundaries and most large urban areas are made up of numerous smaller local governments. Political dynamics often urge the amalgamation or separation of communities, while service efficiencies usually urge agglomeration of urban populations to enhance efficiencies (Bettencourt and West, 2010). Bettencourt further promotes the agglomeration of urban areas with minimal effective borders as they show that cities scale super-linearly (~1.15) for economy, while they scale sub-linearly (~0.85) for infrastructure costs (Bettencourt, 2013). In other words, if externalities associated with increased density, e.g. congestion, are addressed, doubling a city's effective size more than doubles the economy and wealth generation, and does so for less than a doubling of infrastructure costs (and probably material flows) (Batty, 2013).

Challenges of boundaries are exacerbated when service areas do not overlap. For example, the power utility might have a different boundary from waste management, water (resource) supply, waste water collection and transportation services. As outlined in the hierarchy of sustainable cities (Figure 4.1), sustainability increases as cities are able to integrate and justify regional service provision.

The boundary issue is not likely to disappear and service provision borders will regularly change; however, as cities (urban areas) pursue greater sustainability, better rationalization of boundaries should emerge. Similarly, as cities assume a more assertive voice on global sustainability issues (especially risk management), they will be inclined to find a means to speak on behalf of the total urban area. The key driver for this 'common voice' will probably be local residents, as potential efficiencies are better known. Community dispersion will still occur, e.g. dominance of parochial issues, but as the costs are better understood some integration will likely be encouraged.

Key tools are developed here for the urban areas (metros) as they are critical for large sustainability gains in transportation, energy and waste disposal sectors. The broader urban area focus, though, reduces the effective influence individual mayors might have. However, this is usually not an insurmountable problem, for city sustainability through a systems approach (which favours the overall urban agglomeration) is a critical pre-condition for urban sustainable development and therefore an important tool for local governments seeking greater sustainability.

Degrees of Separation

Originally suggested by Karinthy Frigyes in 1929, every person in the world is supposedly connected to each other by no more than six degrees of separation. This friend-of-a-friend and so on helps highlight that this really is a 'small world'. But cities can make a small world seem even smaller. Shortly after the November 2015 terrorist attacks that killed and injured almost 500 victims, informal discussions with a dozen Parisians found that everyone knew someone directly, or had a friend or relative that knew someone, who was killed or injured in the attacks. In cities, even big cities, people are likely connected by no more than a couple degrees of separation.

Rebecca Solnit (2009) in *A Paradise Built in Hell* illustrates through historical calamities in five cities how the human response to disaster is often spontaneous altruism, self-organization and mutual support. In the absence of established institutions of governance and patterns of social behaviour, 'the better angels of our nature' (Abraham Lincoln) frequently emerge in cities despite the mal-intent of a few. Linking better angels across and between cities will be a powerful contribution to urban sustainability.

Cities as Islands

> Tempest-tossed souls, wherever you may be, under whatsoever conditions you may live, know this: in the ocean of life the isles of blessedness are smiling and the sunny shore of your ideal awaits your coming.
>
> James Allen

James Allen (*As a Man Thinketh*, 1902) may have been thinking of Bermuda and its connection to Shakespeare's *Tempest* when he envisaged 'sunny shores' and 'isles of blessedness'. Mark Twain was certainly smitten by Bermuda, opining 'You can go to heaven if you want. I'd rather stay in Bermuda.' Twain stayed for more than half a year on the island and tried to return as frequently as possible.

Even when off the island, Twain fought to keep Bermuda automobile free. James Gordon Bennett, an American newspaper magnate, brought the first automobile to Bermuda in 1906. And even Twain's stature and determinedness would likely not have been enough to stem the wave of cars if it were not for the public support that came in 1908. A notable doctor was thrown from his startled horse reacting to an auto backfiring, and cars were quickly banned as a result of public fury.

But the apparent victory of the 'war on the car' and Bermuda's ban on automobiles was short lived. They were allowed back on the island again in 1946 and the love–hate relationship with cars continues. No one loves them more that the Minister of Finance: personal automobiles are the largest single source of revenue. Duty on the first $10,000 is 75 per cent; duty increases to 150 per cent of value in excess of $10,000. Only one vehicle is allowed per household and nowhere on the island can you drive more than 35 km/h, but even in Bermuda people want their cars. The roads are choked with BMWs and Mercedes – most never having gone beyond third gear.

Bermuda is one of the most beautiful places on earth. Cool breezes, clear turquoise waters, whitewashed roofs, pastel buildings, orange-red Poinciana trees and oleander edge the roads, and, most striking, the beaches really are pink. There are few places as colourful, or as rich, as Bermuda. The island again earned the distinction of having the world's highest average per capita incomes – $107,000 – in 2014 (World Bank).

Like its beauty, Bermuda owes its wealth to geography. With its first shipwreck in 1609[5] (the source for Shakespeare's *The Tempest*) and its connection to trade ever since, Bermuda is one of the few countries that generates almost all its wealth through international trade, namely offshore businesses and tourism. Having only 60,000 citizens, and strong ties with both the UK and US, helps preserve this niche position.

At first blush, Mark Twain was right. Bermuda is paradise, a Disney Land for adults. Residents are aware how fortunate they are and generally keep discontent, racial tensions and ecosystem impacts well hidden. Bermuda generates enough wealth to buy all its food, and just about everything else, off-island. Being isolated and with good researchers and statistics (almost everything has an import duty so tracking material that comes to the island is relatively straightforward), Bermuda is one of the world's best living laboratories.

Bermuda's total land area is 4573 Ha (about 20.5 mi^2). It is one place where 'ecological footprint' can actually be measured. If the boats and planes stopped coming and all the buildings, paved land and golf courses were converted back to agricultural land, estimates are that enough food could be grown to supply 10 per cent of the population of 60,000 (Hayward, Holt Gomez and Sterrer, 1981).

Total global wealth would have to increase 16 times for the rest of the world to live like Bermudians.[6] And then one wonders if there would be the not-so-small problem of needing another 15 planets to supply resources and ameliorate environmental impacts. But Bermuda also gives hope. Its history is inextricably linked to climate and hurricanes. The tempest of 1609 wrecked two ships *en route* to Jamestown, Virginia. Miraculously, all the passengers survived, and built new ships with timbers salvaged from the wrecks and cut down locally. They arrived a couple years late.

Bermuda is brushed or hit by a hurricane every 1.92 years. Hurricane Emily hit the island hard on September 29, 1987. Emily was the fastest-moving hurricane of the century and often considered the first hurricane linked to the Anthropocene's warming climate.

In the wake of major disasters, a wave of altruism and mutual support often arises. The most startling thing about disasters is not merely that people rise to the occasion, but that they can do so with joy, and lasting impact. Nowhere is this more apparent than Bermuda. Bermudians can quibble and agitate with the best of them, but come a hurricane, or other disaster, Bermudians hold strong, like the native Bermudian cedar. Community grows from the shared challenge. This strength of resolve, resilience – social rootedness – will be called on again. This is one more thing Bermuda might be able to trade for its continued wealth.

You cannot get much further from Bermuda without starting to head back than Bali, over on the far side of the world. Almost Bermuda's antipode, Bali is another one of those small islands with an enormous hold on the world's collective imagination.

Hindus believe that Bali, the grandson of Prahlada, is immortal and was a great king that Vishnu respected. King Bali supposedly declared, 'Oh my subjects, your happiness is mine. There will be no room for poverty in Bali's empire. You need not search for heaven for I shall make a heaven of this earth.' Jawarharla Nehru aptly called Bali the 'morning of the world'.

Bali, a small island of 5780 km^2 situated just off the east coast of the larger island of Java, has been continuously inhabited for at least 3,000 years. The island is steeped in a rich confluence of Hinduism and Javanese culture, and more recent influences from China and then the Dutch. Today, as many as a million tourists visit the island's beaches, hotels and occasional cultural wanderings each year.

Living in a relatively closed system, the Balinese adapted. Rice was grown through efficient *subaks*. Some say that the imposed caste system and social pressures, including the naming convention of children, kept families limited to four children or fewer.

If the devil is in the detail, so too is God. The constant fight between good and evil plays out the world over, but in Bali it's represented everywhere in the ubiquitous black-and-white chequered cloth covering statues and decorating the entrances to temples. The Balinese seem to be more aware of how the 'little things' grow through karma into big events, and that what comes around, goes around.

The Hindu philosophy *Rwa Bhineda* symbolizes the balance between good and evil, light and dark, rich and poor, happy and sad. The black and white cloth, or *saput poleng*, adorning the outer layer of Bali's temples catches the mind's eye, urging balance and patience. This simple representation of the balance between good and evil attempts to describe Bali and the world's complexity.

A powerful example of the need to address complexity when working with systems is the Balinese water temples. The community network and technological system that evolved over thousands of years was 'assisted' in the mid-1970s through the provision of high-yield rice varieties, pesticides and chemical fertilizers. Rice yields plummeted with this assistance.

Lansing and Kremer (1993), among others, argued vociferously against agriculture assistance projects. They illustrated how Bali grew irrigated rice sustainably through a complex adaptive system. Anthropologists studying Balinese water distribution systems at the time provided compelling modelling studies that showed how the evolved system optimized yields. The historic system was re-instated and yields were restored.

The Balinese water distribution example highlights the need for a greater appreciation of complexity theory. Network analysis can often improve aid. Programmes that are integrated, long term and incremental will likely yield the most dramatic improvement.[7] Elinor Ostrom supported this approach throughout her career (Ostrom, 1995; 2009; 2014).

The small island states sprinkled about the world's oceans are likely to be the first casualties of climate change. Many of the islands are atolls protected by coral reefs, much of the land just a meter or two above sea level. Already, climate refugees are moving to higher ground. In 2009, the Maldives government, trying to raise awareness of climate change and their precarious geography, held a cabinet meeting underwater.[8]

Kiribati is a tiny speck of land isolated in the Pacific Ocean, 2,000 km south of Hawaii and 5,000 km northeast of Australia. As early as 1994 the island-nation was being helped to build an airport runway. China, Japan, the USA and a few other countries often try to win favour of the small countries. This geopolitical friendship strategy is much about garnering possible votes for things like whaling or recognition for Taiwan, or a host of other issues that might come to the United Nations Generally Assembly. One country one vote, and a few specks of nationalism get a new runway. Kiribati, again serving an iconic role, is also one of the first countries to prepare for climate change.[9]

The Marshall Islands are another one of those tiny places with a big claim to history. Bikini atoll, where the US detonated more than 20 nuclear warheads in the late 1940s, is part of the Marshall Islands. Majuro, the capital city of about 25,000, has some of the most severe squalor in the Pacific.

The country still seems to be dealing with the cultural aftershocks of the detonations and being under the 'protection' of the US for more than 60 years. Diabetes, alcoholism and – like most of the Pacific islands – suicide are rampant. The grocery stores in the late 1990s had two sections: processed meats and canned pasta, potato chips, chocolate and Doritos in one section; the other section had several huge, open-topped freezers with enormous slabs of unwrapped frozen tuna. The cabin in the small fleet (of one) of Air Marshall Islands' aircraft (before it was grounded permanently for mechanical issues) was divided into two compartments – passengers in the front half, chilled tuna in the back. The tuna mostly headed for Japan.

Islands provide a great view into cultures and natural systems. MacArthur and Wilson (1967) in *The Theory of Island Biogeography* illustrated how the number of species increases exponentially as islands increase in size. This work complemented earlier observations by Darwin, who attributed the large number of finch species in the Galapagos to the isolation of the islands.

In 2013 four former bosses from the Icelandic bank Kaupthing were sentenced to between three and five years in prison for their roles in the country's 2008 banking collapse.[10] Iceland is the only country known so far to have prosecuted and jailed someone for the more than a $20 trillion[11] loss in global wealth, triggered (and many say caused) by subprime lending and other banking and investment irregularities. Again, islands help make things clearer.

Diamond (2005) in *Collapse* reviews ancient cultures like the Anasazi, Maya and Vikings and islands, especially Easter Island, to provide compelling analysis on why societies collapse. Turning this insight to today's challenges, he suggests 12 environmental problems that, if not addressed, could lead to collapse of current societies. These are: (i) loss of natural habitat; (ii) over-harvesting of wild foods; (iii) biodiversity loss; (iv) soil erosion; (v) reliance on fossil fuels; (vi) over-extraction of fresh water; (vii) over-use of earth's terrestrial photosynthetic capacity; (viii) synthetic chemicals and trace metals; (ix) invasive species; (x) greenhouse gas emissions; (xi) unstable population growth; and (xii) metabolism (resource consumption) levels of growing populations.

Despite the scale of today's planetary challenges, Diamond provides cautious optimism and reason for hope. He bases his optimism on three factors. First, these are self-inflicted problems. With sufficient political will they can be solved. Second, there is growing environmental awareness everywhere. Diamond traces this back to *Silent Spring* (Carson, 1962). And, third, our current interconnectedness can serve us well. With modern communication and monitoring systems, all parts of the (global) system can better understand what others are doing, and why.

Gupta (2014) uses Molokai, Hawaii, as a case study to investigate how 'localizing' systems of production and consumption might be associated with improved sustainability. The island's isolation and strong environmental ethos (*aloha aina*) encouraged local residents to live independently, e.g. local produce, and sustainably, e.g. rates of fish catch. These local efforts can abrade against similar sustainability efforts at a state-level, e.g. opposition to 'Big Wind', or even efforts at a national or global scale.

> A Molokai resident advocating for island sustainability rooted in *aloha aina* [love of land] and an industrial ecologist arguing that sustainability cannot exist at anything less than a planetary scale come from very different vantage points. It is essential that we uncover the diversity of meanings attached to the term 'sustainability,' and make explicit the varying goals regarding what it is we are in fact trying to sustain, before we can even begin to think about implementing and evaluating this elusive yet critical concept.

A parallel between cities and Bermuda, Bali, Molokai and other islands is possible. Cities evolve in-place, taking advantage of geography: a strategic port, proximity to fertile land, ease of defence. Cities cannot move out of harm's way. Cities emerge where geography and opportunity combine.

The strength of cities comes from their connectivity and resilience. Initial strength is through the connectivity of residents. This is why big cities have bigger economies – they provide more opportunity for residents to connect. And now the second stage of urban strength and resilience is emerging – connectivity with other cities.

Sustainability between the world's larger cities will require civility and a common purpose. Cities are islands, immobile and rooted in place, but cities are also well connected and part of a global system of systems.

The professional perspective

One of the best opportunities for sustainable development appears to be the nexus between cities and the professions that build and manage them. Planners and engineers and, somewhat more difficult to define, professional development workers, civil servants, and public policy advisors are critical to sustainable cities.

Once planners suggest size and location, civil engineers build the urban infrastructure – roads, buildings, waterways and landfills. The community builds the city's social and economic fabric around this infrastructure. To build a great city, a sustainable city, planners and engineers need to think about more than the location and technical aspects of infrastructure. Planners and engineers, working with the community's input, need to create the foundation for sustainable cities.

Unlike when measuring the strength of concrete or steel, there is no easy metric for the coefficient of public support, nor is there an angle of repose for civic action. No textbook provides the engineer with the tensile strength or modulus of elasticity of a neighbourhood or broader community's motivations or social instincts. Human strengths, like our ability to adapt and innovate and our resourcefulness, are traits not always reliable or easily measured. Neither is it easy to predict the impact of human frailties like fragile egos, insecurities and fears, immediacy of the short term, and our selfishness. This human nature, though, defines the degree of sustainability and quality of life in cities.

Even though measuring human behaviour is difficult, engineers are routinely assigned the task. Every banked curve on the road, balcony railing, pipe sizing and roof truss has a built-in factor of safety that balances human behaviour, natural systems and cost. To engineer is to define risk and then apply a factor of safety against that risk. Engineers do this routinely for the stent in an aortic valve, a car's braking system, and in the bolts holding together the baby's crib or a roller coaster.

Systems like climate, nitrogen and phosphorous cycles, biodiversity, economies and healthy communities are more complex than buildings, roads or engines, yet engineering principles still need to apply. To ignore them in these more complex systems is far riskier.

Sustainable development seems akin to the factor of safety every engineer incorporates into problem solving. But instead of only determining how safe the building's foundation is from collapse, a 'factor of sustainability' should also look at the activity in context of what else is going on around the building locally and globally, for at least the next few decades.

> And the reality
> Between the notion
> And the act
> Falls the shadow

T.S. Eliot

Professionals such as planners and engineers, especially those charged to help build cities, need to apply bio-physical and social science considerations to ensure a safe and resilient operating space for culture and economy. This often requires working in the shadows – moving forward without all the information and balancing professional 'certainty' with social licence and cost estimates (financial and other). The search for sustainability for everyone starts from a myriad of beginnings, and is influenced by many things. However, with a common purpose, simple signposts and community support, planners and engineers, as part of effective teams, can support sustainable development. Engineers, planners, architects and scientists are key agents for greater sustainability (Petroski, 2010; ASCE, 2006).

A myriad of professional disciplines are integral to urban operations. In addition to law, healthcare, education and finance, plus urban planners and civil engineers, a few key professions are worth noting. These include risk managers, public policy advisors and development workers.

Risk – the effect of uncertainty on objectives (ISO 31000) – is routinely managed by many disciplines, including the engineering profession. Risk-informed decision making (RIDM) rose in prominence through application by NASA and nuclear regulatory authorities. As system complexity grew, and highly unlikely but significantly impactful events required quantification and response planning, the risk management community developed tools and communication strategies (Table 3.1). RIDM enables better targeting of inspections to reduce risks and oversight costs.

Tools such as RIDM and probabilistic risk assessment became more widespread, particularly with regard to financial markets, food and drug assessments, and climate risk. The role of risk managers is growing as they attempt to better quantify emergent risks as these risks – terrorism, increasing inter-connectivity, sea level rise and greater wind-storm intensity – grow as more people live in cities.

Quantifying potential risks offsets the cognitive limitations of the human mind, which tends to apply a 'bounded rationality' to risk. Humans tend to discount the risk of extreme events, e.g. drunk driving, and often overstate minor risks, e.g. vaccine side effects.

For example, following the September 2001 terrorist attacks that killed 246 airline passengers (plus 2,731 people on the ground), Americans were more afraid to fly and many took to driving instead. Gigerenzer (2004) found that 1,595 Americans were killed in car crashes as a direct result of switching from flying to driving (post 9-11). Engineers (risk quantification and minimization) and sociologists (risk communication and cognition) have an important role in better defining risk and protecting development gains against growing risks.

Risk management is growing in importance as sustainable development requires more comprehensive incorporation of risk into current decision making (e.g. through casualty insurance). Climate risk, for example, is growing. Direct costs of disasters have risen from $75 billion in the 1960s to more than $1 trillion in the last decade (Bakhtiari, 2014). Fawcett et al. (2015) describe how countries negotiating within the UNFCCC framework need to assess global temperature increase from a probabilistic risk perspective, e.g. likelihood of temperatures reaching a 4°C increase, rather than only a deterministic one, e.g. temperatures not exceeding 2°C.

Professionals engaged in long-lived (35+ years) urban infrastructure face increased uncertainty. Historic risk profiling may not be applicable and needs to be better differentiated at the individual city level (Gagnon, Leduc and Savard, 2008). How this is quantified and communicated to the public is a rapidly evolving field. Professionals who function in a manner similar to today's operating engineers that monitor the infrastructure of the world's larger urban areas, e.g. power plants, water supply and treatment, and telecommunications networks, are needed to better monitor local urban systems. This would enable greater integration of urban risk management and enhanced resilience as a key component of sustainable development (Goldberg and Somerville, 2014).

For example, the world's larger urban areas should have authorized 'city-systems engineers' similar to how the Rockefeller Foundation is supporting chief resilience officers at 100 world cities, and how large-scale power plants require on-site authorized power engineers. This engineer(s) should monitor and report on the city's (urban area) material flows and baseline indicators. Global risk managers need to increasingly assess interconnected risks and routinely build resilience in targeted cities.[12]

Professionals who serve as public policy advisors and development workers are critical in building sustainable cities. Top civil servants are routinely called on to oversee the planning, finance and management of urban infrastructure. They may work in local, state–provincial, national or even international echelons. Local pressures, e.g. 'not-in-my-backyard' (NIMBY), social operating licenses, financing arrangements such as public–private partnerships (PPP) and debt finance, and political imperatives suggesting priority in one region over another all need to be balanced.

Developing optimum urban infrastructure is difficult. Every city is rife with examples of sub-optimum solutions. In Toronto, the Sheppard Subway line, which was largely instigated through political pressure, has one of the lowest rider-shares of any heavy-duty subway. A surface rapid-transit line would have met requirements far more cost effectively.

In Shanghai, the $1.2 billion-plus Maglev Train connecting Pudong International Airport to downtown Shanghai operates at about 20 per cent capacity. In Mumbai, the rigid adherence to an exceptionally low floor-area ratio (FAR – one of the lowest in the world for such a large city) leads to much greater urban sprawl and higher costs of infrastructure provisions.[13] São Paulo, Brazil's largest city, is so congested – with a public transit system unable to meet demand and 6.2 million personal cars – that the city boasts the world's second-largest helicopter fleet as the affluent scramble to commute. Dakar makes up just 0.3 per cent of Senegal's total land area, yet is home to most of the economy, national agencies and more than 20 per cent of the country's population, most of which lives in informal, unplanned settlements. The city experiences frequent flooding, in recent years in 2005, 2009 and 2012 especially so. The impact of haphazard planning, with routine and severe flooding, is so pervasive that the city has inordinate difficulty in capturing potential benefits associated with urbanization and economic development.

Development agencies are often criticized for supporting poor infrastructure choices with insufficient consideration of benefits, and who might share them, and full costs – environmental, social and economic. Myriad vested interests are associated with large-scale costly infrastructure. Much of this infrastructure concentrates in, or serves residents and businesses of, cities. In larger cities there is much discussion between various levels of government, potential users and expected fees, and recuperation of associated increased land value, that accompanies infrastructure development. Professionals need to ensure that clear, relatively easily understood metrics are provided with all proposed infrastructure and major public policy.

Professionals also need to place a premium on good-quality data. As W. Edwards Demming said, 'without data you're just another person with an opinion', and 'In God we trust. Everyone else bring us data.' Data should be open by design and collected and published without bias.

Building better cities – the role of engineers and other professions

Large-scale, long-lived urban infrastructure (civil works) often acts as the 'bones' of a city, locking in urban form and much of a city's metabolism. London's Underground (1863), San Francisco's Golden Gate Bridge (1933) and Rome's street alignment illustrate this well. Associated key infrastructure also establishes the prowess of cities, e.g. the Erie Canal and New York City, Changi Airport and Singapore, and the St Lawrence Seaway and Montreal.

As early as 1771, John Smeaton self-declared himself a 'civil engineer' wanting to differentiate his work from the more common military engineer. Since then, civil engineers have had an enormous influence on the shape of cities and the way cities use resources. Recognizing this influence, engineers have attempted to quantify impacts. Poveda and Lipsett (2014) outline more than 600 existing approaches to sustainability assessment (mainly for buildings and urban infrastructure projects). The degree to which buildings are rated and measured is almost opposite to what information cities typically have on their energy supply. Sustainability assessments on urban energy supply are serious shortcomings in most cities. Information is needed on levels of greenhouse gas emissions, security of supply and transmission, energy intensity of local residents and businesses, and rates of increase, or decline (including conservation).

Engineers are well versed in the application of a factor of safety to their designs. A similar process in the design and application of a factor of sustainability is proposed. The aggregate impact of infrastructure projects is measured as it relates to sustainability for that specific city and globally (proposed initially for world's largest, or 'Future Five', cities – those with expected populations of 5 million or more by 2050). Sustainability cost curves, similar to environmental assessments, are proposed for all large-scale long-lived (beyond 2050) infrastructure projects.

The growth of professions

As early as the Middle Ages, guilds started to form in European towns and cities. Guilds were associations of merchants and craftsmen that controlled their craft locally. They oversaw trade, usually through a letters patent from a monarch or other authority. Cities typically had as many as 100 guilds. Around 1200, guilds gave rise to universities in cities like Paris, Bologna and Oxford. Although guilds still exist today, they reached maturity around 1300, and remained prominent into the late eighteenth century.

Jean-Jacques Rousseau, Adam Smith and Karl Marx, among many others, criticized guilds as barriers to free trade, innovation and business development. Rent seeking and protection of influence over public service were common. As nation states assumed the role from cities for overseeing trade, guilds lost much of their influence. For example, with the French Revolution, Le Chapelier Law of 1791 abolished guilds in France. The functions of guilds were taken up by trade unions, universities, copyright and patent protection, and professions.

Along with the guilds, the doctorate appeared in medieval Europe as a licence to teach at a university. Doctoral training was often a form of apprenticeship to a guild. The term 'doctor' originally referred to the Christian authorities who taught and interpreted the Bible. The right to grant a *licentia docendi* was originally the sole purview of the church; the Pope granted to the University of Paris in 1231 the licence to teach and award doctorates. The first professions were divinity, medicine and law.

The University of St Andrews, in Scotland, founded in 1413, is thought to be the first institution to issue professional degrees (of medical doctor, MD). Universities slowly moved away from the control of church and guilds and now in most countries control issuance of professional degrees needed as a prerequisite for professional membership. Professionals now usually need sufficient autonomy from political and corporate influence, a degree from an accredited university, minimum experience requirements, licensure in the related professional association, on-going good conduct, colleague control, and a code of conduct and ethics.

In 1818, the Institution of Civil Engineers was founded in London, and received a Royal Charter in 1828, formally recognizing civil engineering as a profession. In the US engineering licensure began in 1903 in Wyoming as a way to slowly tame the Wild West. Engineering and land surveying were licensed together as a way to bring consistency and order to land development and equal access to water rights.

*****

As the quitting-time horn sounded on the afternoon of August 29, 1907, the Quebec Bridge – nearing completion after four years of construction – collapsed. Earlier that same day, local engineer Norman McLure, after writing letters outlining his concerns of key structural members, had finally travelled to New York to meet with supervising engineer Theodore Cooper. The Phoenix Bridge Company had disputed McLure's earlier concerns, claiming the beams must have been bent before installation. McLure finally convinced Cooper of the seriousness of the situation, and Cooper immediately telegraphed Quebec: 'Add no more load to bridge till after due consideration of facts.' But it was too late: 75 workers lost their lives that day.

The collapse of the Quebec Bridge was catalytic in giving rise to professional engineering in Canada. A few years after the collapse, Professor Haultain of the University of Toronto contacted Rudyard Kipling, asking him to prepare a ceremony for newly graduate engineers commensurate with the need to temper engineering influence and hubris with ethics and obligation. Kipling enthusiastically responded with 'The Ritual of the Calling of an Engineer' and the inaugural Iron Ring Ceremony was held April 25, 1925 at the University Club of Montreal. The first permanent local chapter, or 'camp', started a week later at the University of Toronto on May 1, 1925.

Kipling received the Nobel Prize in Literature in 1907, the same year the bridge collapsed. Born in India in 1865, he is to date the youngest person ever to win this prize. In 1907, the world's cities were home to just 250 million people (about 15 per cent of the world's population at the time), and the world's overall combined wealth was less than $2.5 trillion. Today, about 3.5 billion people live in cities, and our total wealth, almost all of which resides in and is created through our cities, is more than $250 trillion.

Kipling often commented on India's teeming streets and 'chock-a-block' crowds. He was in India when the population was about 270 million people and the country's biggest city, Mumbai (then Bombay), had 750,000 inhabitants. What would he say today upon learning that India will soon overtake China as the world's most populous country? Mumbai, the city of his birth, is on track to be the world's largest city in 2050, with some 40 million people.

If Kipling were alive today, he would likely be horrified with how much damage we've created in the last 65 years, and, despite our new wealth, how Herculean a task we face to build our cities and societies in a way that protects the planet and provides a dignified and honourable life for all. And if asked again to write a ceremony for graduating engineers, Kipling would probably better reflect today's imperatives – much greater inclusion of women, and expanding the call to other professions, and to other countries.

Professionals graduating today will see urban populations double during their careers. Technology and innovation progress exponentially. Yet our social norms, the hardwiring of our brains and our behaviour change only linearly. Engineers, along with all other professionals, urgently need to develop better ways of working together.

George Washington, Thomas Jefferson and Abraham Lincoln, all great leaders, were professional land surveyors before entering politics. They often held to their professional roots when buffeted and battered by circumstance. Such leadership is urgently needed today.[14]

A personal perspective

Everyone has a personal story of sustainability. How we weave these stories together, into community strands, city-strands, and hopefully a strong and inclusive global tapestry, will determine our success in bringing about sustainable development.

Similarly to how the overweight man knows he should lose a few pounds, the smoker or heavy drinker knows moderation is key, or the man whose family life is crashing about his ears, fragility and incompleteness are part of our existence. This 'frailty thy name is human' is part of the foundation of all our lives, and our collective response to sustainability. Most people, most cities, most countries, know what needs to be done to make things more sustainable. Finding and nurturing the will, individually and collectively, is usually the main challenge to bring about greater sustainability.

The parents of a starving child, farmers facing yet another drought, slum dwellers flooded again, the rich aware of, and worried about, keeping their good fortune: everyone has a different perspective on sustainability (Trapenberg-Frick,

Weinzimmer and Waddel, 2014). Cities like Toronto and Dakar, agencies like the World Bank and UN, and professions like planning and engineering are made up of individuals. Their historical perspective as well as their individual and collective vision, their hopes for tomorrow and especially their will to act is the foundation of sustainable development. The view of sustainable development is influenced by where the observer stands.

> It was six men of Indostan
> To learning much inclined,
> Who went to see the Elephant
> (Though all of them were blind),
> That each by observation
> Might satisfy his mind

John Godfrey Saxe

Sustainable development comes in many forms and is often shaped by personal biases, circumstances and fleeting glimpses of something big. The term is so overused, it's like responding 'Fine' when asked how we're doing even, if we are anything but fine at the time. Answering 'Fine' defers a serious discussion. As employees, as professionals, as parents and partners, we often say 'Fine' and hope for the best.

However, deep down, like that once-in-a-round well-hit golf shot, or the way we feel at our first kiss of true love, we know sustainable development when we see it, or feel it. At its core, sustainable development is about equity and the pace of gratification.

To get to that larger place of sustainable communities and a sustainably hospitable planet, sustainable development must first come in some eight billion individual shades of grey. Black and white certainty is rare. There is much *me* with subtle nuances, insecurities and justifications in sustainability.

First-person writing is usually frowned upon. However, your indulgence please. Perhaps a little background and context is warranted, because as hard as we might try we cannot completely take *me* (or *you*) out of the sustainability discussion. Recognizing the potential bias is important.

My search for sustainability began with smatterings of a few memorable moments, mostly environmental. Camping when I was a kid with my family at Sandbanks Park on Lake Ontario (when the beach was cleaner and the park was called the Outlet), we were oblivious to any sort of understanding of environmental cause and effect. My brother and I would whine when our father kept us from riding our bicycles in the thick cloud behind the park's truck as workers drove around spraying for mosquitoes in the calm of dusk. The other 'lucky' kids would weave in and out of the fog of water vapour, pesticides and diesel fuel. This, of course, was also the time of leaded gasoline, PCBs and Agent Orange for the home garden.

Growing up in Trenton, Ontario, my brother, cousins and I would catch fish at the mouth of the Trent River just a few hundred metres downstream of the

Domtar plant, one of the largest point source polluters in Canada. A little further downstream, the fishing at the effluent pipe of the cold storage food processing plant was particularly good, especially for sluggish carp that we sold to the Chinese restaurant for 25 cents. We scoffed when the 'Know Your Limits' fish consumption restriction signs started going up in the 1970s – we weren't pregnant or nursing, after all.

Later, a few breathtakingly beautiful places stick in my mind: the beaches of Bermuda, Hawaii and the Greek Isles; hiking down to the base of the Grand Canyon; scuba diving on the Great Barrier Reef; the terraced rice paddies of Bali and Tana Toraja; seeing an elephant and giraffe in the wild; Alaska's ruggedness; the cherry blossoms of Washington; standing on the edge of Yasur Volcano on Tana Island in Vanuatu; the enormity of Sitka spruce, hemlock and cedars on the Queen Charlotte Islands (now Haida Gwai); Banff, Jasper, Yoho and Kootney Rocky Mountain Parks; being serenaded by wolves in Wood Buffalo National Park; seeing a moose on my first canoe trip in Algonquin Park.

So too a few memorable performances by humans: the ceiling of the Sistine Chapel; the Beat Retreat in Hamilton, Bermuda; Rembrandt's Night Watch and the love and light in the portrait of his wife Saskia; my only visit to the Vienna Opera House; Machu Pichu; Cirque du Soleil; Van Gogh's 'Sunflowers' and 'Blue Irises'; the Taj Mahal; a café break in Milan or Paris.

A powerful catalyst that still makes me think about environmental management was driving up for my first co-op work term at Red Lake, a gold-mining town in Northern Ontario. My colleague Kirk and I were driving at least 90 kilometres an hour with the windows closed when we crossed the Wabigoon River. We gagged on the stink. Amazed, we had to check it out, so we quickly parked the Suburban on the side of the road and clambered down to the river's edge. We were more than 40 kilometres downstream from the Dryden pulp mill and still the river was black and viscous as it tumbled over a beautiful large waterfall. The stench was overpowering. I tossed a rock on the white foam of an eddy and the rock just stayed there. Surely this was wrong. Uncertainty with a smidge of anger was seeded in my mind.

A couple of work terms later, in the summer of 1984, I was floating on Lake Erie drill rigs developing natural gas wells as the government's safety rep. After some 20–30 hours of aimlessly waiting, I would lean over the side of the rig, usually in the middle of the night, to verify that the tell-tale white clouds of cement were in the water. The excess cement would signify that the casing in the fracked well should be fully cemented into bedrock.

That summer I ate very well, 'learned about Africa' as I read every published Wilbur Smith book and watched *General Hospital* and *Ryan's Hope* with the off-duty drill-hands. Horizontal drilling wasn't common back then and fracking was fairly tame compared to today's more aggressive methods, but I still wondered why the US side of the lake wasn't being developed due to environmental concerns while the Canadian side had third-year-student inspectors.

Prior to working on Lake Erie, I spent two co-op work terms for the Ontario Geological Survey driving around southwest Ontario managing exploratory boreholes, including one at the base of the Don Valley brickyard quarry in the middle of Toronto. The government wanted to determine the potential energy reserves in the province's underlying oil shale. The world's oil rush can be traced largely to southern Ontario, where the first commercial oil well was developed in Oil Springs in 1858, a full year before the more famous Titusville oil well in Pennsylvania.

I graduated a geotechnical engineer, and got lucky – a job in Alberta's oilfields. Living in Alberta is useful for every Canadian, especially one from central Canada. Even a country as seemingly homogenous as Canada has intense regional differences. Like the men of Indostan, the location of your vantage point changes the view significantly.

Working in the oilfields allowed me to pay off my student loans, and I loved the freedom of the two-weeks-on/one-week-off work schedule. In a week off, you could see a lot of wilderness, and the Rocky Mountains surely have to be one of the most beautiful places on earth. But I was uneasy. There are few sectors more rapacious than the resource industry.

This is where the story can veer off in several directions. Simply by using the word 'rapacious' to describe the oil and gas industry, you, the reader, have a signpost on my attitudes. Will this sustainability discussion be an environmental rant, you may wonder? Or will I backtrack, admitting I knew full well how the gasoline in my car that took me to all those wondrous wilderness hikes came from that same oil industry? Herein lays the challenge of sustainable development and its shades of grey. Our circumstances shape our sense of sustainability.

One of the things that got me thinking most about sustainability was the Brundtland Commission's report *Our Common Future*, published in 1987. I had read about the report in some newspaper or magazine and special ordered a copy from Guelph's Bookshelf Café (there was no Amazon, or indeed internet, then). The book did a great job of advocating the term sustainable development that was effectively introduced in the IUCN's 1980 World Conservation Strategy. *Our Common Future* convinced me of the merits and need for sustainable development. There, in one easy-to-read report, was a cogent argument admonishing us to figure out how to get along with each other and with the planet.

Right around the time of reading *Our Common Future*, I gave my first public talk. The talk – more of a discussion – was with Guelph's University Women's Club at the house of their president, Brenda Elliot. As I had just joined the city as Waste Management Coordinator I gave my pitch on why recycling was important and how using blue boxes would be a great first step to help the environment. The University Women's Club, along with the local 'Public Interest Research Group' (a member of the loosely knit collection of PIRGs started by Ralph Nader), was agitated about the city's plans to build a waste incinerator adjacent to the University of Guelph.

Brenda, the staff at the Ontario-PIRG and I hit it off well. Yes, I represented the city's efforts to build an incinerator in their backyard, but my bosses and city council saw my job as first and foremost to divert waste from needing to be landfilled or incinerated. Guelph was one of the few cities in Canada that had full control over collection and disposal of its waste, and therefore had a direct financial interest to reduce the amount of waste needing to be disposed. The more waste diverted, the longer the landfill would last.

City residents took to the call 'reduce, reuse and recycle' with vigour. The blue box diversion programme exceeded everyone's expectations and residents quickly looked for more comprehensive approaches. We studied the idea to launch Canada's first wet/dry waste diversion programme (my master's thesis). A park was even established to recognize the size of forested area saved in the first year of the programme (in theory) by recycling paper: Preservation Park, a 27-hectare forest in the city's south end. The area was twinned with the purchase, on 'behalf of the children of Guelph', of Monteverdi Rain Forest in Costa Rica. This was the time of the first big debt-for-nature swaps. A commemorative plaque at the entrance to Preservation Park has a short note on how the city's recycling programme contributed to sustainable development and is emblazoned with 'Think Globally, Act Locally'.

From the start of Guelph's recycling programme, many citizens asked how they could do more to help the environment: 'Recycling is easy. What's next?' So, instead of just encouraging people to use recycled-content paper and low-flow showerheads that were often hard to find, Brenda Elliot and I started in 1987 'For Earth's Sake', North America's first retail store to sell exclusively environmentally friendlier products. We even tried to develop a comprehensive impact rating system, giving impact ratings from 'cradle to grave' for the products we sold. We invited comments from our customers: we got two.

Challenges to the concept of the store quickly emerged. For example, one of our customers, more knowledgeable than us, pointed out that the ground covers we were selling as alternatives to grass lawns contained purple loosestrife, a noxious alien species. And selling stuff to help the environment can only go so far. The products made in developing countries that we sourced through Ten Thousand Villages, and foodstuffs from Fair Trade made sense. So too did kits to adopt a whale or buy an acre of rain forest. Books worked well, and (sort of) children's plush WWF 'endangered animals', where part of the proceeds went to help protect the threatened animal's habitat. But selling for sustainability is a challenge – the rent needed to be paid, and I got a job as waste manager in Bermuda. Brenda went on to run for political office. She won, and immediately became Minister of the Environment for the Province of Ontario. One of her first assignments was to fire Maurice Strong as CEO of the province's Ontario Hydro. For Earth's Sake was sold at a loss and the two of us went on to search for sustainability elsewhere.

A highlight of my career was sitting down one afternoon with A. J. Casson, the then-last surviving member of the Group of Seven artists. I had approached Mr Casson to write a letter of encouragement for Guelph's citizens to recycle. Mr Casson had spent part of his youth in Guelph and had just announced his support of the North Channel Preservation Society's bid to stop silica mining in the La Cloche hills near Killarney Park (100 km south-west of Sudbury). The high-quality silica was sought for glass manufacturing. So 'Why not promote recycling instead?' I thought.

Mr Casson is one of the few people I ever met who did not see sustainable development through shades of grey. We sat in his beautiful home on Rochester Avenue in Toronto. I didn't know it at the time, but I took deep comfort in his certainty, which was probably an important source for his art. He wisely opined, 'Cutting the trees is one thing. They'll grow back. But mining the hills – that's something very different.'

While I was secretary for the Wellington Waste Management Committee that was looking to site a new landfill, mainly for Guelph's garbage, people opposed to the proposed landfill picketed my house, complete with placards and signs admonishing 'Don't do it Dan.' Ken Danby (what is it with artists?) lectured me in public as he worried about a proposed landfill site he thought too close to his idyllic 47-acre 1860s Armstrong Mill estate. (Ken Danby bought the run-down mill in 1967, it was sold to Jim Balsillie in 2011 after the former died of a heart attack in Algonquin Park in September 2007, aged 67.) His 'Summer Solstice' remains one of my favourite paintings. When I look at the jack pine in that painting anchored to the weathered outcrop of Canadian Shield, I sense Mr Danby's connection to his family, friends and sense of place. The deeper the roots, the stronger the tree.

A few years before trying to find a new landfill for Guelph, I had a co-op work term with Gartner Lee Associates, the consulting engineering firm, contracted to do much of the work for the Ontario Waste Management Corporation (OWMC). OWMC spent more than $200 million to try to find a hazardous waste site. Due to intense local opposition, a site was never developed, and wastes were eventually trucked to Alberta, across the US border, and elsewhere (a much riskier option than disposal in Ontario). The opponents to OWMC and the angry residents near Guelph and Alma, Wellington County, as well as those opposed to wind turbines, compost facilities and all manner of change, can be incredibly effective. That seems to be both good and bad.

While in Guelph I helped to start Canada's first Round Table on Environment and Economy and initiated the country's first municipal Green Plan. The Round Tables emerged from Our Common Future and there truly was benefit in getting differing, but constructive, opinions around a common table. The Green Plans were precursors to 'Agenda 21s' launched at the Rio UNCED Conference in 1992 (Canada's first national Green Plan was released by Prime Minister Mulroney December 11, 1990; 'Local Agenda 21s' were brought forward at Rio with the support and insistence of Maurice Strong and Jeb Brugmann, ICLEI's first Secretary General).

While travelling overseas, I've worked in a few of sustainable development's hotspots. Searching for gross domestic happiness in Bhutan while trying to avoid the surly feral dogs guarding the entrance of Thimpu's Swiss Café. Pondering how so many used Land Rovers could end up in Nauru, along with the world's highest rates of obesity and stripped soil cover (mined for the guano). Island hopping in the Marshall Islands, Kiribati, Samoa, Vanuatu, Fiji and Federated States of Micronesia while listening to residents express their fears about climate change. Looking for brown tree snakes in Guam and only seeing a McDonalds. Trying to keep lions out of the garbage dumps and hippos out of the wastewater treatment ponds in Zambia's parks. Working in the slums of Mumbai, Jakarta, La Paz and Lusaka. Marvelling at the mix of *dolce faniti* and governance challenges in Italy. Checking out the back-end of China's manufacturing rush while wandering around the country's garbage dumps and checking the wastewater flowing out of a few factories; marvelling at the number of women all collected in one place making running shoes in Indonesia. Or perhaps the slightly more fortunate ones – mainly Filipino – lining Orchard Boulevard in Singapore on Sundays as they enjoyed their only day off from being a servant. Attending a conference in Riyadh and asking why the few stoic women couldn't even have coffee with the men.

Visiting Robben Island in Cape Town, I wondered at the influence one person can have by staying true to convictions. This was reinforced when visiting Kolkata and standing at the side of Mother Teresa's tomb. Or on the other side of India in Ahmedabad and seeing where Gandhi started his long salt walk and too-short career. Sitting in the kitchen of Willem Van Loon's ancestral home in Amsterdam and wondering, as many Indonesians do, how he and the VOC, the world's first publicly traded company that he helped start in 1602, and the tiny Netherlands could colonize a country as large as Indonesia. Sensing the potential energy of cities like Kunming, Shanghai, Rio de Janeiro, São Paulo and Johannesburg. Sitting in the same lobby of Washington DC's Willard Hotel where apparently Ulysses S. Grant started the practice of 'lobbying'. Joining yet another UNFCCC 'conference of the parties' or Rio+20 and wondering how there can be so much talk about sustainable development with so few genuine results.

I've tried to learn from sustainable development leaders like some of the world's well-intentioned NGOs, entrepreneurs, managers of companies like Unilever, Philips and even Wal-Mart. I've had coffee, shared offices, attended conferences and lunchtime talks, and met with gurus like Robert Goodland, Karl-Henrik Robèrt, Ismael Seregeldin and Maurice Strong. The paths of many of these leaders often crossed through the World Bank.

The World Bank is to sustainable development what McDonalds is to fast food. The Bank's motto of 'Our Dream is a World Free of Poverty' could just as easily be 'Sustainability: Supersize Me'. No agency has more resources, more passionate and qualified staff, more governments willing to be part of an experiment, or more of a mandate to figure out what sustainable development is and how this holy grail of development should be implemented. Critics of the Bank are legion, some with grounds, many without – or at least without credible alternatives. Searching for sustainability while working at the World Bank is like drinking from a fire hose.

While living in Bermuda, I got into the habit of reading one-week-old (and therefore free) copies of *The Economist* magazines on the beach. This is the only reason I ended up joining the World Bank: I serendipitously saw an ad for the Bank's Young Professionals Program with a specific mention of the need for solid waste management expertise. 'Hey,' I thought. 'Maybe I could get an interview and a free flight to Washington.' I'd never been. I didn't know much about the

Bank nor its mandate, and my longest overseas trip to that point had been with my parents to visit my mother's family in the Netherlands.

I was ambivalent about applying to the World Bank. A born procrastinator, I kept putting off answering the long application form and providing my own essay on 'what does development mean to me'. Serendipity intervened again though. The last possible day to complete the application was a Sunday – I would have to courier the package first thing Monday to meet the deadline. I made a deal with my [now] ex-wife (who really didn't want me to apply): if it rained on Sunday I would fill out the form. If it was sunny we would go to the beach and forget about Washington. It rained. I got the interview, and the job, and intensified my search for sustainability.

For me, working at the World Bank came with some uneasiness. When Guelph's local newspaper heard of my taking the job there was an editorial about how 'Dan was selling out'. A friend sent me the words to Bruce Cockburn's 'They Call it Democracy'. The refrain, about the dirty IMF not giving a f—k about people's lives, still plays in my head. The World Bank always gets lumped in with the IMF, but it is a catchy tune.

My search for sustainability began well before the World Bank, but the World Bank certainly 'upped the game'. Some of the world's toughest questions on sustainability are asked of Bank Task Team Leaders, while being grilled by managers and lead advisors about a proposed investment project or research paper. This is then fleshed out with in-country government and community representatives. Rarely is the whole picture viewed, and there are usually clouds of obfuscation and never enough time for a proper sighting. Like triage in the emergency room, Bank teams are expected to be passionate about helping people, but, foremost, to be professional, credible and backed by facts. They must prioritize, and show how they will measure impact, and focus on implementation. After a loan is signed, that focus can quickly blur as conflicting priorities arise, and people are forced to move on to the next task.

The Bank occasionally acts as if it is chasing the latest fitness fad, looking to buy a new piece of exercise equipment or trying the latest miracle diet rather than sticking to the hard stuff, like eating more vegetables and fewer sweets, drinking less booze and going for morning jogs. Anyone who's worked at the Bank long enough will have passed through at least one re-organization. The re-organizations are longer spaced than in government agencies, or certainly the private sector. Management is risk adverse, directors look out for their assigned countries first, and Bank staff is somewhat coddled, many with a sense of entitlement, so 'corporate tectonics' leads to rare but strong, earthquake-like changes. Nevertheless, the dust settles quickly, and the work – and flow of money – is rarely interrupted. With China's and other BRICs (the emerging economies of Brazil, Russia, India and China) ascendance, the Bank's relevance is waning. This is probably unfortunate, as many of the Bank's tasks, such as impartial data collection and observation of the global commons, would need to be assigned somewhere else if the Bank did not exist. The World Bank has a critical role to play for at least the next 50 years – it may just be different from the one it provided for the last 60 years.

Bermudians have a great way of defining the world's mobile creative class: expats are said to be 'missionaries, mercenaries or misfits'. Organizations like the World Bank and UN agencies are staffed by transients with their G4 visas and green cards. Lives are grafted on to the local community, usually through the quick-growing roots of staff members' children, or the desire for a better retirement than in their country of origin. Most of the staff members are not immigrants – they are guests.

Commenting on something as complex and locally contextual as sustainable development is challenging, especially when mainly viewed from the window of a moving taxi, train or airplane. Yet international expats have a unique view – broader than deep, but usually with robust technical and economic underpinning. There may be those who 'dream of a world free of poverty', but there are also those who are hired to get on with making it happen, and almost always they are local residents. Finding that person and then finding a way to help him or her is usually the best bet for greater sustainability.

Saints are sparsely distributed throughout the world. They do not seem to have a preponderance to be in NGOs or international organizations, or even in local schools or health clinics. One of the largest collections of ex-Peace Corps volunteers is probably at the World Bank (not that Peace Corp volunteers have a higher proclivity to sainthood). So too a few formerly rabid NGO members who now wield significant influence in places like the UN and World Bank. By and large, they are not disillusioned, but they have become very adept at shadow boxing and working through a seemingly unending palate that still lets them paint, but mainly in muted colours and shades of grey. Statistically, there are as many saints at the World Bank as anywhere else – they just get paid better at the Bank.

'If men were angels, no government would be necessary' said James Madison. Nor would the World Bank, IMF, United Nations or WTO be necessary, as all development would be sustainable.

The term sustainability, or sustainable development,[15] is now a red flag to the bull of the likes of Fox News, the National Post and other right-leaning media outlets. Some, like Tom DeWees and Rep. Dennis Hedke (R) have even called for an outright ban of the term. Amazingly, in 2013, Kansas tried to outlaw the term from usage in the state. An iconic lightening rod, the term has become somewhat of everything to everyone, and for many people nothing much. Strange, though, that a term supposedly so vacuous can yet instil such passions. The concept should be simple: improve, or maintain, the quality of life for as many people as possible today, without diminishing the opportunity of future generations to do the same. However, the devil really is in the detail.

Our personal experiences, cultures and current security (and safety) determine our individual perspectives on sustainable development. Combining all of these within an agency or community, city or even a country, is how we shape current efforts toward sustainable development. The search for sustainability continues.

Even an agreement on what we are searching for remains elusive. The risk of delay is high.

Sustainable development is supposed to be like a stable three-legged stool with balanced weighting between social, economic and environmental considerations. After more than thirty years of thinking and searching for sustainability, and working with some of the world's best engineers, social scientists, economists and environmentalists, I feel no closer to durable solutions. I do know that the best answers and activities are those that are developed locally and take root in an organic way, although, so far, rarely do they grow tall enough to change the landscape.

*****

Some of the most powerful *social* drivers to shape my version of sustainability are chance encounters, for example, those with perhaps the most beautiful woman I've ever seen and two of the most pathetic children.

The woman was a *pumulung*, a waste picker, at the garbage dump in Semarang, Indonesia. This was my first trip to Indonesia. I was still reeling at the things I was seeing: the poverty, the environmental degradation, the needs, and the amazing hospitality and good nature of Indonesians. The garbage dump, several hectares in extent, was covered in acrid smoke from the constant fires. There were a few cows and hundreds of *pumulung* scratching through the detritus hoping to find enough of value to keep going for another day or two. I had scrambled to the bottom of the steep hill to look for leachate, the contaminated water flowing out of the base of the hill (there was a lot of it), and was climbing back up to my waiting colleagues. There she was. We both emerged from our own little clouds of smoke, with about as disparate backgrounds as any two people could ever have. We both smiled. She had perfect white teeth. She was gorgeous, despite being dressed in rags, filthy and likely harbouring a few debilitating viruses and parasites. She responded with a laugh and a gracious smile to my limited *selemat pagi*. And then just as quickly she was gone. How could she be so beautiful and seemingly so happy?, I wondered. And how on earth could I help her, if indeed that was my job? My colleagues teased me when I told them of my sighting – my *hutu sampah*, garbage ghost, or angel, they joked, but every now and then I wonder where she is now.

The two children that introduced me to sustainable development were continents apart but bound together by their fierce determination and instinct to survive.

I knew nothing about international travel, or development for that matter, when I joined the World Bank. I was just a garbage man, familiar with local government and the provision of basic urban services in rich countries. Here I was on my first big trip, in Harare, Zimbabwe, with a day to sightsee before my boss arrived. I wandered around the city checking out the Lonely Planet's suggested stops. Things were fairly quiet as I walked through the main market, since it was a Sunday. I had fended off most of the touts and beggars, but there was one cute little girl, maybe 4 or 5 years old. She had followed me a good 10 minutes, every now and then banging me with her plastic bowl and pointing to her mouth and gaunt stomach. I hadn't been able to change money at the hotel (and it was before globally ubiquitous ATMs). The smallest bill I had was a US $20. I was so close to giving her the bill – she was so cute, so insistent.

When telling my boss the story the next day she stopped me with an intense look when I mentioned the girl and the $20 bill.

'You didn't give her the money?' she interrupted.

I shook my head, and she sighed. 'Twenty dollars is enough to get a girl that young killed. A few people were probably watching for what you might give her.'

The second child, a boy in Delhi, India, begging for money between cars stopped at a traffic light, was about the same age as the little girl in Zimbabwe, maybe a year or two older. His legs were horribly mangled, sticking out at unnatural angles. He would never walk. He weaved in and out of traffic on a makeshift board with small wheels, pushing along with his broken and blackened hands. 'Wow, that's sad,' I commented to my companion, Kapil, as we watched the determined boy pass by the stopped cars, barely visible through the exhaust.

'What's even sadder', Kapil offered, 'is that he probably wasn't born that way. His parents – not knowing what else to do – did that to his legs so he would be pathetic enough to beg.'

The Monday morning of that same first trip to Harare, my boss Cecile and I took a taxi to the World Bank office. When the driver dropped us off he was unable to provide change. The fare was about $2, but we had been unable to get local currency at the hotel, and the smallest bill each of us had was still a $20. The driver became more and more agitated as Cecile chastised the guy for not having change, telling him he would have to come to the hotel later in the day to get paid. As the situation deteriorated I finally gave the insistent driver a $20 bill and asked him to deliver the change to the hotel later. Cecile admonished me, saying I'd never see that money, and my actions would only encourage the driver not to have change the next time. Later that day, though, a well-worn envelope was pushed under my hotel room door: in it were two $5 and eight $1 bills.

*****

Working at the World Bank is one of the best places to learn about *economics*, the next leg of our sustainability stool. For example, visiting Cirebon, a modest-sized Javanese city of a few million people about 200 kilometres east of Jakarta, was the first time I was a team leader. We were developing a large loan in what was traditionally Asian Development Bank 'territory', mostly for water supply and low-income neighbourhood improvements. On the first day of the trip we met people in one of the fishing communities, or *kampungs*. 'What are your biggest concerns and thoughts about the community?' we asked. The sea was just a few hundred meters away, and the smell of rotting fish and waste water intense. A man holding a crying baby – a rare sight in Indonesia – stood in the background. Someone in the crowd pointed to him and indignantly complained about local crime. A thief had apparently stolen his fishing boat earlier that week. One of the government officials with us asked the man to come forward. The man sheepishly told us his story while his neighbours nodded their heads in agreement and interjected at particularly poignant spots.

With every effort to hold back tears, he told us that the crying baby's mother, his wife, had left a couple weeks ago to work as a maid in Saudi Arabia. He wouldn't see her for at least a year. His boat had been stolen a few days after she left: his only means of making a living. True, the human spirit is indomitable, but it sure can use help every now and then. We took a collection among ourselves and gave the man somewhere between $50 and $100. I felt it was a weak gesture then. Today, if the same thing happened, I'm sure we would approach KickStarter or some other crowdfunding platform to try to raise enough money for a new boat.

That little baby will now be almost twenty. I wonder how she's doing. Indonesia's GDP has increased from $2,000 per person when I first saw her to about $5,000 today. Things are much better. The country has enjoyed considerable economic growth. But did it do *her* any good? Is she rich enough not to have to be a maid away from home for years at a time?

*****

When thinking about the third part of sustainability and the *environment* I remember a few years after that trip to Cirebon flying between Temika and Merauke, in Irian Jaya, Indonesia (now Papua). I had a window seat and a great view of the Ajkwa River, about 70 kilometres downstream from the world's largest Grasberg copper and gold mine, up in the mountains. All vegetation was dead for more than a kilometre on either side, and the water was a soupy grey sludge as it carried the mine tailings to the sea. These are toxic and the fine grains suffocate living things – fish, plants … the river kills it all.

When visiting Temika you could not avoid hearing the rumours, many substantiated, of atrocities against the indigenous community. We weren't allowed off the plane as it refuelled: this was just a few months after ABRI and McMoRan security officers had shot and killed 37 protestors. The contracted military is extremely effective at suppressing dissent associated with the mine. Freeport McMoRan, the mine's developer, is Indonesia's largest tax payer, providing about $1 billion a year to the country's tax base. However, this comes with a very high social and environmental cost.

The first politician I ever discussed environment and jobs with, in the early 1980s, was Mayor Neil Robertson of Trenton, Canada. My father was the City Engineer at the time. We had a great dinner over steaks and garlic at Carman's in Toronto. The mayor and my dad were in the city for an AMO (Association of Municipalities Ontario) conference, and I was still in university. A month or two earlier the Ministry of Environment had produced a list of Canada's largest polluters. The Domtar plant, the smell of which everyone in Trenton knows well, and one of the city's largest employers, was top. In 1962, Domtar's predecessor, Dominion Tar, abandoned its Cape Breton operations, leaving behind its contribution to the hazardous waste at the Sydney Tar Ponds. The mayor wondered over dinner how hard to push for a clean-up in Trenton, if it would mean losing jobs. He genuinely wanted both – jobs and a clean environment – but he saw them at odds with each other.

Mayor Robertson was leaning toward saying little. Trenton then, and still today, needed all the jobs it could get. Domtar has since merged with the larger Weyerhaeuser and is still one of Trenton's main employers. The plant still stinks.

Notes

1 To date, these global negotiations are best illustrated through the UN Conference on Environment and Development (UNCED) held in Rio de Janeiro, Brazil, in 1992, which resulted in 'Agenda 21' (Local Agenda 21 for local governments), and subsequent Rio+5, Rio+10 and Rio+20 conferences. The Rio+20 meeting in June 2012 provided an outcome document 'The Future We Want' negotiated between 180 participating nations. Similar global accords are reflected in the Millennium Development Goals (signed September 2000) and the Sustainable Development Goals (signed by 193 countries September, 2015). The UN's IPCCC efforts to negotiate a climate change accord grew out of the 1992 UNCED conference, with subsequent 'conference of the parties', e.g. COP21 in Paris December 2015. Arguably these efforts have yielded minimal durable and comprehensive attainment of the necessary conditions for sustainable development. Rio+20, the biggest UN event ever organized (with some 45,000 participants), was widely derided for achieving little in tangible commitments toward sustainable development. This book has its genesis in the author's attendance as a World Bank delegate at Rio+20 in 2012.

2 Billionaires list from *Forbes* magazine (March, 2015). Wealth of richest 1 per cent from Oxfam, 2015. Two measures of wealth are used (and often interchanged): income and retained assets. Income tends to be more easily measured and is particularly relevant for the poorest. Retained wealth tends to provide a better measure for the wealthy as land values (and other retained capital) are particularly important measures for urban residents (where land values are a significant driver of local economies).

3 Mining and resource extraction is less than 10 per cent and agriculture less than 5 per cent of Canada's GDP; Statistics Canada, 2014 (www.statcan.gc.ca/tables-tableaux/sum-som/l01/cst01/gdps04a-eng.htm).

4 Term often attributed to Congressman Tip O'Neil's *All Politics is Local: And Other Rules of the Game*, 1995.

5 The *Sea Venture* was on her maiden voyage *en route* to provision starving settlers in Jamestown, VA, when wrecked on Bermuda's reef by a hurricane (all passengers survived).

6 See Table 2.1 The projected total global wealth increase from 2000 to 2100 is more than 13 times.

7 The issue of complexity theory, the Balinese rice programme and network analysis is well documented in *Aid on the Edge of Chaos* by Ben Ramalingam (Oxford University Press, 2013). (The challenge of cities is peripherally mentioned – the lessons appear readily transferrable.)

8 BBC News, Saturday October 17, 2009.

9 Kiribati bought 6,000 acres of land in Fiji to protect its food security and President Anote Tong predicted Kiribati will become uninhabitable from rising sea levels in 30 to 60 years (*New York Times*, March 28, 2014).

10 BBC News, December 12, 2013.

11 Based on the $10.2 trillion loss in the US alone (estimated by John Carney, Business Insider, 3 February, 2009) and similar capital drops around the world.

12 Sustainability and safety is enhanced at an individual city level through a greater focus on resilience (system review, long-term, self-regulating, dynamic) that encompasses, rather than replaces, risk management (single risks, short-term security, direct interventions, continuous oversight) – from Erisman et al. (2015), *Nature*.

13 A. Bertaud (2011) Mumbai FAR/FSI conundrum; available at http://alain-bertaud.com/

14 Reprinted with permission and adapted from 'Letters to a Young Engineer' 2015, University of Ontario Institute of Technology.

15 Sustainability is defined here as the operational state of a system, e.g. urban or global economy or wetland that ensures maintenance of key attributes (productivity and processes). Sustainable development as a political construct endeavors to maximize human well-being (current and future generations) while safeguarding the productive capacity of planetary systems.

References

American Society of Civil Engineers, 2006. *The Vision for Civil Engineering in 2025*. Reston, VA: American Society of Civil Engineers.

Angel, S., Parent, J., Civco, D., Blei, A. and Potere, D., 2011. The Dimensions of Global Urban Expansion: Estimates and Projections for All Countries, 2000–2050. *Progress in Planning*, 75, pp.53–107.

Bakhtiari, S., 2014. Risk Management: A Powerful Instrument for Sustainable Development. *OIDA International Journal of Sustainable Development*, 07(05), pp.95–104.

Batty, M., 2013. A Theory of City Size. *Science*, 340, pp.1418–19

Bettencourt, L. and West, G., 2010. A unified theory of urban living. *Nature*, 467, pp.912-913.

Bettencourt, L., 2013. The Origins of Scaling in Cities. *Science*, 340, pp.1438–41.

Diamond, J., 2005. *Collapse: How Societies Choose to Fail or Succeed*. London: Penguin.

Fawcett, A.A., Iyer, G., Clarke, L.E., Edmonds, J.A., Hultman, N.E., McJeon, H.C., Rogelj, J., Schuler, R., Alsalam, J., Asrar, G.R., Creason, J., Jeong, M., McFarland, J., Mundra, A. and Shi, W., 2015. Can Paris Pledges Avert Severe Climate Change? *Science, Science Express*, November 26, 2015. DOI: 10.1126/science.aad5761

Fabry, J., Hansen, B., Walker, D., Liverman, K., Richardson, P., Crutzen, J. and Foley, A., 2009. Safe Operating Space for Humanity. *Nature*, 461, pp.472–5.

Gagnon, B., Leduc, R. and Savard, L., 2008. Sustainable Development in Engineering: A Review of Principles and Definition of a Conceptual Framework. *Groupe de Recherche en Économie et Développement International Working Paper 08–18*.

Gigerenzer, G., 2004. Dread Risk, September 11, and Fatal Traffic Accidents. *Psychological Science*, 15(4), pp.286–7.

Goldberg, D. and Somerville, M., 2014. *A Whole New Engineer: The Coming Revolution in Engineering Education*. Douglas, MI: ThreeJoy Associates, Inc.

Gupta, C., 2014. Sustainability, Self-reliance and Aloha Aina: The Case of Molokai, Hawai'i. *International Journal of Sustainable Development & World Ecology*, 21(5), pp.389–97.

Hayward, S.J., Holt Gomez, V. and Sterrer, W., eds, 1981. *Bermuda's Delicate Balance: People and the Environment*. Hamilton, Bermuda: Bermuda National Trust.

Hoornweg, D., Sugar, L. and Trejos Gomez, C.L., 2011. Cities and Greenhouse Gas Emissions: Moving Forward. *Environment & Urbanization*, 23(1), pp.207–28.

Kennedy, C., Stewart, I., Facchini, A., Cersosimo, I., Mele, R., Chen, B., Uda, M., Kansal, A., Chiu, A., Kim, K., Dubeux, C., La Rovere, E., Cunha, B., Pincetl, S., Keirstead, J., Barles, S., Pusaka, S., Gunawan, J., Adegbile, M., Nazariha, M., Hoque, S., Marcotullio, P., Otharán, F., Genena, T., Ibrahim, N., Farooqui, R., Cervantes, G. and Sahin, A., 2015. Energy and material flows of megacities, *Proceedings of the National Academy of Sciences*, 112(19), pp.5985–90.

Lansing, S. and Kremer, J., 1993. Emergent Properties of Balinese Water Temple Networks: Coadaptation on a Rugged Fitness Landscape. *American Anthropologist*, 95(1), pp.97–114.

MacArthur, R. and Wilson, E. O., 1967. *The Theory of Island Biogeography*. Princeton, NJ: Princeton University Press.

Meadows, D., Randers, J. and Meadows, D., 2004. *Limits to Growth: The 30-Year Update*. White River Junction, VT: Chelsea Green Publishing.

Meadows, D., 2008. *Thinking in Systems: A Primer*. White River Junction, VT: Chelsea Green Publishing.

Ostrom, E., 1995. Incentives, Rules of the Game, and Development. In *Proceedings of the Annual World Bank Conference on Development Economics 1995*. Washington, DC: The World Bank.

Ostrom, E., 2009. A General Framework for Analyzing Sustainability of Social–Ecological Systems. *Science*, 325(5939), pp.419–22.

Ostrom, E., 2014. A Polycentric Approach for Coping with Climate Change. *Annals of Economics and Finance*, 15(1), pp.97–134.

Petroski, H., 2010. *The Essential Engineer: Why Science Alone Will Not Solve Our Global Problems*. New York: Alfred A. Knopf.

Poveda, C. and Lipsett, M., 2014. An Integrated Approach for Sustainability Assessment: The Wa-Pa-Su Project Sustainability Rating System. *International Journal of Sustainable Development & World Ecology*, 21(1), pp.85–98.

Rockström, J., Steffen, W., Noone, K., Persson, Å., Chapin, F.S., Lambin, E., Lenton, T.M., Scheffer, M., Folke, C., Schellnhuber, H., Nykvist, B., de Wit, C.A., Hughes, T., van der Leeuw, S., Rodhe, H., Sörlin, S., Snyder, P.K., Costanza, R., Svedin, U., Falkenmark, M., Karlberg, L., Corell, R.W., Fabry, V.J., Hansen, J., Walker, B., Liverman, D., Richardson, K., Crutzen, P. and Foley J., 2009. Planetary Boundaries: Exploring the Safe Operating Space for Humanity. *Ecology and Society*, 14(2).

Solnit, R., 2009. *A Paradise Built in Hell: The Extraordinary Communities That Arise in Disaster*. London: Penguin.

Steffen, W., Richardson, K., Rockström, J., Cornell, S., Fetzer, I., Bennett, E., Biggs, R., Carpenter, S., de Vries, W., de Wit, C., Folke, C., Gerten, D., Heinke, J., Mace, G., Persson, L., Ramanathan, V., Reyers, B. and Sörlin, S., 2015. Planetary boundaries: Guiding human development on a changing planet. *Science*, 347(6223).

Trapenberg-Frick, K., Weinzimmer, D. and Waddel, P., 2015. The Politics of Sustainable Development Opposition: State Legislative Efforts to Stop the United Nation's Agenda 21 in the United States. *Urban Studies*, 52(2), pp.209–232.

World Commission on Environment and Development, 1987. *Our Common Future*. London, Oxford University Press.

2 Sustainable development for cities and citizens

The earth's is a story of change and adaptation. For example, during the mid-Cretaceous, some 100 million years ago, temperatures were 8° to 15°C warmer than today (Figure 2.1). A host of tropical flora and fauna, like ferns and alligators, lived in warm, shallow seas at what is today Siberia and Canada's Arctic. During the Cretaceous, the mean atmospheric concentration of CO_2 was about 1,700 ppm. The Jurassic period of 200 million to 145 million years ago, which preceded the Cretaceous, was equally warm, and is best known as the Age of Reptiles, when dinosaurs roamed the earth. By the beginning of the Jurassic, the supercontinent Pangaea had begun to rift into smaller landmasses.

The Cretaceous period ended abruptly about 66 million years ago when a meteorite is believed to have impacted the Yucatan Peninsula. With widespread extinction, especially of reptiles (the end of dinosaurs), the Cretaceous gave way to the Cenozoic – also known as the Age of Mammals.

More recently, the earth's geology and climate is a story of Ice Ages. The earth has had at least five major glaciations.[1] The last one, the Quaternary (Pleistocene), started about 2.6 million years ago, and saw several advances and retreats of major ice sheets covering much of the Northern Hemisphere.[2] Currently, the world is experiencing an interglacial period, and is still in an Ice Age because at least one permanent ice sheet (Antarctica) has continuously existed for the last 2.6 million years. The current relatively warm and stable inter-glacial Holocene has enabled humanity to practice agriculture and prosper for the last 10,000 years.

Sustainable development is an integral part of human history. Table 2.1 provides a historical timeline of sustainable development, tracing its origins back to the beginning of the Holocene (about 11,700 years ago), when climate stabilized to what largely exists today. The stable climate supported the emergence of human settlements, domestication of plants and animals, and human populations flourished across the world. Total human population at the start of the Holocene was likely around 5 million, up from about 2 million 50,000 years ago (Lowe and Walker, 2014). With a more stable climate and the introduction of agriculture and tools, the human population grew quickly to about 300 million at the start of the Common Era, and about 500 million by 1600.

Human impact on the natural environment was significant as far back as the start of the Holocene. Human predation likely extirpated more than half of all

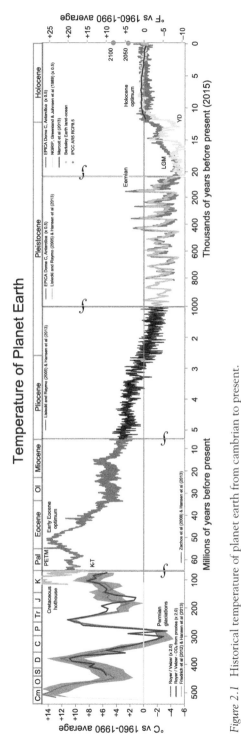

Figure 2.1 Historical temperature of planet earth from cambrian to present.

Source: Fergus, 2014.

megafauna (> 40 kg), especially in Americas and Australia. Unease over declining wildlife populations must have dogged humans as early as predation began; however, the relatively small populations and ability to move to areas with more plentiful resources (or kill and overthrow competing tribes) limited concerns over the shift to the Anthropocene.

The Anthropocene (the 'Era of Humankind') started in the late eighteenth century (based on CO_2 and CH_4 in ice cores), when human impacts started to bring about irrevocable changes to the planet's key systems, as evidenced through stratigraphic records (Crutzen, 2002). The emergence of permanent settlements is a key turning point in the overall scale of human impact on the natural environment.

Economic development

In reviewing sustainable development and its underpinnings of economic development, a key historical point occurs at the Industrial Revolution. Around the turn of the eighteenth to the nineteenth century, people, particularly those in Britain and Europe, started using significantly more resources (especially fossil fuels), and they became very rich. Figure 2.2 highlights the massive growth of wealth in Western industrialized countries. Around 1800, China's and India's economies (as shown by share of global GDP), traditionally the world's largest for the preceding 2,000 years, were quickly eclipsed.

Prior to 1800, the average human spent about $3 per day. Today, that amount is over $100 per day (in constant dollars). And world population increased from less than a billion at the start of the nineteenth century to more than seven billion people today (Table 2.1). This massive increase in wealth was less likely a function of the Industrial Revolution, imperialism or urbanization than it was a reflection of changing attitudes and the new Enlightenment ideas of human dignity and liberty. Making money in trade and mercantile, opening markets and empowering a rapidly growing middle class, or 'Bourgeois', were the key drivers of wealth generation (McCloskey, 2011).

The overthrow of the medieval guild system was an indispensable early step in the rise of freedom in the Western world (Friedman, 1962). Today, on a smaller scale, and mainly emerging in cities, new initiatives such as Uber taxis and Airbnb accommodations are the source of similar disruption. Much of this is enabled through the Internet, and often bypasses existing licensing and regulatory requirements.

'Creative destruction' (aka Kondratiev waves) with periodic advances in large-scale technology, as outlined by Schumpeter (1942), set societies on paths to prosperity. Wholesale changes through new technologies are of sufficient scale to overcome inertia and entrenched interests. The broad deployment of technologies is enabled by shifts in 'social tectonics' and organizational reforms. For example, several types of automobiles existed for decades prior to widespread adoption of Ford's Model T. The periodicity between Schumpeter's waves is declining. Cities are key drivers for much of this innovation – both the need for, and provision of, innovation.

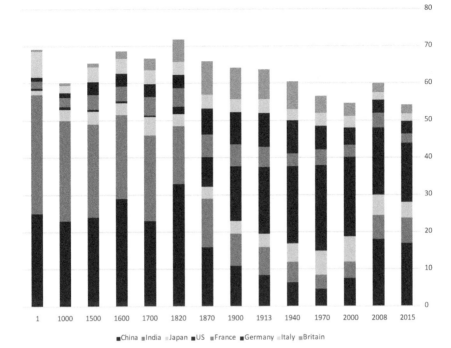

Figure 2.2 A history of world GDP (percentage of total, 1990 $ at PPP/*PPP (2016 international $).

Source: The Maddison Project (2013); adapted from *The Economist*, 2010; *data from The World Bank, 2015.

The 'rich is good' mindset, with a vibrant middle class and technological advances, is well reflected in the more affluent countries of the OECD. China's 1978 economic liberalization, and India's similar opening up in 1991, is now promoting similar wealth creation in Asia. Growing cities, the wealth to finance necessary urban infrastructure, and associated urban growth and environmental degradation are side effects (and at times drivers) of the massive increase in wealth.

An important 'chicken-and-egg' aspect of this growing wealth is the concomitant development of major civil (urban) infrastructure. This can be highlighted in London and Amsterdam, for example. As wealth increased, sanitation, drainage and transportation systems grew in lock-step. Building cities facilitated more wealth generation, which in turn led to more city building.

GDP became the main measure of economic development; however, many questioned its merits as a metric to fully reflect a society's overall well-being.

Table 2.1 Timeline of sustainable development (emergence of the Anthropocene)

~ 200,000 years ago: appearance of modern Homo sapiens.

~ 74,000 years ago: massive volcanic eruption of Mt Toba, Indonesia, believed to have contributed to 1,000-year 'volcanic winter' and global cooling of some 3°C. Populations decline; genetic 'bottleneck' with fewer than 10,000 humans worldwide.

50,000–10,000 BCE: Quaternary Period (Pleistocene to Holocene within the Cenozoic Era); megafauna extinctions (more than half of all species >40kg, especially Australia and Americas – human predation a significant contributor). ~ 11,700 years ago, last Ice Age ends, giving rise to modern climate era and flourishing of humanity (considered start of the Holocene); sea level 120 m below current levels. Rock pigeons believed to be first domesticated animals about 10,000 years ago, when human population ~1 million. Early Anthropocene ~ 8000 BCE (from agriculture).

7000 BCE: Jericho (pop. 2,000) thought to be longest continuously inhabited city.

~ 5500 BCE: human population 5 million.

4000 BCE: Feng Shui philosophy of harmony between environment and physical landscape.

3500–1500 BCE: invention of writing in Mesopotamia, Egypt and central China.

3000 BCE: Knossos, Crete, believed to establish first landfill (midden); ~ invention of the wheel in Southeast Asia.
3000 BCE: origins of Hinduism.

500 BCE: Athens introduces law requiring waste be dumped at least a mile from city; Sun Tzu's The Art of War and strategy of resource use and planning; noticeable ecological decline of the Fertile Crescent.
c.600–400 BCE: Birth of Siddhartha Gautama, Buddha, in Lumbini, Nepal.
c.500 BCE: End of compilation of the Jewish Torah.
c.400 BCE–100 CE: Compilation and canonisation of the Tanakh (Jewish Bible).

220–206 BCE: Qin Shi Huang, the first Emperor, builds major part of the Great Wall of China – some parts constructed as early as the 7th century BCE.

202 BCE: Travel begins on the Silk Road.

300 CE: Beginning of the Golden Age of Hinduism.

c.350: First complete copy of Bible with New Testament.

c.376: Influx of Goths into the Roman Empire, thought to be pivotal point in its decline.

c.650: Quran first compiled by Uthman, the third Caliph.

c.825: First appearance in print of numerical analysis by mathematicians al-Khwarizmi and al-Kindi (introduction of algebra, trigonometry, imported to Italy by Fibonacci 300 years later).

859: Fatima al-Fihri founds first degree-granting university in Fez, Morocco.

960–1279: Song dynasty flourishes in China; first to use of paper currency; earliest use of inoculations against smallpox, spreads to Ottoman Empire (becomes widespread post-1721 when Mary Wortley Montagu – wife of British Ambassador to Turkey – inoculates her own children).

1215: Magna Carta establishes English constitutional tradition.

1271: Marco Polo, aged 17, sets off to Asia with his father and uncle.

1347: Stora Kopparberg, Sweden, oldest commercial corporation, receives Royal Charter.

c.1350: Middle Ages end and the Renaissance begins in Europe (ends ~ 1550).

1366: City of Paris forces butchers to dispose of animal waste outside of the city.

1388: English Parliament forbids throwing of garbage into ditches, rivers and waters.

c.1400–1800: Hanseatic League of cities in northern Europe supports commerce and defence; replaced largely by emergence of nations, e.g. Sweden, Denmark, Netherlands, UK, Germany.

1413: University of St Andrews founded, likely the first to issue professional degrees (MD).

1440: Guttenberg's printing press established (the Bible first book printed).

1472: Italy's Banca Monte dei Paschi di Siena opens (oldest surviving bank).

1492: Columbus lands on Hispaniola and sets up first New World settlement at Santo Domingo.

1500: Approximately 14,500 languages spoken in the world – there are fewer than 7,000 today.

1517: Martin Luther begins the Protestant Reformation.

1522: Magellan ends first voyage around the world.

1532: Niccolo Machiavelli's The Prince written.

c.1540: Evidence of atmospheric pollution from colonial mining in Peru and Bolivia.

1543: Nicolaus Copernicus publishes De revolutionibus orbium coelestium (On the Revolutions of the Heavenly Spheres)

1570–1620: Noticeable drop in CO_2 emissions linked to death of some 50 million indigenous Americans, triggered by arrival of Europeans, and forests reclaiming 65 million Ha of abandoned agricultural lands.

1602: Dutch East India Company founded, leading to world's first stock exchange in Amsterdam (shares returned approx. 16% p.a. 1602–50).

1607: Founding of Jamestown VI, oldest of the original 13 colonies and key conduit for invasive species, e.g. dandelions, tobacco, earth worms, honey bees, purple loosestrife, common sparrow.

1609: Bank of Amsterdam established, thought to be the first modern central bank; Hugo Grotius publishes Mare Liberum proposing international waters, leading to UK and France declaring territorial waters of 5 km (effective cannon range).

1637: Height of tulip mania; single bulbs sold for as much as 10 times annual salaries (generally recognized as first example of a 'speculative bubble').

1640: Isaac Walton's The Compleat Angler (fishing and conservation) written; first global convergence of the value of silver, standardizing the metal's value.

1648: Treaty of Westphalia and the rise of modern system of states; end of Thirty Years' War.

1651: Thomas Hobbes' Leviathan written.

1662: Extinction of dodo bird, Mauritius.

1665–6: London's 'great plague' kills 100,000; the great fire begins September 2, 1666 in Pudding Lane and burns for four days, leaving some 200,000 homeless.

1670: Hudson Bay Company established (world's largest landowner with 15 per cent of North America).

1679: Antoni van Leeuwenhoek in a letter to the Royal Society suggests earth's maximum carrying capacity is 13.4 billion humans.

1690: Gov. William Penn requires Pennsylvania settlers to preserve one acre of trees for every five acres cleared; publication of John Locke's Two Treatises and Essay Concerning Human Understanding.

1700: Per capita GDP ~ $170; average life expectancy ~ 36 years; start of tea being a major commodity in England; ~5% of global ice-free land intensively used by humans.

1720: In India, hundreds in Khejadali killed trying to protect trees from the Maharaja of Jodphur (considered origins of twentieth-century Chipko movement).

1755: Immanuel Kant's Universal Natural History and Theory of the Heavens published.

1775: Percival Pott, an English surgeon, observes that chimney sweeps develop cancer through contact with soot (first recognition of environmental factors and cancer).

1762: Jean-Jacques Rousseau argues in The Social Contract for city-states and personal freedoms. Voltaire's writings (1731–64) critique European politics (esp. French).

1771: John Smeaton (who built Eddystone Lighthouse) declares himself first 'civil engineer'.

1776: Adam Smith's The Wealth of Nations published.

1770s–1830s: Beginnings of the Industrial Revolution in Britain (textiles, steam power, iron); peak of transatlantic slavery.

1779: The possibly fictitious Ned Ludd (Edward Ludham?) allegedly destroys textile machinery, giving rise to Luddite movement; Johann Friedrich Blumenbach divides the human species into five races (Caucasian, Mongoloid, Malay, Negroid, American – Australoid added 1940s and Capoid early 1960s).

Table 2.1 Continued

1781: James Watt patents a steam engine.

1788: James Hutton's Theory of the Earth; or an Investigation of the Laws observable in the Composition, Dissolution, and Restoration of Land upon the Globe published; Royal Society of Edinburgh founded (credited as start of modern geology, although Abu al-Rayhan al-Biruni, 973–1048, was one of the earliest geologists, with works including writings on the geology of India).

1798: Thomas Malthus's An Essay on the Principles of Population published.

1791: Le Chapelier Law abolishes guilds in France.

1795: Immanuel Kant's Perpetual Peace published.

1800: Per capita GDP ~ $200; average life expectancy ~ 40 years.

1807: Britain bans African slave trade; steamship invented.

1815: Mt Tambora, Indonesia, erupts, killing 90,000, globally precipitating 'year without a summer'; Congress of Vienna and the end of Napoleonic Wars in Europe; William Smith publishes geological map of Great Britain; Rhine Commission – the world's oldest international organization – established.

1817: First roller coaster opens in Paris (with wheels locked to track); prior to this were similar ice sled rides in St Petersburg.

1818: Baron von Drais patents Laufmaschine (bicycle), developed to replace horses that starved during Mt Tambora's volcanic winter.

1820: Approximate start of fossil fuel- (coal)-driven aspects of Industrial Revolution; atmospheric CO_2 concentration ~ 280 ppm; global population 1 billion.

1830: Charles Lyell's Principles of Geology published.

1836: Ralph Waldo Emerson's Nature published.

1842: Edwin Chadwick's report Sanitary Condition of the Labouring Population of Great Britain supports the 1834 Poor Law Act.

1845: John Snow produces London's 'ghost map' linking cholera to a contaminated water source; Alexander von Humboldt's Volume I of Kosmos published.

1846: First mechanically drilled oil well, Baku, Azerbaijan (Oil Springs, ON dug by hand in 1858 and Titus, PN percussive drill and 'oil gusher' in 1859 – led to today's commercial oil industry).

1848: Jules Dupuit (an economist and engineer) credited with first use of cost–benefit analysis; Public Health Act in Britain begins waste regulation (amended 1875 assigning duty to local authorities); Karl Marx and Friedrich Engels write The Communist Manifesto.

1850: First submarine telegraph cable (English Channel); Atlantic Ocean bridged eight years later (Newfoundland to Ireland).

1853: First international meteorological conference (Brussels); US Navy recommends standardized measurement protocols (US Weather Bureau established in 1870, Meteorological Services Canada in 1871, International Meteorological Organization in 1873).

1854: Chief Seattle's famous open letter (speech), including 'Man did not weave the web of life, he is merely a strand in it. Whatever he does to the web, he does to himself'; Elisha Otis demonstrates his 'fail safe platform' at the Crystal Palace of New York's World Fair – start of modern elevators (first passenger elevator 488 Broadway, NY, 1857); Henry David Thoreau retreats to the woods near Concorde, MA and pens Walden.

1855: Limited Liability Act, UK; Thomas Cook offers first international tour package.

1858: Alfred Wallace publishes on natural selection; Charles Darwin writes The Origin of Species (1859); year of the 'Great Stink' in London – Parliament commissions Joseph Bazalgette to build London's sewer system.

1862: First products made from plastic (widespread manufacture begins in the 1930s); John Ruskin's Unto This Last published; Louis Pasteur establishes germ theory.

1863: London's tube opens (first in world); John Tyndall gives public lecture On Radiation Through the Earth's Atmosphere, explaining the greenhouse effect; International Committee of the Red Cross, one the first global NGOs, established.

1864: George Perkins Marsh's Man and Nature: Physical Geography as Modified by Human Action published.

1865: International Telegraph Union – first global regulatory agency.

1866: Ernst Haeckel, a German zoologist, coins the term ecology.

1869: Suez Canal opens.

1872: Yellowstone Park established (Yosemite in 1890); Robert Smith describes acid rain.

1884: Greenwich Mean Time established.

1885: Banff Park established; Canadian Pacific Railway completed.

1886: George Grinnell founds the Audubon Society.

1888: Nikola Tesla sells his patent for polyphase AC induction motor to George Westinghouse (Westinghouse and Tesla win bid, over Edison and DC power, to light World Expo in Chicago, 1893).

1889: Eiffel Tower (324m) overtakes Washington Monument as world's tallest structure; overtaken in 1930 by the Chrysler Building, New York.

1889–90: Global flu pandemic (1,000,000 dead).

1890: American bison face extinction, likely fewer than 1,000 animals (est. 60,000,000 in 1491).

1891: Telluride, CO first community to receive AC supplied (hydro) electricity.

1892: Sierra Club starts (Henry Senger of Berkeley and John Muir).

1893: New Zealand becomes first country to give women the right to vote.

1895: Gillette invents first disposable razor.

1896: Svante Arrhenius, a Swedish chemist, calculates how changes in levels of atmospheric CO_2 could alter temperature through the greenhouse effect (Nobel Laureate 1903); Hamilton, ON and Buffalo, NY receive transmitted AC (hydro) electric power (from DeCew Falls and Niagara Falls respectively – ends the first 'standards war' in favour of AC transmission over DC); first modern Olympics.

1898: Gifford Pinchot, US Secretary of Interior, encourages 'wise use'.

1899: Thorstein Veblen coins the term conspicuous consumption.

1900: Global GDP $2 trillion (about $680 per capita); average life expectancy ~ 48 years; less than 15% of world's population urban.

1901: First awarding of Nobel Prizes.

1902: Willis Carrier invents air conditioning.

1903: Wright brothers' inaugural flight.

1905: The term smog coined by Henry Des Voeux in London.

1906: Vilfredo Pareto (Italy) observes that 80% of land is owned by 20% of his compatriots.

1907: Francis Galton, after visiting a London livestock fair, publishes in Nature on the uncanny accuracy of 'crowd sourced' weight estimate of an ox (1198 lb vs mean of 1207 lb).

1908: Ford's first Model T.

1909: Canada–US Boundary Water Treaty, leads to International Joint Commission 1912 and Niagara River Water Diversion Treaty 1950; President Theodore Roosevelt convenes North American Conservation Conference (US, Canada, Newfoundland, Mexico).

1912: Alfred Wagner introduces concept of 'Continental Drift', corroborated by Tuzo Wilson, in theory of plate tectonics ('Evidence from Islands on the Spreading of Ocean Floors', Nature 1963 – term Pangaea coined in a 1927 symposium); Corrado Gini publishes Variability and Mutability (leading to Gini coefficient).

1913: First household refrigerator.

1914: Panama Canal opens; last known passenger pigeon, a female named Martha, dies at the Cincinnati zoo; first scheduled commercial passenger flight.

1915: Ecological Society of America founded, followed by Ecologists Union (1946) and Nature Conservancy (1950).

Table 2.1 Continued

1917: October (Bolshevik) Revolution in Russia.

1918: Fritz Haber receives Nobel Prize for the synthesis of ammonia.

1918–20: Global flu pandemic (75,000,000 dead).

1920: League of Nations established by Treaty of Versailles (USA abstains).

1925: General Motors and Standard Oil spokesmen claim in Public Health Service hearings there are no alternatives to leaded gasoline as an anti-knock additive (Scientific American reported in 1918 that alcohol–gasoline was 'universally' expected for anti-knock).

1927: Sir Arthur Tansley coins the term ecosystem; global population 2 billion; development of the television.

1929: Aluminium foil invented; Swann Chemical Company develops PCBs; Wall Street crash; Alexander Fleming discovers penicillin.

1930: Mahatma Gandhi leads Salt March from Ahmedabad to Dandi; Sigmund Freud publishes Civilization and its Discontents.

1930s: Franklin D. Roosevelt's New Deal includes strong ecological component (designed to overcome soil erosion).

1931: Floods in China (up to 4 million deaths).

1933: Gerhard Domagk synthesizes prontosil (Nobel Laureate 1939), ushering in wide spread use of antibiotics; convention on the preservation of fauna and flora.

1936: US Corps of Engineers initiates use of cost–benefit analysis (e.g. Federal Navigation Act).

1937: Last known Balinese tiger shot.

1939: First jet plane, German He 178; at World's Fair, New York, General Motors promotes 'Futurama', the 'new and attractive' (car-dependent) suburbs.

1942: Joseph Schumpeter publishes Capitalism, Socialism and Democracy and coins the term creative destruction; Oxfam founded; invention of the computer.

1943: Aerosol can invented.

1944: Bretton Woods Conference – IMF and World Bank created (GDP becomes a standard metric for a country's economy); von Neumann and Morgenstern's Theory of Games and Economic Behavior published.

1945: United Nations established (replaces the League of Nations, 45 member nations); UNESCO established (November convening conference held at Institute of Civil Engineers, London); first test detonation of atomic bomb (Trinity site, New Mexico, July 16) – nuclear testing provides clear global stratigraphic marker between 1945 and 1963, when Nuclear Test Ban takes effect after some 500 nuclear blasts; World War Two ends – more than two-thirds of today's 195 countries did not exist as sovereign states or within existing boundaries.

1946: Ten Thousand Villages, Mennonite Central Committee, begins selling locally sourced socially preferable products; convention for regulation of whaling; Electronic Numerical Integrator and Computer, ENIAC, announced (based on Alan Turing's 1936 paper).

1947: International Organization for Standardization (ISO) founded in Geneva (replaces the International Federation of the National Standardizing Associations founded in 1926); Canadian Wildlife Service; UN introduces international guidelines of economic indicators (by country); Marshall Plan announced; GATT formed.

1948: IUCN founded in Fontainebleau; IMF publishes first balance of payments manual; Organization for European Economic Cooperation (OEEC) created (mainly to administer the Marshall Plan) – reformed to Organization for Economic Cooperation and Development (OECD) in 1961.

1949: Aldo Leopold, A Sand County Almanac (introduces 'land ethics'); NATO established.

1950: Two Canadians at Union Carbide invent polyethylene garbage bags; 84 countries; approximate start of 'the great acceleration' – massive increase in materials such as black carbon, cement and plastic; 30% of world's population urban.

1952: London's 'great smog' leaves at least 4,000 dead.

1953: Hooker Chemical sells Love Canal site to Niagara Falls School Board for $1 with a deed that explicitly declares presence of waste. Niagara Falls Gazette extensively chronicles waste issue 1976–8. In August 1978 President Carter declares the site a Federal Health Emergency (along with Times Beach, MI. Love Canal largely responsible for creation of US site remediation 'Superfund').

1954: First nuclear power plant, Obninsk, USSR; Harrison Brown's The Challenge of Man's Future published.

1955: Watson and Crick publish double helix structure of DNA; Bandung Conference launches Non-Aligned Movement; first McDonald's restaurant opens.

1956: Minamata disease (mercury poisoning) first discovered in Minamata, Japan; first use of intermodal shipping on Ideal X (Newark to Houston), now about 17 Mn containers worldwide regulated by ISO 668 (dimensions) and ISO 6346 (labelling); Hubbert's peak theory (and curve) introduced in 'Nuclear Energy and the Fossil Fuels' to American Petroleum Institute.

1957: Thalidomide first marketed in Germany (causes more than 10,000 birth defects worldwide before drug sales discontinued in 1962); Asian flu leaves 2,000,000 dead; European Economic Community (EEC) replaces the European Coal and Steel Community (1951); Sputnik satellite launched.

1958: John K. Galbraith's The Affluent Society published.

1959: Moses Abramovitz questions if GDP accurately measures a society's overall well-being; Antarctic Treaty.

1960: Vance Packard's The Waste Makers published; OPEC founded by Iran, Iraq, Kuwait, Saudi Arabia and Venezuela; global population 3 billion; 91 countries worldwide.

1961: World Wildlife Fund (WWF) founded, Switzerland (internationally changes names to World Wide Fund for Nature in 1986 but WWF US and Canada maintain original name); Lewis Mumford's The City in History: Its Origins, its Transformations, and its Prospects published; Jane Jacobs, The Death and Life of Great American Cities (introduces the term 'social capital'); Yuri Gagarin first person to orbit the earth.

1962: Rachel Carson's Silent Spring and Thomas Kuhn's Structure of Scientific Revolutions published; launch of the first communications satellite.

1963: Martin Luther King's 'I Have a Dream' speech in Washington, DC; global human population growth peaks at 2.19% per year; Edward Lorenz publishes a paper Deterministic Nonperiodic Flow, giving rise to the 'Butterfly Effect'; issuance of the first Eurobond.

1964: Norman Borlaug director of International Wheat Improvement Program, Mexico (leads to 'Green Revolution', receives 1970 Nobel Peace Prize); Olivetti's personal computer (PC) launched at New York's World Fair.

1965: Oxfam launches 'Helping-by-Selling'.

1967: Environmental Defense Fund (goes to court to stop Suffolk Co. Mosquito Control Commission from spraying DDT); Torrey Canyon oil tanker runs aground near Cornwall, UK; Churchman introduces the term wicked problem; European Community replaces EEC.

1968: Publication of Paul Ehrlich's Population Bomb; Garrett Hardin introduces Tragedy of the Commons (follow-on essay in 1976, carrying capacity as an ethical concept, 'Lifeboat Ethics'); Aureilio Pueccei founds the Club of Rome; Hong Kong flu leaves 1,000,000 dead; first UN Biosphere Conference in Paris (hosted by UNESCO); World Federation of Engineering Organizations (WFEO).

1969: Friends of the Earth; Pollution Probe, Toronto; Cuyahoga River, OH catches on fire again (leads to Clean Water Act, Great Lakes Water Quality Agreement, US EPA); Icelandic herring stock collapses; Canada's Pearson Commission on World Bank and international development (leads to IDRC); Neal Armstrong steps on the moon; first Boeing 747.

1970: International Development Research Center (Gov. of Canada); first Earth Day(s) (coins the term 'sustainable society' – some 20 million people participate peacefully in US); 134 countries in the world.

Table 2.1 Continued

1971: Greenpeace starts in Vancouver – replaces Don't Make a Wave Committee, 1970; International Institute of Economic Development (London, UK); Rene Dubos and Barbara Ward's Only One Earth published; Ralph Nader et al.'s Action for Change launches more than 100 college campus Public Interest Research Groups; Pierre Wack begins scenario planning at Royal Dutch Shell; OECD recommends 'polluter pay principle'; UN Conference on the Human Environment, Stockholm (114 countries participate, 109 recommendations including creation of UNEP); Klaus Schwab founds the World Economic Forum (WEF) in Geneva; Médecins Sans Frontières founded in France, receives Nobel Peace Prize 1999; first email.

1972: UNCHE held in Stockholm launches UN Environment Program (Maurice Strong chairs UNCHE and first Executive Director of UNEP); Club of Rome publishes Limits to Growth; BRAC (formerly Bangladesh Rural Advancement Committee); first 'blue marble' photograph of earth from Apollo 17; Goldsmith and Allen Blueprint for Survival; convention for protection of world cultural and natural heritage; Archie Cochrane publishes Effectiveness and Efficiency: Random Reflections on Health Services, on the Importance of Using Evidence to Provide Equitable Health Care.

1973: OPEC oil crises; E.F. Schumacher publishes Small is Beautiful; Ignacy Sachs founds the International Research Centre on Environment and Development (CIRED) in Paris; women in Himalayan villages begin the Chipko movement to protect trees from commercial logging; Convention on International Trade in Endangered Species of Wild Fauna and Flora (CITES) adopted; MARPOL Convention (pollution from shipping); first handheld mobile phone demonstrated (Motorola).

1974: Rowland and Moilna publish on CFC and ozone (Nobel Laureates 1995) – data on CFCs from James Lovelock; Club of Rome's Mankind at the Turning Point; Worldwatch Institute founded by Lester Brown with $500,000 grant from Rockefeller Brothers Fund; Bucharest conference 'Science and Technology for Human Development'; TERI, Tata Energy Research Institute, established in Delhi by Dabari Seth; global population 4 billion.

1975: CITES comes into force; UN-Habitat and Human Settlements Foundation; first UN conference on women and development, Mexico City; MITS Altair PC kits.

1976: Eric Hoffer, The Ordeal of Change published; Body Shop founded by Anita Roddick; OECD releases Guidelines for Multinational Enterprises (voluntary standards for responsible business); Habitat I, Vancouver.

1977: Green Belt Movement starts in Kenya (Wangari Muta Maathai, founder, is awarded Nobel Peace Prize in 2004); Sullivan Principles created to help US companies apply pressure to South Africa to end apartheid; protests in the Philippines lead to the World Bank's withdrawal of support for four dams on the Chico River; Commodore PET.

1978: Lester Brown's The Twenty Ninth Day published; World Bank's first World Development Report (WDR), Prospects for Growth and Alleviation of Poverty; UN-Habitat established (replaces UN HHSF, 1975); China reforms (opens) its economy; year in which Genuine Progress Indicator peaked globally – declining ever since (on average GPI does not increase beyond a GDP/ capita ~ $7000/ca); Manuel Castells' City, Class and Power published.

1979: Three Mile Island nuclear accident; James Lovelock's The Gaia Hypothesis; Ralf Dahrendorf's Life Chances; Greenpeace International, Amsterdam; introduction of China's one-child policy; NTT Japan launches first cellular network.

1980: World Conservation Strategy (IUCN); Our Common Crises (Willy Brandt, chair); first GMO patent issued (a bacterium that digests crude oil – US Supreme Court rules to permit patenting of life forms); The Global 2000 Report to the President, commissioned by Jimmy Carter, released; Mount St Helens erupts.

1981: Bermuda's Delicate Balance (an applied systems approach to people and the environment); start of Ashoka: Innovators for the Public by Bill Drayton.

1982: World Resources Institute (Gus Speth starts with a $15 million grant from MacArthur Foundation); UN General Assembly approves World Charter of Nature; Our Common Security (Olof Palme, chair); Internet protocol (TCP/IP) introduced as standard protocol on the ARPNET; Latin America debt crises.

1983: Grameen Bank established, Bangladesh; WCED created; H.T. Odum introduces systems ecology (flow of materials); Kitchener first city in Canada to launch Blue Box recycling programme (>80% participation); Development Alternatives, India.

1984: Bhopal chemical leak (10,000 dead, 30,000 injured); Jane Jacobs publishes Cities and the Wealth of Nations; first Worldwatch State of the World; debt-for-nature swap endorsed by Thomas Lovejoy, WWF – first transaction between Conservation International and Bolivia (1987); Third World Network established.

1985: Metropolis city association (HQ Montreal); Antarctica ozone hole discovered; 'Responsible Care', Canadian Chemical Producers; France sinks Greenpeace Rainbow Warrior in New Zealand.

1986: Chernobyl nuclear accident.

1987: Montreal Protocol; Our Common Future (the Brundtland Report); atmospheric CO_2 concentration exceeds 350 ppm; ISO (quality management) 9000 series; global population 5 billion; Conservation International founded.

1988: Intergovernmental Panel on Climate Change created; Chico Mendez assassinated in Brazil; Canada's National Roundtable on Environment and Economy (closed March 31, 2013); Canadian Council of Resource and Environment Ministers (CCREM); Piper Alpha oil production platform, North Sea, explodes, killing 167; Canada–US Free Trade agreement (first of many bilateral trade agreements); E.O. Wilson, Biodiversity pubished.

1989: Stockholm Environment Institute; Exxon Valdez oil tanker runs aground; 'Endangered Earth' Time magazine's 'Planet of the Year'; Berlin Wall falls; Gallopoulos and Frosch popularize the term industrial ecology in special issue of Scientific American, 'Managing Planet Earth'; The Natural Step introduced by Karl-Henrik Robèrt; Basel Convention (controlling shipping of hazardous waste); extinction of golden toad, Costa Rica.

1990: International Institute of Sustainable Development (Winnipeg); ICLEI (HQ in Toronto); Canada's Green Plan for a Healthy Environment (with $3bn over 5 years funding); McDonalds restaurant opens Pushkin Square, Moscow (eventually becomes chain's busiest – est. 40,000 patrons/day – closes 2014, re-opens several months later); 'dolphin safe' labelling for tuna introduced; East and West Germany reunited; Nelson Mandela freed from prison; 166 countries worldwide.

1991: Global Environment Facility, Washington DC; Canadian cod fishery collapses; Government of Canada's National Waste Reduction Handbook; Environment Canada's State of Canada's Environment; Environmentally Sustainable Economic Development – Building on Brundtland, edited by Robert Goodland, Herman Daly, Salah El Serafy, Bernd von Droste; Wuppertal Institute, Germany; 'Acid Rain Treaty' signed between Canada and US; India reforms (opens) its economy; Soviet Union collapses; World Wide Web introduced.

1992: William Rees introduces ecological footprint; 'Earth Summit' in Rio de Janeiro (Agenda 21) – Convention on Biological Diversity signed, comes into force.

1993: Union of Concerned Scientists issues Warning to Humanity; Business Council for Sustainable Development (becomes WBCSD in 1995); Francis Fukuyama, The End of History published.

1993: Robert Putnam's Making Democracy Work; founding of the European Union (replaces EC); Forest Stewardship Council (FSC) founding assembly held in Toronto; first text message.

1994: John Elkington coins the term triple bottom line; Interface (a carpet company) founded by Ray Anderson; CEOs of seven largest tobacco companies state under oath before US House Subcommittee that they believe nicotine is not addictive; NAFTA enacted January 1; Amazon. com founded, first book sold 1995.

1995: World Trade Organization launched (replaces GATT, which commenced 1948); Francis Fukuyama's Trust; first Conference of the Parties (COP1) UNFCCC, Berlin; Graedel and Allenby's Industrial Ecology; Fourth World Conference on Women in Beijing; Ken Saro-Wiwa hanged in Nigeria; first transaction on eBay (broken laser pointer sold for $14.83); 1995 to 2015 > half of all concrete ever produced (50bn tonnes).

1996: ISO 14000 series (environmental management); Habitat II, Istanbul; Ismael Serageldin (World Bank), Sustainability and the Wealth of Nations; first commercial harvest of genetically modified crop; first cloning of a mammal (Dolly the sheep).

Table 2.1 Continued

1997: Kyoto Protocol adopted December 11; launch of Journal of Industrial Ecology; Global Reporting Initiative (GRI – sustainability guidelines released in 2000); Costanza et al. publish The Value of the World's Ecosystem Services and Natural Capital; Janine Benyus Biomimicry; WRI, Resource Flows: The Material Basis of Industrial Economies; forest fires burn more than 5 Mn Ha (largest global total in human history).

1998: Hunter and Amory Lovins with Ernst von Weizsäcker publish Factor Four (call to double wealth while halving resource consumption); Google launched; WBCSD-WRI GHG protocol; UN-Habitat and World Bank sign MOU to establish Cities Alliance (incl. 20 City Development Strategies first 3 years); European Union blocks imports of GMOs.

1999: Amartya Sen's Development as Freedom; Donella Meadows, Twelve Leverage Points (system intervention); Dow Jones Sustainability Indexes; Seattle anti-globalization protests; global population 6 billion; Euro introduced.

2000: Hernado de Soto, The Mystery of Capitalism published; Paul Crutzen (Nobel Laureate) with others popularizes the term Anthropocene (the geologic epoch 'Age of Man' to replace the Holocene); UN Millennium Development Goals; Carbon Disclosure Project; Jantzi Social Index (securities, Canada); Yale's Environmental Sustainability Index (becomes Environmental Performance Index, 2006); per capita GDP ~ $6500, global total ~ $41 trillion (total wealth $117 trillion – Credit Suisse); average life expectancy ~ 78 years; 187 countries; mineral extraction alone displaces ~ 57bn tonnes per year of sediments, exceeding the natural rate of riverborne sediment transport ~ threefold; ~ 55% of global ice-free land intensively used by humans, wild area down to 25% - was ~ 50% wild in 1700.

2001: 9/11 terrorist attacks; China joins WTO; Enron scandal; Human Genome Project publishes working draft; start of the Acumen Fund by Jacqueline Novogratz; Stockholm Convention on Persistent Organic Pollutants.

2002: Global Reporting Initiative; Hindu–Muslim violence in Gujarat leaves more than 1,000 dead; terrorist bombing in Bali; Chechen rebels take hostages in Moscow theatre, 116 dead; international Fairtrade certification mark launched – worldwide use, except US; ~ 1bn internet connections; Braungart and McDonough's Cradle to Cradle: Remaking the Way We Make Things; about 500m PCs in use worldwide.

2003: World Bank's WDR, Sustainable Development in a Dynamic World; US and Britain launch war against Iraq; European heatwaves (70,000 dead); first Skype connection.

2004: Facebook launched; HIV/AIDS pandemic peaks (started approx. 1960 Congo Basin, traversing through Kinshasa, 30,000,000 dead); China surpasses US as world's largest generator of solid waste; terrorist attacks in Spain, 200 dead; Chechen terrorists take 1,200 school children hostage, 340 dead; ASCE, Sustainable Engineering Practice, with WFEO – followed by The Vision for Civil Engineering in 2025 (2006).

2005: Royal Academy of Engineering publishes Engineering for Sustainable Development: Guiding Principles; Hurricane Katrina; C40 cities association begins (London); Millennium Ecosystem Assessment; Walmart adopts global sustainability strategy; Ellen Johnson-Sirleaf becomes Africa's first female head of state (Liberia); London hit by terrorist attacks, 52 dead, more than 700 wounded; Jared Diamond's Collapse; first video posted on YouTube.

2006: Stern Review (makes economic case for climate action); Danish newspaper challenges Muslim prohibition of images of the Prophet Muhammad by publishing cartoons; Iraq sees severe civil strife between Sunnis and Shiites; bombing in Mumbai commuter trains kills more than 200; Porter and Kramer (HBR), Strategy and Society: The Link Between Competitive Advantage and Corporate Social Responsibility; first tweet, 'just setting up my twttr'.

2007: Al Gore's An Inconvenient Truth wins Academy Award (IPCC and Gore share Nobel Peace Prize); iPhone unveiled; Tesco, a UK grocer, pledges CO_2 labelling for all products (discontinued 2012).

2008: Some global food prices increase 43%; US financial markets tumble (global recession begins, $20 trillion+ global wealth lost); world passes 50% urban mark; 1bn PCs in use worldwide.

2009: ISO 31000 (risk management) series; G20 Pittsburgh Summit – leaders call for phasing out fossil fuel subsidies; Copenhagen climate negotiations (COP 15) fails to reach agreement (cities play key role); Elinor Ostrom receives Nobel Prize in Economics for her work on governance of the commons; China overtakes US as world's largest GHG emitter; first year more items connected to the internet than people living (launches 'internet of things' – number of connected devices doubles every ~ 5 years); Sustainability Consortium founded.

2010: Deepwater Horizon oil spill, Gulf of Mexico; Nagoya Protocol (Convention on Biological Diversity) and Cartagena Protocol (Biosafety); more than 400 die in massive Pakistani flooding; G8 pledges to double aid to Africa to $50bn/year, cancel debt, and open trade; WBCSD Vision 2050.

2011: Arab Spring starts in Tunisia; world population exceeds 7 billion (last 1 billion took only 12 years, next 1 billion expected within ten years); COP17 climate negotiations in Durban yield mixed results (framework for future agreement beyond Kyoto); Osama bin Laden killed; South Sudan declares independence (Africa's 54th country, UN's 193rd member); Norway hit by terrorist attacks; Occupy Movement starts September in New York City; western black rhino hunted to extinction.

2012: Rio+20 strives (unsuccessfully) for an agreement to 'greening' the world's economies; Russia joins WTO; in Pakistan 14-year-old Malala Yousafzai shot in the head; 'Lonesome George', last known specimen of the Pinta island tortoise, dies.

2013: Word Federation of Engineering Organizations (WFEO) Model Code of Practice for Sustainable Development and Environmental Stewardship; May 9, daily average atmospheric CO_2 400.03 ppm at Mauna Loa, HI (Ralph Keeling continuously measuring CO_2 concentrations since 1958 – first time concentration exceeds 400); clothing factory collapses in Bangladesh killing at least 900; Edward Snowden admits to leaking classified US intelligence; Saudi Arabia declines seat on UN Security Council; Nelson Mandela dies at age 95; April – average foreign currency exchange reaches $5.3 trillion per day.

2014: Malala Yousafzai awarded Nobel Peace Prize; The New Economy report launched by Nick Stern and President Calderon; McDonalds, Pushkin Square, Moscow, closes; WWF Living Planet report launched (states that between 1970-2014 half of all wildlife lost); ISO 37120; global wealth $262 trillion (Credit Suisse) – 94.5% of wealth held by 20% of adults, $798,000 and above places you in wealthiest 1%.

2015: Launch of SDGs; terrorist attack in Paris; COP21 Paris climate agreement; average concentration of CO_2 exceeds 400 ppm (value likely to be exceeded for rest of century); Steffen et al. update Rockstrom et al. (2009) planetary boundaries; globally annual fossil fuel subsidies exceed $500bn (IEA); Alibaba Group's IPO of $25 billion largest in history.

2016: Habitat III (Quito); SDGs take effect (goals to 2030); UK votes 52% to leave EU.

2022: India's and China's population both expected to reach 1.4 billion; from this point on India world's most populous country (at least for rest of century).

2025: 101 cities expected to have populations over 5 million (~907 million total; up from 691 million in 2006).

2026: Human population likely 8 billion (5bn urban); atmospheric CO_2 ~ 434 ppm; >100bn devices connected to internet.

2042: Human population likely 9 billion (6.3bn urban); atmospheric CO_2 ~ 483 ppm (author's estimate).

2050: 122 cities expected to have populations over 5 million (~1.4bn; 181 cities with populations over 5 million expected by 2100 – total population ~ 2.8bn).

($ – constant 2015 US$).
Source: Hoornweg (2015).

The need for social and environmental development

This massive growth in wealth had negative consequences. For the first time, humans were using enough resources, and generating enough collateral pollution, to alter planetary ecosystems. The human economy generated enough CO_2 to modify the relatively stable climate of the Holocene. The rate of species extinction increased two-orders of magnitude from pre-industrial levels. Local impacts – water pollution, air quality and species predation – were severe. London, for example, one of the world's wealthiest cities, as recently as 1952 still had 'great smog' events killing 4,000 (Table 2.1).

Another concern is that over the last 50 years of wealth increase inequality has also grown. Inequity (real and perceived) is emerging as a serious concern (Piketty and Saez, 2014). Associated dissatisfaction may curtail economic growth and foster social unrest.

Most discussions on inequity focus on wealth (capital and daily expenditures). Variation across countries can be significant; for example, the Gross National Incomes of the richest and poorest countries are $220 in the Democratic Republic of Congo versus $106,920 in Bermuda (2014 values, World Bank). However, other inequities are also important, for example disparities in wealth between residents in the same city, or between urban and rural residents in the same country, or between rights and obligations of ethnic groups, or between genders. Other areas cause concern, e.g. resource consumption such as wildlife harvesting from the commons, or pollution of the oceans and atmosphere. Within and across countries, per capita GHG emissions vary as much or more than variations in wealth.

Prior to 1800, many of the drivers to large-scale environmental and social degradation and today's modern economy were in place (leading to non-'sustainable development'). Around 1800, transatlantic slavery was at its peak; the industrial revolution was in full swing; colonialism was widespread; key 'rules of engagement' for nations existed (e.g. Treaty of Westphalia and Magna Carta); commercial corporations, national and public banks, stock exchanges were in place; communications and trade flourished, e.g. growing quickly upon the printing press (1450); and in Britain and Europe especially, people were intent on growing wealth. An early indication of the power of human greed and its ability to drive speculative bubbles was tulip mania in the Netherlands, where in the 1630s a single tulip bulb could sell for as much as ten times annual salaries (Dash, 2001).

The nineteenth century ushered in far more awareness of the drivers and impacts of wealth creation. New governance systems and economic tools were developed. Perhaps the most impactful aspect of the 1800s is how Britain (and Europe) and then the US economy eclipsed India and then China (Fig. 2.2). This was not so much a reduction in India or China's economy as it was an enormous growth in Western industrialized countries.

Key advances related to development between 1800 to 1900 include: London's cholera epidemic and resulting sewer system (1854); the discovery and use of hydrocarbon-based oil (ca 1850); Jules Dupuit's use of cost–benefit analysis (1848); the British Public Health Act and emergence of local authorities as key providers of public health (1848); the international meteorological conference and recommendation of standardized measurement protocols (1853); the Limited Liability Act (1855); the first subway system (London 1863); the opening of Suez (1869) and Panama (1914) canals; polyphase AC electricity (1888); and elevators (1854).

The nineteenth century also saw environmental awareness grow, with the establishment of Yellowstone and Banff parks (1885), Ralph Waldo Emerson's *Nature* (1836), Alfred Wallace's and Charles Darwin's work on the evolution of species (1858), publication of the basis of the 'greenhouse effect' (1863), and start of the Audubon and Sierra clubs (1886 and 1892 respectively).

The 1900s was when humanity powered the Anthropocene in earnest, and began to understand the enormity of the task to bring humanity within natural ecosystem boundaries (Waters, et al., 2016). In 1900, global GDP was some $2 trillion (about $640 per capita), and life expectancy for the 1.65 billion people alive then was about 48 years. By the close of the twentieth century, population had grown to more than 6 billion, global GDP had increased more than 80-fold to about $41 trillion ($6500 per capita) and life expectancy had increased to a remarkable 78 years. Atmospheric CO_2 values were 369.5 ppm and growing by more than 2 ppm per year.

A few iconic developments of the 1900s warrant special notice. These include: the invention of air conditioning (1902), Ford's Model T (1908) and the first household refrigerator (1913); the global flu pandemic of 1918–20 (75 million dead); the First and Second World Wars (1914–18, 1939–45); the establishment of the League of Nations (1920), which was replaced by United Nations (1945); the establishment of the IMF and World Bank (1944); the ISO's founding in Geneva (1947), replacing the International Federation of the National Standardizing Association (1926); and IUCN (1948).

Several events, particularly in the second half of the century, garnered public attention. These included: London's great smog killing 4,000 in 1952; Minamata disease (mercury poisoning) in 1956; Thalidomide-induced birth defects starting in 1957; the impacts of DDT, illustrated in Rachel Carson's *Silent Spring* (1962); Cuyahoga River again catching on fire (1969); the OPEC oil crisis (embargo) in 1973; Rowland and Molina sound a warning about CFC and ozone in 1974; Love Canal (1976); Bhopal chemical leak in 1984; Chernobyl nuclear accident in 1986; and Exxon Valdez (1989), among others.

As awareness of environmental degradation, social inequality and challenges to the global economic model grew, agencies and NGOs flourished. A few of these include: Ecological Society of America (1915), which became the Nature Conservancy in 1950; Oxfam (1942); Ten Thousand Villages (1946); World Wildlife Fund (1961); Environmental Defense Fund (1967); Friends of the Earth and Pollution Probe (1969); Canada's International Development Research Center (1970); Greenpeace (1971); the start of the UN's Conference on Human Environment and the establishment of UNEP (1972); TERI (1974);

Body Shop (1976); Habitat I in Vancouver (1976); Greenbelt Movement in Kenya started by Wangari Muta Maathai (1977); World Resources Institute (1982); Grameen Bank and WCED (World Commission on Environment and Development), created in 1983; Intergovernmental Panel on Climate Change (1988); Stockholm Environment Institute (1989); International Institute for Sustainable Development in Winnipeg (1990); and Global Environment Facility (1991).

Seminal publications included: Aldo Leopold's *A Sand County Almanac* (1949); E.F. Schumacher's *Small is Beautiful* (1973); Lester Brown's *The Twenty-Ninth Day* (1978); James Lovelock's *Gaia Hypothesis* (1979); John Elkington coining the term 'triple bottom line' in 1994; Hunter and Amory Lovins and Ernst von Weizacker describing *Factor Four* that called to double wealth while halving resource consumption (1998); the IUCN's *World Conservation Strategy* (1980); and the start of a global discussion on sustainable development through publication of *Our Common Future* (1987).

The history of sustainable development

Jericho (9,000 years ago), Rome, Athens, Mesopotamia and the Song dynasty in China ushered in much of today's Common Era. Progress in development objectives was relatively modest up to about 1800. For example, human life expectancy was 36 years in 1700, and grew by only about 10 per cent during the 100 years to 1800 (up to 40 years). Yet several observers were already issuing warnings. Malthus (1798), for example, warned of exponential population growth in a world of linear agricultural production.

A few decades later, witnessing the destruction wrought by European settlers, Chief Seattle pleaded for environmental respect, and cautioned: 'Man did not weave the web of life, he is merely a strand in it. Whatever he does to the web, he does to himself' (1854).

When reviewing the history of sustainable development, a few key markers emerge. The concept was well established far earlier than may be expected, with early glimpses available in areas such as timber harvest rates in Germany (c.1713) (Grober, 2007), the Constitution of the Iroquois Nation governance structure requiring consideration for future seventh generations (some 500 years ago), and cooperative rice farming in Bali (more than 1,000 years ago).

Within the last 50 years, sustainable development as a concept is largely a reaction to the unprecedented growth in wealth and resource consumption in the 'western industrialized grouping' (Hoffer, 1976; Schaffartzik, et al., 2014). This increase in resource consumption and resulting pollution is now being replicated by China and India, and, within a couple of decades, will be in Sub-Saharan Africa.

Important early responders to wealth generation and resource consumption (with related globalization and population growth) include Aurelio Peccei forming the 'Club of Rome' in the late 1960s. One of the Club of Rome's first tasks was to commission researchers at MIT to model population growth and resource consumption. The resulting *Limits to Growth* (1972) was harsh in its warning of pending 'over shoot'. The follow-on, *Mankind at the Turning Point* (1974), had a more positive slant, yet the message was still a stern warning of impending resource consumption, population growth and ecosystem damage overwhelming the planet's carrying capacity. This work was further advanced through the IUCN[3] World Conservation Strategy (WCS, 1980), considered to be one of the earliest modern documents to use the term 'sustainable development'.

The IUCN's WCS was instrumental in launching similar UN-commissioned work, starting with the Brandt Commission's (after Willy Brandt, former Prime Mister of Germany) 'Program for Survival and Common Crises' (1980), and followed by the Palme Commission's (Olaf Palme was former Prime Minister of Sweden) 'Common Security' (1983). In December 1983, Javier Perez de Cuellar, UN Secretary General, asked Gro Harlem Brundtland (former Prime Mister of Norway) to chair a WCED focusing on 'long-term environmental strategies for achieving sustainable development by the year 2000 and beyond'.

Leading to the 1980 review by the World Conservation Strategy was work by influential researchers like Garrett Hardin, who introduced the concept of the *Tragedy of the Commons* in 1968. The main concern raised in this work was 'over population'. This was consistent with the *Limits to Growth* findings that typically applied exponential population growth scenarios. Prime Ministers Brandt, Palme and Brundtland shared socialist party affiliations, a distinction apparently not lost on other world leaders such as Ronald Reagan and Margaret Thatcher (Drexhage and Murphy, 2000).

Our Common Future popularized the term sustainable development with a succinct definition of 'development which meets the needs of the present without compromising the ability of future generations to meet their own needs' (World Commission on Environment and Development, 1987). Launch of the report coincided with the successful Montreal Protocol for ozone depleting substances and a growing general awareness in public opinion for greater environmental protection (at least in North America and Europe). The report catalysed this public awareness and support. For example, countries, regions and cities quickly established follow-on Round Tables on Environment and Economy (Canada's national Round Table started in 1988). In 1989, *Time* magazine declared 'Endangered Earth' its 'Planet of the Year' (the first time a person was not selected) (Mitcham, 1995).

The same 1989 Special Edition 'Managing Planet Earth' of *Scientific American* that discussed industrial ecology contains an article by Ruckelshaus (former head of US EPA and US representative on WCED) reflecting on his experience as a co-author of *Our Common Future*. He called for three things to facilitate sustainable development: (1) strengthening of institutions and financial support, especially for UNEP; (2) reliable information – agency/-ies to research and provide credible public information; and (3) better integration of overseas development assistance. For example, he cited parts of Africa being served by 82 international donors and 1,700 private organizations. In 1980, Burkina Faso, population 8 million, had 340 independent aid projects underway.

Numerous researchers contributed to the analytical underpinnings of sustainable development. Several suggest the need to transform the concept from global to regional scale with a focus on the fabric of buildings and transportation (Baccini, 1996). Others specifically review high-income lifestyles that often accompany urbanization (Weisz and Steinberger, 2010). Household incomes are strongly correlated with embodied energy and overall energy and material flows in cities (Huang, Yeh and Chang, 2010; Duchin and Levine, 2013). Urban form and building design is also very important (Kennedy et al., 2009).

Ehrlich (1994) concentrated on humanity's total energy consumption, suggesting this was the key factor leading to species extinction. The current degree of planetary over-reach is high, leading to calls that 'humanity's unsustainable footprint' be halved (Hoekstra and Wiedmann, 2014), suggesting that the Anthropocene requires we move beyond sustainable development (Benson and Craig, 2014). Glasby (1995) argues that 1 billion global population is the 'sustainable level'. This is obviously an unrealistic objective, as the UN continues to project that human population will exceed 10 billion by 2100.

Related to sustainable development, Cole, Rayner and Bates (1997) provided an empirical analysis with environmental Kuznet curves, stating the curves can only be relied on for local air pollution. They showed that wealth reduces pollution, but only when people are directly impacted, therefore an alternative approach to hoping affluence will address global pollution is needed.

On August 4, 1987, the 42nd Session of the UN General Assembly accepted the WCED's work *Our Common Future*. The General Assembly largely endorsed the report's recommendations, and, along with growing public support in many countries, political support was channelled through the UN Conference on Environment and Development (UNCED) in Rio de Janeiro, June 2–14, 1992. Government officials from 178 countries arrived, plus 20,000 to 30,000 individual representatives (the date coincided with the 20-year anniversary of the Stockholm Conference).

Key achievements of the 1992 Rio (UNCED) meeting included: (i) adoption of the Rio Declaration with 27 principles of sustainable development, including 7 on 'common but differentiated responsibilities'; (ii) issuance of 'Agenda 21' (and city-targeted 'local Agenda 21s'); (iii) establishment of UN Framework Convention on Climate Change (UNFCC); (iv) the Convention on Biological Diversity; (v) the non-legally binding Statement of Forest Principles; and (vi) creation of the Commission on Sustainable Development later that year. The Rio Summit was successful in capturing the world's attention and engagement. Virtually every world leader attended, despite George H. W. Bush's admonishment prior to the event that 'The American way of life is not negotiable.' The event also spun off important parallel initiatives (some still lasting), e.g. the World Business Council on Sustainable Development.

Ten and twenty years later, Rio+10 and Rio+20 were arguably much less successful than the 1992 event. Rio+20 occurred just after major global economic retrenchment, and Rio+10 was complicated with climate negotiations and political transitions in several key countries.

As part of the WCED discussions on sustainable development, a key focus was on equity of resource consumption and system efficiency of Western industrialized countries, compared to low-income countries (Holden, Linnerud and Banister, 2014).

Maurice Strong and many others, through discussions on sustainable development, admonished Western Industrialized Countries to use fewer resources and share more wealth (Brown, 1978). The political underpinnings of sustainable development were further entrenched since the first Rio conference in 1992. Negotiations on various aspects of sustainable development often bifurcate along different groups; e.g. wealth transfer, trade flows, regional alliances. The last 20 years of progress on sustainable development is largely measured through geo-political positioning and agreements (Zaccai, 2012). The recent Paris Conference of the Parties (COP21) highlighted well an emerging trend of 'working coalitions'. These *ad hoc* coalitions are likely to increase in number and stature.

While sustainable development is mostly an optimization process with ongoing political undertones, sustainability is the application of efficiency and resilience to material flows and quality of life. Quality of life is mostly a local issue (Putnam, 1988), although minimum health and social norms are proposed through the SDGs (Sachs, 2012). Energy and material flows analysis is often likened to 'societal metabolism', with cities having the largest appetites.

Material Flows

A key building block of sustainability (and from that sustainable development) is energy and material flows. The availability of resources such as energy, food and water, their use within the economy and their eventual disposal as waste drives most of the science of sustainability and debate over sustainable development.

Wolman's influential 1965 *Scientific American* article described the earth as 'a closed ecological system' and introduced the 'metabolism of the city' as an important early contribution to the concept of urban metabolism. This was well detailed in *The Metabolism of a City: The Case of Hong Kong* by Newcombe, Kalma and Aston (1978). This was further refined through Frosch and Gallopoulos's field of 'industrial ecology' (1989).

The World Resources Institute (1997) supported early material flows work with a detailed analysis of resource flows (primary) and materials intensity in Germany, the Netherlands, the USA and Japan. WRI followed this report with a call for material intensity accounts for countries.

Material flows assessment was taken one step further when assessing the '1.7 kg microchip'. A 2 g computer chip required fossil fuel (1600 g), chemicals (72 g), water (32,000 g) and elemental gas (700 g) to manufacture (Williams, Ayres and Heller, 2002). These vicarious or embodied emissions represent a significant contribution to overall environmental impacts, especially the impacts of the relatively affluent and high-consuming urban resident (Krausmann, 2009).

A 177-country material flows assessment (1950 to 2010) found material consumption ranged from 4.5 t/cap/a in Sub-Saharan Africa to 14.8 t/cap/a in

Western Industrial Grouping countries (Schaffartzik et al., 2014). The global average is greater than 10 t/cap/a (~3 t biomass, 2 t fossil energy carriers, 1 t metal, 4 t construction materials, and 200 kg industrial minerals). In terms of total material use, Asia overtook the Western Industrial Grouping in 1995, and now uses 50 per cent of the world's material resources.

Material flows have been assessed from the perspective of small island states, e.g. Trinidad and Tobago (for five decades) (Krausmann, Richter and Eisenmenger, 2014), cities, e.g. the stock of copper in Vienna (180 kg/cap) versus Taipei (30 kg/cap) (Kral et al., 2014) and countries, e.g. the material stock for Japan (310 t/cap) versus the US (375 t/cap) (Fisherman, 2014).

An emerging field of material flows is embodied emissions and inter-connectedness, and at-times increased vulnerability of supply chains (O'Rourke, 2014). Embodied resource flows can be as high as a third of overall global flows (Duchin and Levine, 2013).

Efforts to foster sustainability require clear awareness of material flows (Anderberg, 1998). Risks of flow interruption need to be known and ameliorated (Ferrão and Fernandez, 2013). Cities are particularly vulnerable, as energy, food and water supply can be disrupted, and long-term economic vulnerabilities manifest over material provisioning (Kennedy and Hoornweg, 2012). As much as possible, these material flow analyses should be for the urban conurbation, and should be regularly provided in an apolitical means, e.g. engineering schools and remote sensing.

Challenges ahead

In addition to pending geopolitical concerns, social depravations and more than one billion people in poverty, planetary system boundaries appear to have been crossed. The two of greatest immediate concern are loss of biodiversity and climate change. Nitrogen-use levels have also crossed a safe boundary and a recent update of the 2009 planetary boundaries assessment argues that land-use changes have too (Steffen et al., 2015).

Significant climate variance is expected and climate is projected to move to a state continuously out of bounds of historical variability in 2047 if a business-as-usual approach is followed (with massive societal disruptions) (Mora, 2013). Along with the World Bank, PricewaterhouseCoopers in its 2014 Low Carbon Economy Index predicts 4°C warming, the 2015 Paris COP21 negotiations notwithstanding.

An approaching state shift in earth's biosphere is projected (Barnosky et al., 2012), arguing for the need to develop local and global early warning systems. Some researchers warn that climate change must not blow conservation off course (Tingley, Estes and Wilcove, 2013), as ecosystems have already been significantly impacted from biodiversity loss (Cardinale et al., 2012). The complexities of environmental–social challenges and inability to provide an integrated public policy response give concern. This global public policy conundrum is exacerbated, since world population is not likely to stabilize this century (Gerland et al., 2014). Population estimates are 7.2 billion in 2050 and 10.9 billion in 2100 (Cohen, 2006), the key determinant being Africa.

Researchers suggest that scenarios with 80 per cent reduction of GHG emissions for low-carbon cities are unlikely (Mohareb and Kennedy, 2014). More specifically, reviews of Swiss lifestyles found that the goal of 2000 Watts per person could be achieved, but not the 1 tonne CO_2 per person (Notter, Meyer and Althaus, 2013). Globally, GHG emissions increased 8.8 Gt CO_2e from 1995 to 2008 (30.5 Gt to 39.3 Gt) (Arto and Dietzenbacher, 2014). The main driver was consumption, not population growth. This is readily apparent through municipal solid waste generation rates – these are increasing significantly around the world (Hoornweg, Bhada-Tata and Kennedy, 2013; 2014).

GDP has increased more than threefold since 1950 (De Long, 1998), but genuine progress indicator (GPI) has actually decreased since 1978 (Kubiszewski et al., 2013). Life satisfaction in 17 reviewed countries has not improved since 1975 and GPI per capita does not increase beyond a per capita GDP ~ $7,000.

Globalization has so far largely been driven by diesel engines and gas turbines (Smil, 2007). GHG emissions associated with these activities are still accelerating and with large populations, such as East and South Asia and Africa, yet to fully join the global marketplace, pressure for emissions to increase will grow.

Glimpses of hope

Buhaug and Urdal (2013) use an empirical analysis since 1960 for 55 major cities in Asia and Africa to ascertain if increasing urban population leads to social disorder. On the contrary, they found that urban disorder is primarily associated with lack of consistent political institutions, economic shocks and ongoing civil strife. Other encouraging findings suggest that in assessing 'Sustainable Energy for All' (i.e., universal access; doubling the share of renewables; improving energy efficiency by more than 2.4 per cent per year, rather than historic 1.2 per cent per year improvement) is compatible with maintaining a 2°C global warming threshold (Rogelj, McCollum and Riahi, 2013).

From 2003 to 2012, reductions in particulate matter were responsible for one-third to one-half of total monetized benefits of all US environmental interventions (Dominici, Greenstone and Sunstein, 2014). This suggests priorities that are fully consistent with efforts to reduce GHG emissions. In addition to reducing GHG emissions, East Asian co-benefits in reducing PM 2.5 and ground-level ozone are 10–70 times marginal costs in 2030, reducing approximately 1.3 million deaths in 2050.

Urban ecology is an important means to connect city residents to local and global imperatives. Interdisciplinary research on sustainable development is particularly valuable, especially with regard to urban settings (Ferraro and Reid, 2013).

Surowiecki (2005) in *The Wisdom of Crowds* discusses how in the TV show *Who Wants to be a Millionaire?* the polled studio audience selects the correct answer 91 per cent of the time (Ask the Expert is correct just 65 per cent of the time). This work is consistent with Galton (1907), who observed uncanny accuracy of 'crowd-sourced' weight estimates of an ox at the Plymouth County Fair.

Adaptation to rising sea levels is a (legitimate) concern for many coastal cities. However, in many cases, groundwater extraction and the associated settlement can be an order of magnitude greater than potential sea-level rise (Hinkel et al., 2014). Reducing groundwater extraction is obviously not easy, as many demands exist, but curtailing extraction to sustainable recharge rates is plausible through city-based policy and enforcement, and theoretically easier than hoping for changes to global sea-level regimes. Much can be done today by nervous coastal cities to strengthen their resilience significantly.

With regard to food production, projections to 2050 suggest possible sustainability of the agriculture system in light of growing global food demand (Tilman, Cassman and Matson, 2002; Tilman et al., 2011). As a function of per capita real income from 2005–2050 a 100–110 per cent increase in global crop demand can be expected. Two routes are possible – extensification and intensification. Extensification would require ~ 1 bn Ha of land, release 36t/y GHGs and use ~ 250 Mt/y of N, while intensification would require a much more modest ~ 0.2 bn Ha clearing, release ~ 1 Gt/y GHG emissions and use ~225 Mt/y of N. Estimates for global land use, water and fertilizer use to 2050 are reasonably well quantified (Odegard and van der Voet, 2014). A key aspect is the demand side – wastage and use of animal products. Feeding future potential populations is possible but challenging. With less-resource-intensive diets and improved productivity, especially in Africa, the planet could sustainably feed 9 billion people (Springer and Duchin, 2014).

Potential broad-based business support is emerging and enhanced (local) business involvement in city development is particularly noteworthy as this often provides more innovation (Macomber, 2013). Kanter (2012) provides a four-part plan to enrich innovation ecosystems: (1) link knowledge and venture creation; (2) link large and small enterprises; (3) improve linkages between education and employment; (4) link leaders across sectors. The work is developed for the business sector, but readily transferrable to cities.

Porter and Kramer (2006) provided a seminal paper outlining the benefits to corporate profits and market share through corporate social responsibility (CSR). They raise an implicit warning against potential vehemence of a stakeholder group not necessarily reflecting the importance of an issue.

Other encouraging developments from a city's viewpoint of sustainable development includes looking at services like solid waste management from a systems perspective, e.g. including district heating, electricity, vehicle fuel, agricultural practices, movement toward circular economy (Eriksson, 2005). As cities adopt integrated systems approaches, (sustainable development) benefits accrue, e.g. the economic insurance value of ecosystem resilience (on urban systems) (Baumgartner and Strunz, 2014), and reduce environmental risk (Kessler, 2014).

In some areas eco-regions and their adaptive capacity have been mapped and overlain with cities in these ecosystems, highlighting the value of local ecosystems (ideally intact), especially in growing cities (Watson, Iwamura and Butt, 2013). This work is backed up with plot distribution of threatened species, which varies by city location (Pimm et al., 2014). Therefore particularly strategic cities could have an important role in protecting local (and global) biodiversity. Supporting these efforts is emergence of value of ecosystem resilience (Baumgartner and Strunz, 2014). The insurance industry, e.g. Swiss Re and Munich Re, are adapting quickly to impending threats to key infrastructure and providing the means to quantify (fiscally) unsustainable behaviour.

The role of cities

A systems approach is suggested and 'city' for the largest urban areas is defined as the urban agglomeration. In most cases the urban area, or city, is made up of several local governments. Typically, the mayor that represents the largest local government within the city (urban area) presumes to speak for the city internationally. Many services overlap and are provided by various utilities, and state, provincial and national governments. The boundaries of cities (urban areas) are presumed to be fluid and the process suggested here accommodates changing boundaries of targeted cities.

From a systems perspective, clear, agreed-to populations and boundaries of most urban agglomerations do not yet exists. This is bewildering, as cities (urban areas) are the world's most important drivers of economy and ecosystem impacts. Political boundaries, which are much more arbitrary and transient, usually take precedence over analysis of the urban agglomeration. For any sort of materials flow analysis (arguably a pre-condition for research on sustainability), as much as possible the complete urban boundary needs to be defined (Ausubel and Waggoner, 2008). The urban agglomeration is the unit of analysis for example in transportation, waste disposal, water supply and energy generation.

Urbanization reflects humanity's desire to live together in denser, more connected, wealthier communities, with greater life-chances and material consumption (Dahrendorf, 1979). Urbanization is now the single largest driver of the global environment, economy and, increasingly, societies and structures of governance. Cities, and their impacts and opportunities, are driving much of today's global dialogue.

Humanity's relationship with cities is, however, often strained. Referenced as early as the Quran and Genesis, in the beginnings of civilization, the punishment meted for murder was exile, divorce from the land, restless wandering and city building.[4] Cities were for the transient populations, the restless, and thought to be impermanent.

Cities are driven by connectivity as supported by mobility and density, therefore focusing on employment density rather than population density is preferred. In the European Union, for example, transport CO_2 emissions correlate much more closely with land use (density) than with population or GDP. City boundaries should be set by mobility characteristics – boundary decays exponentially with physical mobility boundaries (Pan, et al., 2012).

Cities are also critical portals to global trends, economies and material flows. The spread of HIV-1 in human populations highlights this well (Faria et al., 2014). The key role Kinshasa played as the portal for spread of the disease and connection to the rest of Congo, Africa and the world by rail, boat and road is evident. When reviewing global systems and the flows of wealth, energy, ideas and opportunity, the critical role of cities is quickly evident. A few 'global cities' have a particularly influential role (Sassen, 1991). When hoping for global adoption of product use, or artist popularity, about 50 cities act as 'global portals'. The cities proposed for inclusion here include all of the world's 'portal cities'. Presumably, similar to other global trends and material flows, if sustainability was anchored in these key cities, it would quickly spread globally.

Cities (as local governments) are often fiscally constrained. The World Economic Forum (2013) provides a detailed investment report suggesting that 'green growth' needs about $5 trillion per year to keep to 2°C warming scenario.[5] This would almost entirely be spent within urban areas. The estimate is corroborated by Kennedy and Corfee-Morlot (2013), who estimated global infrastructure needs 2015 to 2050, including buildings and vehicles: ~ $6.7 trillion per year, following a 'business-as-usual' scenario. Incremental costs of low-carbon infrastructure are on the order of $70 to $450 billion per year, i.e. less than a 5 per cent additional cost.

These values are consistent with McKinsey Global Institute estimates of $57 trillion between 2013 and 2030 (in 2010 prices). Values vary by what is included and not, and methods of finance; however, a reasonable estimate is that between 2015 and 2050 global civil works (urban infrastructure) expenditures will exceed $200 trillion. These estimates include remediation of potential flood losses from rising sea levels and storm events projected to be $63 billion per year by 2050 (Hallegatte et al., 2013).

Finance is, however, only one of the many needs of cities. Other key pillars include governance, infrastructure and neighbourhoods (Kennedy et al., 2005). Cities rarely achieve all objectives simultaneously. More than anything, the development of sustainable cities is a challenge to human organizational capacity (technology and finance needs are secondary).

Bettencourt (2013) and Bettencourt et al. (2007), reflecting on the origins of Schumpeter's creative destruction, highlight the disconcerting need for a marked increase in the pace of innovation in cities to keep up with growing populations. New technologies facilitate emergence of new cities overtaking older cities (Brezis and Krugman, 1997). Examples include the decline of Pittsburg (subsequent rise came after 1997), Leiden and Haarlem the Netherlands, and Manchester, Birmingham and Sheffield in the UK.

Cities as complex, scalable systems

Bettencourt (2013) argues that cities are 'first and foremost large social networks' with 'agglomerations of social links' that 'enable social interactions to form and persist'. This 'social amalgamation' supports a city's primary role to 'expand connectivity per person' and 'strive for social inclusion'.

Cities are natural systems that evolve spontaneously in human societies, 'as natural as beehives and coral reefs'. The essence of a city is of a built canvas that enables residents to construct the social linkages needed to maximize their personal and collective economy, culture and utility. Cities also by their design of density and connectedness are the most efficient form for material distribution, hence the similarities with naturally evolving coral reefs and beehives. We do well when we mimic nature.

Two thoughts give pause to this 'essence of a city': Sigmund Freud (1930) and the compelling case he makes in *Civilization and its Discontents* and economist Ralph Dahrendorf (1994) and his argument that sustainable development poses a contrast between 'life chances' (opportunities of living or potentials for decision) versus 'ligatures' (established bonds of the individual to society) (Keiner, 2006).

Freud believed that civilization (i.e. cities) exists to 'curb the irrevocable ill will within the hearts of man'. Freud argues convincingly in *Civilization and its Discontents* that civilization is paradoxically our largest source of happiness and unhappiness. Man has 'immutable instincts' and unlike bees and fish we are much more able to act upon these baser instincts.

Dahrendorf's exploration of ligatures and life chances need to be addressed when investigating sustainable cities – humans have traditionally moved to cities to increase life chances, all the while being anchored, and at times held back, by ligatures and social norms. Cities will fail if they cannot foster connectivity and inclusion along with economic opportunity.

Aristotle in particular presciently noted in *Politics* that people are the most *political* (= urban) of all animals. We may be an urban species, but globally we only just passed the 50 per cent urban mark. Many of our political constructs and social norms still retain a rural bias. As we shift from a rural to urban mindset and build our new cities, we will do well to keep nature in mind.

> That which is not good for the hive cannot be good for the bees.
>
> Marcus Aurelius

Complex adaptive systems behave according to three basic properties: (i) they show diversity and individuality of components with localized interactions and evolutionary processes; (ii) they are hierarchical and self-organizing; (iii) they exhibit non-linear processes, multiple stable states and threshold effects (Lubell, 2015).

Big cities count. Big 'sustainable cities' count even more, and in the pursuit of sustainable development there is a premium on larger cities. Scalability of cities explains much of this – double the size of a city, and you obtain 1.2 times the benefits at about 0.8 times the (infrastructure) cost (Bettencourt et al., 2007; Bettencourt, 2013). When building cities for an additional 2.5 billion people over the next 35 years, these savings in infrastructure costs will be enormous (and probably a pre-condition for sustainable development).

The value of 'trunk infrastructure' in large cities as they grow (scale upward) is significant. This 'bigger, better' infrastructure is not usually easy to provide, as almost all cities grow in place. They are constrained by historic land use patterns and urban form. Retrofitting trunk infrastructure is much more difficult than building it first and letting the city grow around the in-place urban services (this type of growth is also more difficult to finance).

Key implications for urban planning and sustainable cities as highlighted include: (i) trunk, or critical, infrastructure needs to serve the entire urban agglomeration, or whole city; (ii) the 'engineering practices that think of the city as a machine' need to be ameliorated by 'seeing the city as a whole' and building infrastructure to 'first and foremost facilitate social networks'; (iii) networks of infrastructure 'should be decentralized where possible'; (iv) the price of land rises faster with population size than average incomes (this wealth creation should be tapped to raise funds for needed infrastructure); and (v) 'policies that increase the supply of land per capita or reduce transportation costs will tend to create cities that are less dense and that require higher rates of energy consumption' (Bettencourt, 2012).

Physicist Geoffrey West of the Santa Fe Institute likens the emerging science of cities to organized complexity where they offer a more effective approach to urban planning. West apparently likes to say they are just doing 'Jacobs with the math', referring to Jane Jacobs and her early cities work (1961). Cities are complex adaptive and dynamic systems. The key themes emerging from the science of cities include:[6]

- Cities generate economic growth through networks of proximity, casual encounters and economic spillovers.
- Cities can generate large efficiency gains (environmental benefit).
- Cities perform best economically and environmentally when they encourage human-scale connectivity.
- Cities perform best when they adapt to human psychological dynamics and patterns of activity.
- Cities perform best when they offer some control of spatial structure to residents.

A growing emphasis in the new science of cities is the role of networks and hierarchies in material and energy flows (Batty, 2013).

A general 'rule of thumb' emerges: as cities double in population, innovation, patents and economy scale super-linearly ($\sim$1.15), while infrastructure scales sub-linearly ($\sim$0.85) (Bettencourt and West, 2010). Through the constructal law, cities mimic growth of natural systems and exhibit criticality of hierarchy (Bejan and Zane, 2012). The constructal law states that societal flows emerge and evolve according to the same principles as all other natural flows. Hierarchy evolves as a means to enhance flow and benefits the entire system – all constituent components also benefit. Mathematical patterns of complexity and the fractal nature of urban morphologies is helping to strengthen the science of cities (Samet, 2013).

Kenworthy (2006) provides 10 key dimensions for the 'eco-city' (sustainable city):

- The city has a compact, mixed-use urban form that uses land efficiently and protects the natural environment, biodiversity and food-producing areas.
- The natural environment permeates the city's spaces and embraces the city, while the city and its hinterland provide a major proportion of its food needs.
- Freeway and road infrastructure is de-emphasized in favour of transit, walking and cycling infrastructure, with a special emphasis on rail. Car and motorcycle use are minimized.
- There is extensive use of environmental technologies for water, energy and waste management – the city's life support systems become closed loop systems.
- The current city and sub-centres within the city are human centres that emphasize access and circulation by modes of transport other than the automobile, and absorb a high proportion of employment and residential growth.
- The city has a high-quality public realm throughout that expresses a public culture, community, and equity and good governance. The public realm includes the entire transit system and all the environments associated with it.
- The physical structure and urban design of the city, especially its public environments, are highly legible, permeable, robust, varied, rich, visually appropriate and personalized for human needs.
- The economic performance of the city and employment creation are maximized through innovation, creativity and the uniqueness of the local environment, culture and history, as well as the high environmental and social quality of the city's public environments.
- Planning for the future of the city is a visionary 'debate and decide' process, not a 'predict and provide' computer-driven process.
- All decision-making is sustainability-based, integrating social, economic, environmental and cultural considerations as well as compact, transit-oriented urban form principles. Such decision-making processes are democratic, inclusive, empowering and engendering hope.

Sustainable development is debated mostly in cities. The science and systems engineering of cities is evolving fast. Current non-sustainable levels of materials-use (as seen through impacts of polluting by-products) are driven mostly by the lifestyles of today's urban citizens. Solutions must therefore be targeted mostly to cities, and are most likely to originate from people in cities.

Table 2.2 Waves of innovation and economic activity

1785 ~ 1845	water, power, textiles, iron, mechanization ('First Industrial Revolution')
1845 ~ 1900	steam, rail, steel, mass-production, start of electricity ('Second Industrial Revolution')
1900 ~ 1950	electricity (ubiquitous), chemicals, internal combustion engine
1950 ~ 1990	petrochemical, electronics, aviation ('Third Industrial Revolution')
1990 ~ 2020	digital networks, software, new media, cyber-physical systems ('Fourth Industrial Revolution')

Note declining periodicity between waves, starting at 60 years in 1785, likely declining to 10–15 years by mid-twenty-first century. 2020 ~ 2040 likely genomics and biological applications. Adapted from The Economist and World Economic Forum.

Notes

1 Major Ice Ages: Quaternary (2.6 Ma–present); Karoo (360 Ma–260 Ma); Andean–Saharan (450 Ma– 420Ma); Cryogenian (800 Ma–635 Ma); Huronian (2400 Ma–2100 Ma).
2 The Pleistocene epoch (of the Quaternary period) saw at least four major ice advances and retreats in North America: Wisconsin (13,000 to 60,000 years ago); Illinoian (140,000 to 350,000 years ago); Kansan (500,000 to 640,000 years ago); and Nebraskan (780,000 to 900,000 years ago). Names denote location of furthest glacial advance.
3 The International Union for Conservation of Nature was founded in 1948 as the world's first global environmental organization. Now headquartered near Geneva, Switzerland, IUCN has 200+ government and 900+ NGO members, 11,000 voluntary scientists, and regularly issues a 4-year 'Global Programme' (latest 2012 to 2016) to frame its ongoing work programme.
4 'And Cain went out from the presence of the Lord, and dwelt in the land of Nod, on the East side of Eden. And Cain knew his wife; and she conceived, and bore Enoch: and Cain built a city, and named the city after his son, Enoch' (from Genesis 4:16–17). Nod is considered 'the land of wandering'.
5 Of the ~ $114 trillion required to 2030, WEF estimates by sector are: $26.4trn – water; transportation vehicles – $21trn; buildings – $13trn; telecom – $12trn; power generation – $10.1trn; roads – $8trn; industry – $5.8trn; rail – $5trn; transportation – $5trn; agriculture – $2.5trn; airports – $2.3trn; forestry – $2.1trn; ports – $800bln.
6 Michael Mehaffy, CityLab, *The Atlantic*, September 19, 2014.

References

Anderberg, S., 1998. Industrial Metabolism and the Linkages Between Economics, Ethics and the Environment. *Ecological Economics*, 24, pp.311–20.
Arto, I. and Dietzenbacher, E., 2014. Drivers of the Growth in Global Greenhouse Gas Emissions. *Environmental Science and Technology*, 2014, 48(10), pp.5388–94.
Ausubel, J. and Waggoner, P., 2008. Dematerialization: Variety, Caution, and Persistence. *Proceedings of the National Academy of Sciences*, 105(35), pp.12774–9.
Baccini, P., (1996). Understanding Regional Metabolism for a Sustainable Development of Urban Systems. *Environmental Science and Pollution Research*, 3(2), pp.108–11.
Barnosky, A., Hadly, E., Bascompte, J., Berlow, E., Brown, J., Fortelius, M., Getz, W., Harte, J., Hastings, A., Marquet, P., Martinez, N., Mooers, A., Roopnarine, P., Vermeij, G., Williams, J., Gillespie, R., Kitzes, J., Marshall, C., Matzke, N., Mindell, D., Revilla,

E. and Smith, A., 2012. Approaching a State Shift in Earth's Biosphere. *Nature*, 486(7), pp.52–8.

Batty, M., 2013. *The New Science of Cities*. Cambridge: MIT Press.

Baumgartner, S. and Strunz, S., 2014. The Economic Insurance Value of Ecosystem Resilience. *Ecological Economics*, 101, pp.21–32.

Bejan, A. and Zane, J., 2012. *Design in Nature*. New York: Anchor.

Benson, M. H. and Craig, R. K., 2014. The End of Sustainability. *Society and Natural Resources*, 27(7), pp.777–82.

Bettencourt, L., Lobo, J., Helbing, D., Kuhnert, C., West, G., 2007. Growth, Innovation, Scaling and the Pace of Life in Cities. *Proceedings of the National Academy of Sciences*, 104(17), pp.7301–6.

Bettencourt, L. and West, G., 2010. A Unified Theory of Urban Living. *Nature*, 467, pp.912–13.

Bettencourt, L., 2012. Cities. *Science – Special Edition*, 337, August 10, 2012.

Bettencourt, L., 2013. The Kind of Problem a City Is. *SFI Working Paper: 2013-03-008*.

Bettencourt, L., 2013. The Origins of Scaling in Cities. *Science*, 340(6139), pp.1438–41.

Brezis, E. and Krugman, P., 1997. Technology and the Life Cycle of Cities. *Journal of Economic Growth*, 2, pp.369–83.

Brown, L., 1978. *The Twenty-Ninth Day: Accommodating Human Needs and Numbers to the Earth's Resources*. New York: Norton.

Buhaug, H. and Urdal, H., 2013. An Urbanization Bomb? Population Growth and Social Disorder in Cities. *Global Environmental Change*, 23, pp.1–10.

Cardinale, B., Duffy, J., Gonzalez, A., Hooper, D., Perrings, C., Venail, P., Narwani, A., Mace, G., Tilman, D., Wardle, D., Kinzig, A., Daily, G., Loreau, M., Grace, J., Larigauderie, A., Srivastava, D. and Naeem, S., 2012. Biodiversity Loss and its Impact on Humanity. *Nature*, 486(7), pp.59–67.

Cohen, B., 2006. Urbanization in Developing Countries: Current Trends, Future Projections, and Key Challenges for Sustainability. *Technology in Society*, 28, pp.63–80.

Cole, M., Rayner, A. and Bates, J., 1997. The Environmental Kuznets Curve: An Empirical Analysis. *Environment and Development Economics*, 2, pp.401–16.

Crutzen, P., 2002. Geology of Mankind. *Nature*, 415(6867), p.23.

Dahrendorf, R., 1979. *Life chances: Approaches to Social and Political Theory*. London: Weidenfeld & Nicolson.

Dash, M., 2001. *Tulipomania: The Story of the World's Most Coveted Flower and the Extraordinary Passions it Aroused*. New York: Three Rivers Press.

De Long, J., 1998. *Estimates of World GDP, One Million B.C.–Present*. Department of Economics, U.C. Berkeley.

Dominici, F., Greenstone, M. and Sunstein, C., 2014. Particulate Matter Matters. *Science*, 344, pp.257–9.

Duchin, F. and Levine, S., 2013. Embodied Resource Flows in a Global Economy: An Approach for Identifying the Critical Links. *Journal of Industrial Ecology*, 17(1), pp.65–78.

Drexhage, J. and Murphy, D., 2000. Sustainable Development: From Brundtland to Rio 2012 (Background Paper). In: International Institute for Sustainable Development, High Level Panel on Global Sustainability. United Nations Headquarters, New York, September 19, 2010.

Ehrlich, P., 1994. Energy Use and Biodiversity Loss. *Philosophical Transactions: Biological Sciences (The Royal Society)*, 344, pp.99–104.

Eriksson, O., Reich, M., Frostell, B., Bjorklund, A., Assefa, G., Sundqvist, J., Granath, J., Baky, A. and Thyselius, L., 2005. Municipal Solid Waste Management from a Systems Perspective. *Journal of Cleaner Production*, 13, pp.241–52.

Faria, N., Rambaut, A., Suchard, M., Baele, G., Bedford, T., Ward, M., Tatem, A., Sousa, J., Arinaminpathy, N., Pépin, J., Posada, D., Peeters, M., Pybus, O., and Lemey, P., 2014. The Early Spread and Epidemic Ignition of HIV-1 in Human Populations. *Science*, 346(6205), pp.56–61.

Fergus, G., 2014. *Temperature of Planet Earth* [graph].

Ferrão, P. and Fernandez, J., 2013. *Sustainable Urban Metabolism*. Cambridge: MIT Press.

Ferraro, E. and Reid, L., 2013. On Sustainability and Materiality: Homo Faber, a New Approach. *Ecological Economics*, 96(C), pp.125–31.

Fisherman, T., Schandl, H., Tanikawa, H., Walker, P. and Krausmann, F., 2014. Accounting for Material Stock of Nations. *Journal of Industrial Ecology*, 18(3), pp.407–20.

Freud, S., 1930. *Civilization and Its Discontents*. Eastford, CT: Martino Publishing.

Friedman, M., 1962, *Capitalism and Freedom*. Chicago, The University of Chicago Press.

Keiner, M., ed., 2006. *The Future of Sustainability*. Rotterdam: Springer.

Frosch, R., and Gallopoulos, N., 1989. Strategies for Manufacturing. *Scientific American*, 261(3), pp.144–52.

Galton, F., 1907. Vox Populi. *Nature*, 75, pp.450–51.

Gerland, P., Raftery, A., Ševčíková, H., Li, N., Gu, D., Spoorenberg, T., Alkema, L., Fosdick, B., Chunn, J., Lalic, N., Bay, G., Buettner, T., Heilig, G. and Wilmoth, J., 2014. World Population Stabilization Unlikely this Century. *Science*, 346(6206), pp.234–7.

Glasby, G., 1995. Concept of Sustainable Development: A Meaningful Goal? *The Science of the Total Environment*, 159, pp.67–80.

Grober, U., 2007. Deep Roots: A Conceptual History of 'Sustainable Development' (Nachhaltigkeit). Discussion papers // Beim Präsidenten, Emeriti Projekte, Wissenschaftszentrum Berlin für Sozialforschung, No. P 2007-002.

Hallegatte, S., Green, C., Nicholls, R. and Corffee-Morlot, J., 2013. Future Flood Losses in Major Coastal Cities. *Nature Climate Change*, 3, pp.802–6.

Hinkel, J., Lincke, D., Vafeidis, A., Perrette, M., Nicholls, R., Tol, R., Marzeion, B., Fettweis, X., Ionscu, C. and Levermann, A., 2014. Coastal Flood Damage and Adaptation Costs Under 21st-Century Sea-Level Rise. *Proceedings of the National Academy of Sciences*, 111(9), pp.3292–7.

Hoekstra, A. and Wiedmann, T., 2014. Humanity's Unsustainable Footprint. *Science*, 344(6188), pp.1114–17.

Hoffer, E., 1976. *The Ordeal of Change*. Cutchogue, NY: Buccaneer Books.

Holden, E., Linnerud, K. and Banister, D., 2014. Sustainable Development: Our Common Future Revisited. *Global Environmental Change*, 26, pp.130–39.

Hoornweg, D., Bhada-Tata, P. and Kennedy, C., 2013. Waste Production Must Peak this Century. *Nature*, 502, pp.615–17.

Hoornweg, D., Bhada-Tata, P. and Kennedy, C., 2014. Peak Waste: When Is It Likely to Occur? *Journal of Industrial Ecology*, 19(1), pp.117–28.

Hoornweg, D., 2015 (updated 2016). *A Cities Approach to Sustainability*. PhD. University of Toronto.

Huang, S-L., Yeh, C-T. and Chang, L-F., 2010. The Transition to an Urbanizing World and the Demand for Natural Resources. *Current Opinion in Environmental Sustainability*, 2, pp.136–43.

Kanter, R., 2012. Enriching the Ecosystem. *Harvard Business Review* [online]. Available at: https://hbr.org/2012/03/enriching-the-ecosystem.

Kennedy, C., Miller, E., Shalaby, A., Maclean, H. and Coleman, J., 2005. The Four Pillars of Sustainable Urban Transportation. *Transport Reviews*, 25(4), pp.393–414.

Kennedy, C., Steinberger, J., Gasson, B., Hansen, Y., Hillman, T., Havranek, M., Pataki, D., Phdungsilp, A., Ramaswami, A. and Villalba Mendez, G., 2009. Greenhouse Gas Emissions from Global Cities. *Environmental Science & Technology*, 43, pp.7297–302.

Kennedy, C. and Hoornweg, D., 2012. Mainstreaming Urban Metabolism. *Journal of Industrial Ecology*, 16(6), pp.780–82.

Kenworthy, J., 2006. The Eco-City: Ten Key Transport and Planning Dimensions for Sustainable City Development. *Environment and Urbanization*, 18(1), pp.67–85.

Kessler, R., 2014. Air of Danger. *Nature*, 509, pp.62–3.

Kral, U., Lin, C., Kellner, K., Ma, H. and Brunner, P., 2014. The Copper Balance of Cities: Exploratory Insights into a European and an Asian City. *Journal of Industrial Ecology*, 18(3), pp.432–44.

Krausmann, F., Gingrich, S., Eisenmenger, N., Erb, K., Haberl, H. and Fischer-Kowalski, M., 2009. Growth in Global Materials Use, GDP and Population During the 20th Century. *Ecological Economics*, 68, pp.2696–705.

Krausmann, F., Richter, R. and Eisenmenger, N., 2014. Resource Use in Small Island States: Material Flows in Iceland and Trinidad and Tobago, 1961–2008. *Journal of Industrial Ecology*, 18(2), pp.294–305.

Kubiszewski, I., Costanza,R., Franco, C., Lawn, P. and Talberth, J., 2013. Beyond GDP: Measuring and Achieving Global Genuine Progress. *Ecological Economics*, 93, pp. 57–68.

Lubell, M., 2015. Collaborative Partnerships in Complex Institutional Systems. *Current Opinion in Environmental Sustainability*, 12, pp.41–7.

Macomber, J., 2013. Building Sustainable Cities. *Harvard Business Review*, pp.40–50.

McCloskey, D., 2011. *Bourgeois Dignity and Liberty: Why Economics Can't Explain the Modern World*. Chicago: University of Chicago Press.

Mitcham, C., 1995. The Concept of Sustainable Development: Its Origins and Ambivalence. *Technology in Society*, 17(3), pp.311–26.

Mohareb, E. and Kennedy, C., 2014. Scenarios of Technology Adoption Towards Low-Carbon Cities. *Energy Policy*, 66, pp.685–93.

Mora, C., Frazier, A., Longman, R., Dacks, R., Walton, M., Tong, E., Sanchez, J., Kaiser, L., Stender, Y., Anderson, J., Ambrosino, C., Fernandez-Silva, I., Giuseffi, L. and Giambelluca, T., 2013. The Projected Timing of Climate Departure from Recent Variability. *Nature*, 502, pp.183–8.

Newcombe, K., Kalma, J. and Aston, A., 1978. The Metabolism of a City: The Case of Hong Kong. *AMBIO*, 7(1), pp.3–15.

Notter, D., Meyer, R. and Althaus, H., 2013. The Western Lifestyle and its Long Way to Sustainability. *Environmental Science & Technology*, 47, pp.4014–21.

O'Rourke, D., 2014. The Science of Sustainable Supply Chains. *Science*, 344(6188), pp.1124–7.

Odegard, I. and van der Voet, E., 2014. The Future of Food: Scenarios and the Effect on Natural Resource Use in Agriculture in 2050. *Ecological Economics*, 97, pp.51–9.

Pan, W., Ghoshal, G., Ktumme, C., Cebrian, M. and Pentland, A., 2012. Urban Characteristics Attributable to Density-Driven Tie Formation. *Nature Communications*, 4(1961).

Piketty, T. and Saez, E., 2014. Inequality in the Long Run. *Science*, 344(6186), pp.838–42.

Pimm, S., Jenkins, C., Abell, R., Brooks, T., Gittleman, J., Joppa, L., Raven, P., Roberts, C. and Sexton, J., 2014. The Biodiversity of Species and Their Rates of Extinction, Distribution, and Protection. *Science*, 344(6187), pp.987–97.

Porter, M. and Kramer, M., 2006. Strategy and Society: The Link Between Competitive Advantage and Corporate Social Responsibility. *Harvard Business Review*, pp. 76–91.

Putnam, R., 1988. Diplomacy and Domestic Politics: The Logic of Two-Level Games. *International Organization*, 42, pp.427–60.

Rogelj, J., McCollum, D. and Riahi, K., 2013. The UN's 'Sustainable Energy for All' initiative is compatible with a warming limit of 2°C. *Nature Climate Change*, 3, pp.545–51.

Sachs, J., 2012. From Millennium Development Goals to Sustainable Development Goals. *The Lancet*, 379, pp.2206–11.

Samet, R., 2013. Complexity, the Science of Cities and Long-Range Futures. *Futures*, 47, pp.49–58.

Sassen, S., 1991. *The Global City: New York, London, Tokyo*. Princeton, NJ: Princeton University Press.

Schaffartzik, A., Mayer, A., Gingrich, S., Eisenmenger, N., Loy, C. and Krausmann, F., 2014. The Global Metabolic Transition: Regional Patterns and Trends of Global Material Flows, 1950–2010. *Global Environmental Change*, 26, pp.87–97.

Smil, V., 2007. The Two Prime Movers of Globalization: History and Impact of Diesel Engines and Gas Turbines. *Journal of Global History*, 2, pp.373–94.

Springer, N. and Duchin, F., 2014. Feeding Nine Billion People Sustainably: Conserving Land and Water through Shifting Diets and Changes in Technology. *Environmental Science and Technology*, 48, pp.4444–51.

Steffen, W., Richardson, K., Rockström, J., Cornell, S., Fetzer, I., Bennett, E., Biggs, R., Carpenter, S., de Vries, W., de Wit, C., Folke, C., Gerten, D., Heinke, J., Mace, G., Persson, L., Ramanathan, V., Reyers, B. and Sörlin, S., 2015. Planetary Boundaries: Guiding Human Development on a Changing Planet. *Science*, 347(6223).

Surowiecki, J., 2005. *The Wisdom of Crowds*. New York: Anchor Books.

The Economist, 2010. Hello America. *The Economist* [online]. Available at: www.economist.com/node/16834943.

The Maddison Project, 2013. *Maddison Project Database*. [online]. Available at: www.ggdc.net/maddison/maddison-project/home.htm.

The World Bank, 2015. World Development Indicators Database, The World Bank [online]. Available at: http://data.worldbank.org/indicator/NY.GDP.MKTP.PP.CD.

Tilman, D., Cassman, K., Matson, P., Naylor, R. and Polasky, S., 2002. Agriculture Sustainability and Intensive Production Practices. *Nature*, 418, pp.671–7.

Tilman, D., Balzer, C., Hill, J. and Befort, B., 2011. Global Food Demand and the Sustainable Intensification of Agriculture. *Proceedings of the National Academy of Sciences*, 108(50), pp.20260–64.

Tingley, M., Estes, L. and Wilcove, D., 2013. Climate Change Must Not Blow Conservation Off Course. *Nature*, 500, pp.271–2.

Waters, C., Zalasiewicz, J., Summerhayes, C., Barnosky, A., Poirier, A., Gałuszka, A., Cearreta, A., Edgeworth, M., Ellis, E., Ellis, M., Jeandel, C., Leinfelder, R., McNeill, J., Richter, D., Steffen, W., Syvitski, J., Vidas, D., Wagreich, M., Williams, M., Zhisheng, A., Grinevald, J., Odada, E., Oreskes, N. and Wolfe, A., 2016. The Anthropocene is Functionally and Stratigraphically Distinct from the Holocene. *Science*, 351(6269).

Watson, J., Iwamura, T. and Butt, N., 2013. Mapping Vulnerability and Conservation Adaptation Strategies Under Climate Change. *Nature Climate Change*, 3, pp.989–94.

Weisz, H. and Steinberger, J., 2010. Reducing energy and material flows in cities. *Current Opinion in Environmental Sustainability*, 2, pp.185–92.

Williams, E., Ayres, R. and Heller, M., 2002. The 1.7 Kilogram Microchip: Energy and Material Use in the Production of Semiconductor Devices. *Environmental Science & Technology*, 36(24), pp.5504–10.

Wolman, A., 1965. The Metabolism of the City. *Scientific American*, 213, pp.179–85.

World Commission on Environment and Development, 1987. *Our Common Future*. London, Oxford University Press.

Zaccai, E., 2012. Over Two Decades in Pursuit of Sustainable Development: Influence, Transformations, Limits. *Environmental Development*, 1(1), pp.79–90.

3   The urbanscape

Why cities are at the core of sustainability

Much on sustainable development is written from the perspective of countries, or from one of the multitude of people to have attended some related UN conference. Cities as the single largest drivers of the world's economy, and the single largest generators of pollution and waste, are relatively quiet in the sustainable development debate. This is mostly by design, as cities usually defer to national (or state/provincial) representatives. Local imperatives are often difficult to contextualize in global conversations.

Corporations and countries are usually the main agencies to advocate for and measure sustainability. In the case of planetary boundaries, a global metric is used. Corporations usually pursue sustainable development objectives within the context of market-share protection and enhancement. And as future companies are not able to lobby and promote their perspective, existing corporations implicitly encourage the status quo and sustained profitability. Countries advocating for sustainable development must do so within the constraints of possible regional tensions at home, protection of territorial integrity, and geopolitical considerations. Cities, on the other hand, are increasingly measuring sustainability through service provision standards and local quality of life (well-being).

Measuring sustainability

Countries are transient, cities less so. Heads of state spend considerable efforts safeguarding country borders and powers, mayors less so. For example, two-thirds of today's 195 member countries did not exist in 1945, when the UN was established. Every one of the 120 'Future Five' cities was a large urban conurbation in 1945, most having had continuous human habitation at their location for more than 200 years. The political borders of cities may be as fluid as national borders; however, sustained residency in key urban areas is common for most cities.

Coincidently, nationalism has proceeded at a pace almost as fast as urbanization. Cities drive much of the world's nationalism and their host country's political dynamic (simply through their share of population and economy). Almost every one of the world's largest cities has had its political boundaries changed in the last 70 years by 'senior' levels of government, although in most cases the city is older than the national government (about half the world's countries did not exist in present form before 1945). Cities are a unique and historical confluence of political and material drivers (Angel, 2011).

Most international affairs are driven by countries and their agencies, yet cities generate the wealth and markets that drive and sustain these affairs. Colonialism, for example, affected enormous swaths of geography, yet it was the conversations and raising of finance in cities like London, Amsterdam, Paris, Lisbon, Rome and Madrid that drove much of colonialism.

Governance, or governments, follow a pattern similar to differential equations with primary, secondary and tertiary, or first-order, second-order, third-order application. 'First-order' or community (city) governance should be the most responsive with least distortion and uncertainty. Through habit, much of the world now approaches governance with nations being 'senior' or primary; however, a more apt approach is a hierarchy with the community centre and other levels of government radiating outward. The first level of 'constituted' government is, then, the city. Constitutions may not fully reflect this hierarchy of governance; however, as populations are stressed in future, retrenchment of day-to-day life is likely. Countries may fracture, but cities as urban agglomerations (based on material flows) cannot be further divided. Berlin, for example, was only divided temporarily.

As development and financial aid grew in the twentieth century agreements were structured country-to-country. The term 'third world' emerged during the Cold War as a way to differentiate between OECD countries (first world), Communist-bloc countries (second world) and non-aligned nations (third world). The Non-Aligned Movement was strengthened through the 1955 Bandung Conference; however, between the first use of the term 'third world' in 1952[1] and the late 1980s, third world tended to connote developing and low-income countries. Similar to the vernacular at the time, *Our Common Future* (1987) differentiates by 'Industrialized Countries' and 'Third-World Countries'.

'Third world' and 'developing country' are seen as pejorative by some (IISD 2000), and countries are now more typically defined as high income, middle income (which is occasionally divided into upper and lower) and low income. The level of income is defined by GNI (gross national income) and published every July 1 by the World Bank (and elsewhere). In 1964 the World Bank further simplified country definition to 'Part 1' and 'Part 2', Part 1 countries being those that by and large contributed to IDA (concessional lending of the International Development Agency) and Part 2 those countries eligible for IDA finance. The threshold was initially set at an annual per capita income level of $250 and today stands at $1,045 (World Bank, 2014). 'Middle-income' economies are those with a GNI per capita of more than $1,045 but less than $12,746; 'high-income' economies are those with a GNI per capita of $12,746 or more. 'Lower-middle-income' and 'upper-middle-income' economies are separated at a GNI per capita of $4,125 (2015 fiscal year values based on 2013 actuals).

The history of estimating a country's total economy goes back almost 350 years. William Petty created the first estimate of national income in 1665 (for England, improved 1696 by Gregory King to measure domestic product by income, production and expenditure). Simon Kuznet presented the concept of

GDP to US Congress (National Income, 1929–35). Wassily Leontief further refined the concept through economic input–output models in 1936 (the same year John Maynard Keynes published *General Theory of Employment, Interest and Money* and commissioned J. M. Meade and J. R. Stone to estimate national income and expenditure).

The Bretton Woods organizations (World Bank Group and IMF) established in 1944 likely increased overall usage and familiarity with gross national product (GDP) as a metric for economic output. Lending volumes (and interest rates) and differentiated fees and capital contributions were often defined by GDP levels (as GNI). The use of GDP as a measure of economic output (with most countries pursuing annual growth in GDP) became the common mindset in the last half of the twentieth century. Today, GDP – as a measure of economic output – is likely the most powerful metric driving political processes. Recognizing the limitations of GDP as a measure of a country's progress, other metrics such as genuine progress index (GPI) and human development index (HDI) are regularly tracked.

Sustainable development is not nearly as easy to measure as economic output (GDP). Much of the institutional landscape of sustainable development and its discussion is taken up by countries and their agencies (Dietz, Ostrom and Stern, 2003). The scale may be part of the challenge. The most important metrics in quality of life – employment, education, air quality, safety, mobility, connectivity – can vary markedly across a country, rural-to-urban, and city-to-city. For example, Los Angeles has much different air quality from Seattle; Montreal's unemployment rate differs from Calgary's; Kolkata's educational scores are much lower than Bangalore's.

Countries are broadly managed through macroeconomic tools, e.g. currency, interest rates, import–export controls and standing militaries. These are intended to provide a stable environment for the economy to flourish. The national government's role is largely to protect sovereign territory, redistribute wealth (and hardship), provide peace, order and good government, and facilitate access to the economy's needed inputs, e.g. energy, food and water. Countries on behalf of their cities project power internationally.

Francis Fukuyama (1992; 1995) in *The End of History* and *Trust* argues the long-term superiority of liberal democracies as a stable form of governance, with recognition of the importance (and enhancement) of trust – trust between people, agencies, government and institutions. Elinor Ostrom (1995; 2011) argues for a similar emphasis on trustworthy and effective institutions as a precursor to effective management of the commons. Trust is, however, usually stronger at the local level.

Over the last several decades the United Nations, and its committees and agencies, has arguably played the lead role in defining and pursuing 'sustainable development', particularly from 1987 onward with the publication of *Our Common Future*. The UN (apart from its subnational governmental agency of UN-Habitat) convenes and represents national governments. History for the last few hundred years is usually discussed from the perspective of countries or national factions of major cultures.

The commons is most often envisaged as oceans or shared grazing lands and forests. This perspective may well change, as urban areas emerge even larger in the public psyche. Both well-being and trust tend to be higher in urban areas. Cities also drive culture and economies (where pragmatism takes on greater value). Countries will continue to play a possessive and protective role; however, the emerging 'commons', as shared human space, may well be the city. Connecting these cities and building trust within and among them will be a key geopolitical driver of this century.

In addition to the UN, several key institutions have an important role in defining and encouraging sustainable development. These include: the World Bank and its sister organization the IMF; other international financial institutions (e.g. Asian Development Bank, African Development Bank, Inter-American Development Bank and the new BRICS Bank); OECD, International Organization of Standards; and a host of other institutions, often with specific but critical mandates, such as World Meteorological Association, Red Cross–Red Crescent and International Air Transport Association.

Table 3.1 presents a summary of sustainability metrics. The list is indicative only, as in some areas, for example sustainability rating of infrastructure, there are more than 600 identified metrics (Poveda and Lipsett, 2014). Sustainability measurement, or at least adherence to the concept, started as early as Balinese rice *subaks* (more than 1,000 years ago), governing for 'the Seventh Generation' (500 years ago in the Iroquois Nation) and regulations requiring 'sustainable timber yield' (c.1713 in Germany).

The first known use of cost–benefit analysis is thought to have been by Jules Dupuit in France, evaluating a bridge on behalf of President Bonaparte (1844). The US Corp of Engineers was mandated under the 1936 Federal Navigation Act to apply cost–benefit analysis, a powerful tool for sustainable development, despite the likelihood of debates on (true) costs and benefits. Determining and including externalities is a useful way to increase the robustness of cost–benefit analysis.

King Wangchuck of Bhutan gained notoriety when upon his coronation in 1972 he declared that Bhutan's pursuit would be 'gross domestic happiness'. Several important measures followed, e.g. the World Values Survey that started in 1981 and the UN's Human Development Index.

Systems engineering is an important tool to drive greater sustainability in cities, as well as in other sectors; it is often considered key to modern development (Schlager, 1956). Systems engineering takes a holistic, interdisciplinary and integrated view of complex and usually dynamic systems.

Life cycle assessment (LCA) is thought to have begun in 1969 when Coca Cola retained Midwest Research Institute to compare different types of beverage containers: plastic vs steel, vs glass, vs aluminium. Proctor & Gamble carried out a similar assessment through Franklin Associates in 1988 to compare types of packaging and surfactants. LCA takes a 'cradle-to-grave' view and is now a standard metric in the energy industry, e.g. oil and gas, and consumer products, e.g. Walmart's sustainable product index. LCA, or overall sustainability

Table 3.1 Sustainability: measurement, activities and tools

Approach	Application	Example of implementation
Cooperative Farming	Balinese Rice *Subaks*	Shared water rights integrated with *Tri Hita Karna* (religious tenet emphasizing harmony), practiced more than 1,000 years
Governing for Future Generations	Seven Generations	'In every deliberation, we must consider the impact on the seventh generation ...' – the Constitution of the Iroquois Nations (more than 500 years ago)
Sustainable Yield	Timber Harvest in Forestry	Royal Mining Office (Germany) and Hanns Carl von Carlowitz suggest Nachhaltiger Ertrag (sustained yield) for timber supply (1713)
Statistical Dispersion (Income Equality)	Gini Coefficent	Corrado Gini, Variability and Mutability, 1912, relative distribution (usually used to measure income inequality)
Cost–Benefit Analysis		• Jules Dupuit in France analyses merits of bridge and possible toll rates (for Pres Bonaparte) 1848 • US Corp of Engineers mandated to use C-B analysis in 1936 Federal Navigation Act
Measure of Economy	Gross Domestic Product	• William Petty creates first estimate of national income, 1665 (for England – Improved 1696 by Gregory King to measure domestic product by income, production and expenditure) • Simon Kuznet presents concept of GDP to US Congress (National Income, 1929–35) • Wassily Leontief develops economic input–output model, 1936 (same year John Maynard Keynes publishes *General Theory* and commissions Meade & Stone to estimate national income and expenditure) • Upon coronation, King Wangchuck of Bhutan declares country's pursuit is 'Gross Domestic Happiness' (1972) • UN's Human Development Index (1990)
Measure of Well-being	Gross Domestic Well-being	World Values Survey (started 1981, now available for more than 100 countries)
Product Labelling		• Germany's Blue Angel Programme (1978) • Environment Canada's EcoLogo certified products (1988)
Environmental Agencies	Legislative Establishment	• Canada Water Act (1970); Department of Environment (1971), advocated 'ecosystem management' • US EPA started December 1970
Probabilistic Risk Assessment	Risk-Informed Decision Making	US National Research Council (1982); US Nuclear Regulatory Commission (1983) and NASA

Approach	Application	Example of implementation
Material Flows Assessment	Urban Metabolism	• Wolman, Scientific America (1965); 'Industrial Ecology' (1989) • Urban GHG emissions inventories (approx. 1989)
Equivalency Aggregation	Disability Adjusted Life Year (DALY)	Harvard University develops concept for the World Bank as means to measure overall disease burden (1990)
Strategic Decision Making	Game Theory	• Mixed Strategy Equilibria, zero-sum games (Von Neuman's minimax theorem, 1928) • Tucker's 'Prisoner's dilemma' (1950)
Life Cycle Assessment		• Coca Cola retains Midwest Research Institute in 1969 to compare types of beverage containers • Proctor & Gamble retains Franklin Associates to compare packaging and surfactants (1988)
Systems Engineering		• Schlager (1953) – 'Systems Engineering key to modern development' (key role in engineering) • Interdisciplinary (lifecycle) field of engineering • Schlager 1956 (Bell Telephone Laboratories) • National Council on Systems Engineering (NCOSE, 1990) • 'Limits to Growth', MIT, global ecosystems modelling • 'Ecological engineering' (1962) coined by H.T. Odum – Systems Ecology and energy/material flows 1983
Scenario Analysis and Integrated Assessment		• Herman Kahn and Hudson Institute for scenario planning and public policy (1961) • Royal Dutch Shell scenario planning (1971)
Contingent Valuation	Willingness to Pay	• Surveys proposed by Ciriacy-Wantrup (1947) • NOAA convenes high-level advisory panel on survey methodology (1993)
Social Entrepreneurship		• Ashoka: Innovators for the Public, 1981 • Various – usually individual metrics • Grameen Bank, 1983
Philosophy		• Jeremy Bentham (1748–1832): greatest happiness principle • John Stuart Mill (1806–73): liberty, scientific method, and utilitarianism • Gifford Pinchot (1865–1946): 'conservation ethic' and Wise Use, US Forestry Service • Aldo Leopold (1887–1948): land ethic (e.g. A Sand County Almanac)

Table 3.1 Continued

Approach	Application	Example of implementation
Earth Summit	UN Conference on Environment and Development in Rio de Janeiro, 1992	• 109 heads of state • Agenda 21 (Local Agenda 21) • Outcomes: climate change convention, convention on biological diversity, UNFCCC, reform of GEF, statement of forest principles • 'Common but differentiated responsibilities'
Use of Indicators	Simple indicators	Numerous examples, including Australia's Sustainable Forest Management Framework, e.g., Indicator 1.1.a – area of forest by forest type and tenure
	Compound and complex indicators	World Economic Forum's sustainably adjusted Global Competitiveness Index (GCI)
Assessments	Environmental Impact Assessment (EIA), Social Impact Assessment (SIA)	Standard practice in many countries for all new developments
	Life Cycle Assessment (LCA)	Roundtable on Sustainable Biofuels Fossil Fuel Baseline Calculation Methodology (RSB-STD-01-003-02)
Framework Assessments	European Research Projects	• European Common Indicators (1999–2003) • LASALA – Local Authorities' Self-Assessment of Local Agenda 21 (1999–2002) • Indicators to Assess New Urban Services (2000–2003) • Urban-Nexus (2011–2014)
Equivalence Measurement	Ecological Footprint	• William Rees (1992) • Wackernagel and Rees (1996)
Maintenance of Capital Stocks and Flows	Triple Bottom Line (TBL) Sustainability	The Global Reporting Initiative (GRI) founded in Boston (1997)
Schemes and Standards for Measuring, Assessing, Reporting and Certifying Sustainability		• Montreal Process Criteria and Indicators of Sustainable Forest Management • Forest Stewardship Council – Certification • The Carbon Disclosure Project (2000) • The Standards Map: information on 120 voluntary standards operating in over 200 countries, and certifying products and services in more than 80 economic sectors • ISO 9000 Quality Standards • EcoChoice, Blue Dot, Fair Trade • 'Dolphin Safe' • Jantzi Social Index • Energystar • Acumen (Capital) Fund, 2001

Approach	Application	Example of implementation
(Driver-Impact) Pressure-State-Response (DIPSR)	Pressure-State-Response (PSR)	OECD: Environmental Indicators 2008; Guidelines for Multinational Enterprises (voluntary standards), 1976
Accounting System Approaches	System of Integrated Environmental and Economic Accounting (SEEA)	SEEA Central Framework, adopted in 2012 as an international standard by the United Nations Statistical Commission, supported by the European Commission, FAO, IMF, OECD, UN and World Bank
	Consumption-based Accounting (CBA)	United Kingdom 2011–13 – Department for Energy and Climate Change (DECC) with the University of Leeds, developing a CBA Indicator for GHG emissions
	Supply Chain	Global Forest Watch
Indexes		<ul><li>Dow Jones Sustainability Index, 1999</li><li>Yale's Environmental Sustainability Index, 2000</li><li>Transparency International started by Peter Eigen, 1993</li><li>World Bank's 'Ease of Doing Business' Index launched Nov, 2001</li></ul>
Risk Assessment Dealing with Uncertainty	Risk Assessment and Management	<ul><li>ISO 31000 – Risk Management</li><li>Risk Management – Principles and Guidelines</li></ul>
Subjective Well-being		Cognitive and affective evaluations; Ed Denier (2000) – proposes a US national Index of SWB
Rating of Buildings	Sustainable Buildings	<ul><li>BREEAM (Building Research Establishment Environmental Assessment Methodology, 1990)</li><li>US Green Building Council (1993), LEED (Leadership in Energy and Environment Design, 2000)</li><li>Canadian GBC (2002)</li><li>BOMA (founded 1907) provides advisory services and ratings for building owners</li></ul>
Rating of Cities		<ul><li>GaWC – Globalization and World Cities, Beaverstock et al., 1998 – e.g., London and NYC 'Alpha++'</li><li>Saskia Sassen, The Global City (1991), NYC, Tokyo and London. Now city raking and indices common and widespread, e.g. Mercer Index of Livability, 2000</li><li>WHO 'Healthy Cities Project', 53 indicators from 47 cities (1992–4)</li><li>Mercer (2005), Economist (2005), Siemens Green City Index (started 2009), and others, ranking cities for 'livability', 'quality of life', etc.</li></ul>

Table 3.1 Continued

Approach	Application	Example of implementation
Management Approaches: Adherence to Prescribed Approaches	Best Management Practices (BMP), Codes of Practice; Environmental Management Systems (EMS)	• Cotton Australia's MYBMP, a best management practice tool for Australia's cotton growers • BSI Group – first EMS (BS 7750) • ISO 14000 series (1996); ISO 14001 used by more than 250,000 organizations in 159 countries (ISO, 2010)
	Six Sigma	Motorola introduces quality control scheme, 1988
Cost Curves	Marginal Abatement Cost Curves	Rose in prominence post Kyoto Protocol, e.g., McKinsey Global GHG abatement cost curve to 2030
Adaptive Management		Canadian Environmental Assessment Agency – Operational Policy Statement: Adaptive Management Measures under the Canadian Environmental Assessment Act
Engineering Principles	Strategic Guidance	• *Sustainable Development in the Consulting Engineering Industry*. FIDIC (2000) list of 18 objectives • Clift and Morris (2002), *Engineering with a Human Face*. Dealing with uncertainty; social acceptance
Millennium Development Goals	UN consensus – various metrics, various attainment	• Established September 2000. Eight goals over 15 years to 2015: (i) eradicate extreme poverty; (ii) primary education; (iii) gender equality; (iv) child mortality; (v) maternal health; (vi) combat disease; (vii) environmental sustainability; and (viii) partnership for development
Rio +10	Johannesburg, 2002	Johannesburg Declaration Included some 300 'partnership initiatives' to help achieve MDGs
Scenario Analysis and Integrated Assessment		• Intergovernmental Panel on Climate Change (IPCC) – 5th Assessment Report (AR5) • Shell Oil scenario planning continues
Environmental Performance Index		• Fare et al (2004) apply environmental performance index to sample of OECD countries • Esty and Porter (2005) – National Environmental Performance (data-driven and analytical rigour)
Millennium Ecosystem Assessment (MA) - Ecosystem Services Report		• Millennium Ecosystem Assessment • UK National Ecosystem Assessment 2011

Approach	Application	Example of implementation
Resilience Thinking, Thresholds and Planetary Boundaries		• Resilience Practice: Engaging the Sources of our Sustainability, Brian Walker and David Salt (2012), exploring the application of resilience theory to real-world situations • Rockstrom et al., *A safe operating space for humanity*, (climate change, ocean acidification, ozone depletion, N and P cycles, freshwater use, biodiversity loss, land use – plus pollution and aerosols), 2009. Updated by Steffen *et al* 2015
Measuring City Performance	City Indicators, GCIF (2007)	• Federation of Canadian Municipalities, 'Quality of Life in Canadian Communities' (2001) • European Common Indicators, Towards a Local Sustainability Profile (2003) • The power and potential of well-being indicators. A pilot project by nef (the New Economics Foundation) and Nottingham City Council (2004) • World Bank discussion paper, *The Current Status of City Indicators*. 'City Indicators: Now to Nanjing' presented at WUF3, Vancouver (2006)
Urban Growth Modelling	City Scaling	West and Bettencourt propose city scaling – economy scales super-linearly while infrastructure scales sub-linearly
Emissions Inventory	GHG Protocol	GHG emissions inventory (national, regional and city) – Scopes 1, 2 and 3; ISO 14064 (2006) from WBCSD-WRI (1998)
Adaptive Governance		*Adaptive governance and climate change*, Ronald D. Brunner and Amanda H. Lynch (2010), arguing for decentralized adaptive governance to provide diversity and innovation in addressing climate change
Corporate Social Responsibility		• Various corporate forms, ISO 26000 (November 2010): e.g. Marks & Spencer, Plan A; Body Shop; Patagonia • Sustainability Consortium (2009) – ASU, University of Arkansas and Walmart – product sustainability metrics (now more than 100 member companies)
Engineering Principles	Strategic Guidance	• Shanghai Declaration on Engineering and Sustainable Development. WFEO (2004) – commit to: ethics; interdisciplinarity; education and capacity building; gender issues; international cooperation • Abraham (2006) proposed nine principles • National directives: ICE, UK (2003); IPE, NZ (2004); Eng Aus., IIE, Spain (2005); CSCE and Engineers Canada (2006) • Meadows, Thinking in Systems (2008)

Table 3.1 Continued

Approach	Application	Example of implementation
Engineering Tools	Infrastructure Ratings	• Arup's ASPIRE (2008) with DFID and Engineers Against Poverty • Envision Infrastructure Rating System by ISI • Numerous other tools, e.g., BE2ST, GreenLITES, Greenroads, I-LAST and INVEST • CEEQUAL (UK – 2003)
Rio +20	Rio de Janeiro, 2012	• Billed as largest UN event ever organized • ~45,000 participants (130 heads of state) • Renewing Agenda 21 • 'Green economy roadmap' with SDGs ('The Future We Want') • Larger role for UNEP
Defining Urban Boundaries and Borders	Consultative or Directive	Data, Boundaries, Competitiveness: The Toronto Urban Region in Global Context. Global City Indicators Facility (2013)
Community Indicators	World Council on City Data	Sustainable development of communities: Indicators for City Services and Quality of Life. ISO 37120 (2014)
Sustainable Cities	Guidance Document	• Indicators of the Emerging and Sustainable Cities Initiative, Inter-American Development Bank, 2013 • Certu, European Commission
	Resource Efficient Cities	UNEP – International Resource Panel – 'Decoupling'
Inventories	Global or Regional Assessments	WWF Living Planet Report (2014) – 'half of all global wildlife lost since 1970'
Assessment Tools	Higg Index	• Apparel and footwear products – used by hundreds of organizations • Sustainability Consortium (100+ corporate members, 7 retail sectors)
Modelling, Data Management, 'Smart Cities'	Predictive Analytics	Predictive policing, e.g., Santa Cruz
	Algorithms in Policy Making	Traffic management, e.g., Lyon, Stockholm
	Data Mining and Systems Development	City management through data collection and predictive modelling, e.g., Rio de Janeiro, New York, Kunming
Indexes, continued	Sustainability	Yale's Environmental Sustainability Index (ESI) modified to Environmental Performance Index (EPI), 2005 – national rankings published annually (with WEF)
	Adaptation	Notre Dame – Global Adaptation Index (GAIN) – transferred from Global Adaptation Institute, 2013 – national rankings published annually

Approach	Application	Example of implementation
Sustainable Development Goals	UN consensus, 2015	• Target implementation 2016 to 2030 • 169 targets with 304 indicators • Comprised of 17 goals: (i) end poverty; (ii) end hunger, promote sustainable agriculture; (iii) promote well-being; (iv) quality education for all; (v) gender equality; (vi) sustainable water and sanitation for all; (vii) sustainable energy for all; (viii) economic growth and productive employment work for all; (ix) sustainable industrialization; (x) reduce inequality; (xi) sustainable cities; (xii) sustainable consumption and production; (xiii) combat climate change and its impacts; (xiv) conserve the oceans; (xv) manage lands and halt biodiversity loss; (xvi) inclusive societies and institutions; (xvii) revitalize global partnerships

NB: Ballantine (CitiesToday, October 2014) and Monnen and Clark (2013) list more than 150 benchmarking tools for sustainable cities metrics, e.g., Corporate Knights, Siemens Green City Index, AT Kearney's Global Cities Index, Mercer, ICLEI, C40, Covenant of Mayors, GRI, Eurostat Urban Audit. Poveda and Lipsett (2014) outline more than 600 existing approaches to sustainability assessment (mainly for buildings and infrastructure projects). Adapted from World Economic Forum, Designing for Action: Principles of Effective Sustainability Measurement (2013). European research projects from Moreno Pires et al. (2014). Engineering principles adapted from Gagnon et al. (2008).

assessments, are difficult to carry out, and apparently difficult to communicate in a way that keeps the public engaged. In 2007, the CEO of Tesco, Britain's largest grocer, promised 'a revolution in green consumption' by pledging to put carbon labels on its own 50,000 grocer products. The programme was phased out in 2012 with only 500 products labelled.[2] More recently, LCAs are being (somewhat) streamlined and supported by international standards, e.g. ISO 14040.

Product labelling such as that attempted by Tesco goes back to at least 1978 when Germany's Blue Angel programme began: products with a particularly low environmental impact were permitted to carry a trademarked symbol. Canada's EcoChoice logo provided similar certification starting in 1988.[3] Similar initiatives followed, such as 'dolphin friendly' tuna, and, more recently and more broadly, the Walmart-supported Sustainability Consortium. The Sustainability Consortium attempts to refrain from legislating ecolabels due to the complexity of social-ecological systems (recommending instead better supply of information), and suggests that any sustainable product index should simultaneously consider a broad spectrum of potential impacts, e.g. climate, ecosystems, energy use, efficiency, community well-being through the product's lifecycle.

Scenario planning, largely based on military strategic scenario exercises, attempts to evaluate (model) a dynamic system into the future. Royal Dutch Shell is likely the best known corporate to apply scenario planning. A challenge of scenario planning is the multiplicity of possible events around the world and their potential interactions. Cities are emerging as important clients for scenario planning, especially as it relates to the city's likely impact from, and response to, climate change. This work is also of growing relevance to casualty insurance firms.

A key aspect of sustainable development is risk identification and mitigation. Probabilistic risk assessment (PRA) grew from the aerospace and nuclear industries as a way to evaluate the probability of an event occurring and its potential impact (US Nuclear Regulatory Commission, 1983). PRA estimates the magnitude and likelihood of risk through the basic questions of 'What can go wrong, what would be the consequence, what is the probability?' Risk assessments are now commonly applied to key components of complex systems. In cities, this includes critical infrastructure such as water supply, power, transportation and food distribution. By estimating the likelihood of risk through standard tools such as those used by the insurance industry, impacts to complex systems, e.g. climate change impacting power distribution, quantification of sustainable development becomes possible (risk premiums adjusting to increasingly likely future events).

Partial impacts of risk are measured through a variety of tools. Risk-informed decision making (RIDM) is the most common and comprehensive approach to assess risk to (or from) complex systems (Zio and Pedroni, 2012). RIDM requires consistent metrics for risk impacts as well as probabilistic likelihoods and potential magnitudes. Responding to this demand in the health field, for example, Harvard University developed in 1990 on behalf of the World Bank the risk impact metric 'Disability Adjusted Life Years' (DALY). DALY now serves as a common metric for several sectors.

RIDM is emerging as a key tool in resilience estimation for cities. The Global Adaptation Index (ND-GAIN) estimates risk (and resilience) by country with national rankings published annually. The index was originally launched by Juan Jose Daboub (former Executive Director, World Bank), founding chief executive officer of the Global Adaptation Institute, and is now published annually by University of Notre Dame University.

Similar to ND-GAIN, Yale's Environmental Sustainability Index (ESI) from 1995 to 2005 annually ranked the world's countries by level of sustainability (based on 21 components). The main partners were Yale and Colombia Universities and the World Economic Forum (WEF). The Sustainability Index was shifted to the Environmental Performance Index (EPI) in 2006 and is now published every two years with a key focus on a country's achievement of the Millennium Development Goals and follow-on Sustainable Development Goals (Hsu et al., 2016). EPI[4] is researched and maintained by Yale and Colombia Universities in partnership with WEF. Performance is summarized in effective radar diagrams (Figure 3.1).

'Green buildings' are another important signalling tool for sustainable development (BREEAM, 1990; US GBC, 1993; LEED, 2000). The scope of assessment and degree of lifecycle impacts varies between programmes; however, programmes are merging to a common metric. Most programmes require accreditation of reviewers and fee payment by building developers.

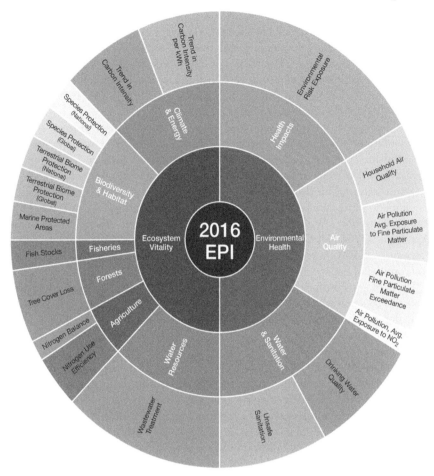

Figure 3.1 2016 Environmental Performance Index.
Source: Hsu et al. (2016).

Broader than buildings the US Institute for Sustainable Infrastructure developed Envision Infrastructure Rating System.[5] Envision contains 5 sections with 60 sustainability criteria. Clevenger, Ozbek and Simpson (2013) review the six most prominent US infrastructure rating tools, including Envision. All six tools have broad similarities; main variations result from differences in attribute weightings. Achievement of sustainability is difficult as no consensus exists on what constitutes sustainability. ASPIRE, developed by Arup Consultants (2008) in partnership with DFID and Engineers Against Poverty, provided a dashboard approach to sustainability similar to other sustainability tools such as the Environmental Performance Index. A major challenge associated with sustainability rating tools is that there are more than 600 existing approaches to sustainability assessment of buildings and infrastructure projects (Poveda and Lipsett, 2014).

The high number of metrics with little consensus on what to measure is a common challenge. In developing a common set of city indicators, the World Bank illustrated in 2007 how among eight pilot cities (São Paulo, Belo Horizonte, Porto Allegra, Bogota, Cali, Montreal, Toronto, Vancouver) 1,100 city indicators were collected annually, yet only 2 were common across all eight cities. This lack of uniformity is largely resolved through issuance of ISO 37120 (International Organization for Standardization, 2014).

The 'ecological footprint' converts environmental impact into a spatial representation (Rees and Wackernagel, 1996). This leads to statements such as 'we need four planets to support today's lifestyle'. Canadians are estimated to have a global ecological footprint of about 7 Ha[6]. In assessing the ecological footprint as a tool for the European Union, researchers identified concerns and recommend using a basket of indicators including the Ecological Footprint (EF), Environmentally Weighted Material Consumption (EMC), Human Appropriation of Net Primary Production (HANPP) and Land and Ecosystem Accounts (LEAC) to monitor de-coupling of economic growth from environmental impacts (Best, 2008).

The ecological footprint based on its widespread use, and adaptation to 'carbon footprint', is a powerful tool. However, caution, or greater specificity, is warranted (Van den Bergh and Grazi, 2013). Carbon emissions as a spatial representation is less effective than presenting carbon emissions as tonnes per capita or per city, corporation or country.

The business community is actively producing sustainability metrics. In addition to specific product metrics such as those from Body Shop, Marks & Spencer and Tesco, industry-wide programmes are also being implemented. The Higgs Index, for example, was developed to largely measure worker health and safety and production impacts in the apparel and footwear sectors. Broader industry-wide initiatives include the Dow Jones Sustainability Index (1999). This is largely based on the Human Development Index. Competitiveness, a subset of sustainability, has been measured and reported annually by WEF since 1979.

The Global Reporting Initiative (GRI, founded 1997), with input from the Coalition for Environmentally Responsible Economies (CERES, founded 1989) and the Tellus Institute (founded 1976), endeavours to have sustainability reporting standard practice for all companies and organizations. The first guidelines were launched in 2000. The second iteration, known as G2, was unveiled in 2002 at Rio+10 in Johannesburg (2002). Version G4 of the guidelines is now available.

Over the last few decades numerous key international guidelines and codes of practice emerged. These are similar to the GRI and include the Equator Principles (banking practices), the Good Practice Guidance for Mining and Biodiversity, Sustainable Forestry Practices, Higgs Index, Carbon Disclosure Project, Consumption Based Accounting Indicators, LEED, FDIC and Sustainability Consortium. Indices are being developed, e.g. the Environmental Performance Index and Global Adaptation Index. Additional indices are being developed in areas such as resilience and security, although the methodological challenges of creating something as comprehensive as an energy security index are considerable (Costanza et al., 1997).

A key metric of sustainable development to 2015 was the Millennium Development Goals (MDGs). The MDGs were mainly socio-economic targets. They were replaced by the Sustainable Development Goals in late 2015.

Progress on the MDGs varied by region and by targets, e.g. not all improved simultaneously. With such heterogeneity the SDGs need to differentiate between inputs and outputs and ideally monitor an integrated approach to sustainable development that combines demography, economics, ecology and epidemiology (Bourguignon et al., 2010). The SDGs could be reframed as a planetary stewardship agreement that includes a new social contract on global sustainability.

When discussing sustainable development, two drawbacks associated with environmental management are typically raised: (1) the implicit assumption that ecosystem responses to human intervention are linear, and (2) the assumption that human and natural systems can be treated independently (Folke et al., 2002). The need for additional sustainable development indicators globally and individually that capture system dynamism, plus progress toward targets and values-based ethics is suggested along with the 'art of long term thinking' and recommend focusing on 'stocks' and 'institutions' (Dahl, 2012; Klauer et al., 2013).

The Sustainable Development Solutions Network proposes four dimensions of sustainable development: (1) the right to develop for every country; (2) human rights and social inclusion; (3) convergence of living standards across countries; (4) shared responsibilities and opportunities.[7]

Some researchers suggest integrating planetary boundaries and global catastrophic risk (Baum and Handoh, 2014). Others argue that climate policies need to use risk management tools to reflect the many sources of uncertainty (Kunreuther et al., 2013). Probabilistic risk assessment is, however, not straightforward, as there is rarely consensus on risk probability and risk tolerance can vary markedly.

The measurement of sustainable development is criticized as 'being vague; attracting hypocrites; and fostering delusions' (Robinson, 2004). 'Sustainability' is more typically used by academia and NGOs as they tend to have concerns that the aspect of development is seen to be synonymous with growth. Sustainable development in government and business is seen to be more managerial and incremental.

Measuring progress toward sustainable development post-2016 needs to recognize key aspects that arguably were not sufficiently measured through earlier metrics, or the MDGs. These local and global metrics need to recognize system-wide dynamism. Achievement of the SDGs will be heterogeneous and will vary spatially and temporarily for all metrics. An example of this would be the need to record Scope 3 (or embodied) GHG emissions by corporations and communities. A full measure of an indicator like biodiversity, GHG emissions, and resilience requires a local and global value.

Another metric that new SDG assessments will need to reflect is risk. As the impacts of non-sustainable development become more pressing and identifiable, risk mitigation and risk insurance will take on a larger role. Risk-informed decision making (RIDM) will likely merge with efforts to enhance sustainability and increased resilience.

Both system-dynamism and the need for flexible yet comprehensive indicators, e.g. Scopes 1, 2 and 3, and the RIDM and sustainability metric are most critical in urban areas. ISO 37120 could play a large role in identifying and collecting these metrics, especially if potential funding is associated with levels and achievement (e.g. green bonds and risk/resilience support).

Box 3.1 *Better data – a team effort*

On a crisp autumn day in 1906, 84-year-old British scientist and statistician Francis Galton visited the Plymouth fair. He headed to the poultry and livestock exhibits and observed a contest to guess the weight of a dressed ox. After the winner was announced, he collected the entry papers. There were 787 accepted entries. The dressed weight of the ox was 1198 pounds. The crowd had amazingly guessed an average weight of 1197 pounds (and a mean of 1207 pounds). Galton was astonished at the crowd's uncanny accuracy and published a letter in *Nature* in March 1907 outlining his observations.

Guessing the weight of livestock is not the only thing to challenge the wisdom of crowds. Jellybeans in a jar: if there's a contest and you can calculate the mean of the guesses, you should enter that number. Collectively, the crowd almost always knows best.

Restaurant reviews, large-group movie reviews, opinions on hotels, eBay participants, or Uber drivers – measure enough of the opinion of the crowd, and the accuracy is likely very good. This can also be seen in sports betting. The race-day odds for the Kentucky Derby or the point spread for the Super Bowl is uncannily accurate.

Several organizations take advantage of this 'two (or preferably more) heads are better than one' approach. The Iowa Electronics Market at the University of Iowa enables people to join the 'crowd' (paying a small membership fee increases accuracy) and entering considered opinions on who might win an upcoming election, or how financial markets might perform. The stock market when working well is a large prediction (or expectations) market.

Transparency International surveys about 3,000 business people to provide corruption rankings in 175 countries. The World Bank provides a similar assessment (and survey) in providing its annual 'Ease of Doing Business' Report. These estimates are not without controversy or discrepancy, but they are sufficiently accurate for considered input to public policy development.

The city sustainability assessments outlined in this book require both accurate and auditable data and professionally peer-reviewed 'best guess' estimates. A hierarchy of data quality is proposed. The best city-based data, when available, is ISO 37120 ('Sustainable development of communities – indicators for city services and quality of life', preferably available and audited by the not-for-profit World Council on City Data). Where cities have not yet provided this data, especially all local governments across a metropolitan area, estimates are made for a metropolitan average. This might include down-scaling of national data until city-specific information is available.

For the more subjective data sets like the indices of biodiversity impact, embodied water consumption, resilience, and land-use changes, partner organizations like WWF and the Notre Dame–GAIN Adaptation Index could assist along with 'crowd sourced' estimates. In selected cities, municipal officials, urban planners and civil engineers, could initially quickly provide accurate estimates for these values, to show proof of concept. A handful of researchers at the Universities of Toronto and University of Ontario Institute of Technology provided early estimates here. As the cities approach to sustainability evolves, a prediction market for key city information is under development.

International agencies working with cities

The following is a partial list of key agencies with international mandates working directly with cities. In the case of WBCSD and WEF, the organization's oversight and funding comes mainly from global corporations. In the case of OECD, UN, World Bank and GEF, oversight and funding comes from national governments. In the case of agencies like C40, ICLEI, UCLG, WWF and the Rockefeller Foundation, funding comes from a variety of sources such as endowments, membership and service fees, and contributions.

Other important organizations working directly with cities include ISO, FDIC and WFEO, IATA, Commonwealth of Nations, Interpol, WTO, EU and la Francophonie, among others. Foreign assistance agencies such as Canada's CIDA and Britain's DFID also work directly with cities.

Many agencies and corporations are emerging or expanding their city-specific initiatives, e.g. C40, Rockefeller Resilient Cities Program, WBCSD's Urban Infrastructure Initiative, World Economic Forum (WEF), Siemens Green City Index, WWF's annual Earth Hour Capital Award, as well as the World Council on City Data (WCCD) and the newly published ISO37120.[8] More should be expected. ICLEI, launched around the 1992 Rio conference, has been a strong advocate for member cities. The proposed Local Agenda 21s (modelled after national Agenda 21s as recommended at the Rio UNCSD) provided comprehensive plans for cities to work toward sustainable development. Similarly, the Cities Alliance provides a compelling starting point for city-specific sustainability through its long-standing City Development Strategy process.

The origins of the World Business Council for Sustainable Development (WBCSD) date back to the 1992 Rio Summit when Stephan Schmidheiny, a Swiss entrepreneur, was appointed chief adviser for business and industry to the secretary general of the UNCED. Schmidheiny convened the forum 'Business Council for Sustainable Development', which then wrote *Changing Course*, introducing the concept of eco-efficiency.

The WBCSD was created in 1995 through a merger of the Business Council for Sustainable Development and the World Industry Council for the Environment and is headquartered in Geneva, Switzerland. The WBCSD has more than 200 corporate members considered leaders in sustainable development (mainly

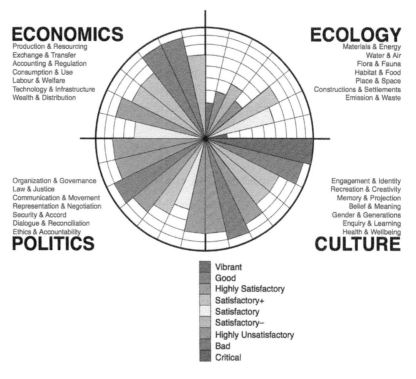

Figure 3.2 Circles of sustainability – Melbourne, Australia.

This image shows the sustainability of the Melbourne metropolis across the four domains of sustainability – economics, ecology, politics and culture – as developed by the UN Global Compact, Cities Programme.

Source: James, 2012.

multinational firms like Engie, Cisco, BP). WBCSD has about 50 full-time equivalent staff and an annual operating budget in the order of $14 million.

Greenpeace was severe in its criticism of WBCSD in its 2011 COP17 lead-up report 'Who's Holding Us Back? How Carbon-Intensive Industry is Preventing Effective Climate Legislation'. Greenpeace argued, 'WBCSD's Executive Committee is a Who's Who of the world's largest carbon-intensive companies who continue to profit from continued inaction on climate change.' Arguably, and there has been much argument, some of the business community has urged movement toward sustainable development and provided credible metrics and signposts on how to proceed as well as any sector.

Two important contributions of WBCSD include 'Vision 2050' and the Urban Infrastructure Initiative.[9] WBCSD's 'Visions 2050' lays out a pathway with nine elements that lead to Visions 2050: (i) people's values (one world – people and planet); (ii) human development (basic needs of all are met); (iii) economy (true value, true costs, true profits); (iv) agriculture (enough food and biofuels through a common Green Revolution); (v) forests (recovery and regeneration); (vi) energy and power (secure and sufficient supply of low-carbon energy); (vii) buildings (close to zero net energy buildings); (viii) mobility (safe and low-carbon mobility); and (ix) materials (no waste).

The Urban Infrastructure Initiative (UII) brought together 14 leading WBCSD-member companies and 10 cities. For each participating city, the main challenges and solutions landscapes were identified. Two key challenges of the UII concept emerged. Some approached cities were reluctant to work directly with WBCSD and its UII member companies. Concerns over potential downstream procurement challenges were raised. Another challenge associated with UII was how to select the member companies and cities, and how to mediate at-times varying objectives.

The World Economic Forum (WEF) was founded by Klaus Schwab in 1971 (and called the European Management Forum until 1987). Headquartered in Geneva, the organization has some 1,000 mostly trans-national member companies, 21 groupings of industry partners, strategic partners and regional partners. WEF is governed by a 14-member board of directors[10] and has about 500 full-time equivalent staff and an annual operating budget of 190 million CHF (US$192m). WEF is well known for its annual Davos meeting.

The WEF began publishing the Global Competitiveness Report in 1979 and the Global Risk Report in 2006. The Forum also publishes an annual Gender Gap Report, and is a key partner with Yale University's annual Environmental Performance Index.

A common criticism of both WEF and WBCSD, and perhaps the OECD (below), is their 'Euro-centric focus'. These organizations are aware of this and are taking steps to remedy, e.g. WEF's annual CEO summit in China. Similar criticisms are levelled at the UN, especially the globally discordant membership of the Security Council (the city association C40 is facing similar challenges with membership), and at the World Bank and IMF, as their presidents are typically appointed by the US and European Union respectively (leaving some 80 per cent of the world ineligible for presidency).

The Organization of Economic Cooperation and Development (OECD) began in 1948 as the Organization for European Economic Cooperation (OEEC). The organization was created mainly to administer the post-World War Two Marshall Plan and was reformed as the Organization for Economic Cooperation and Development (OECD) in 1961. Like the World Bank and UN, the OECD is owned and governed by countries (i.e. their national governments). In the case of OECD and the World Bank/IMF, the organizations are mainly overseen by the ministries of finance from respective countries, while the link to national governments and the UN is usually through ministries of foreign affairs, or their equivalents. For international negotiations such as the IPCC, the majority of country delegations are led by ministers of environment.

The OECD is seen as one of the more credible agencies reviewing regional and national trends and international economic affairs. It played a strong role in recommending the 'polluter pay principle' (1971) and in 1976 released Guidelines for Multinational Enterprises (voluntary standards relating to sustainable development for responsible business). In 2008, OECD began publishing Environmental Indicators for member countries.

An important contribution to cities and sustainable development is the OECD's series of Territorial Reviews, which began in 2001, with 17 national territorial reviews, 30 city (region) and 3 regional reviews, e.g. the Mesoamerican Region (2006). In a few cases, e.g. Switzerland (2002 and 2011), the reviews are periodically updated. Examples of city territorial reviews include Mexico City (2004), Montreal (2004), Toronto (2009), Guangdong (2010) and Gauteng (2011). OECD usually charges a fee for these reviews (about $300,000 per review [personal communications]) and in most cases is able to meet with representatives of national, regional and city officials. The selection of cities and countries undergoing territorial reviews is mostly ad hoc, determined by funding and staff availability.

International finance institutions

Similar to OECD's Territorial Reviews, over the last four years the World Bank completed Urbanization Reviews for China, Colombia, India, Indonesia, Korea, Sri Lanka, Uganda and Vietnam.

The role of international finance institutions (IFIs) and bilateral aid agencies in cities is considerable. These financing agencies likely have more than 3,000 active city-based investment projects around the world at any given time. A typical larger city in a Part-2 (low- or middle-income) member country can easily have more than 100 active international assistance projects supporting key aspects of infrastructure and social development. A recent review of the solid waste sector in Dar es Salaam provides a powerful example for the need to consolidate approaches by external agencies. Over the last 10 years more than 40 international organizations supported solid waste activities in the city. There are more than 10 solid waste master plans, many with differing objectives. In addition, the city has at least 26 reports and unsolicited proposals for energy from waste facilities.[11]

The World Bank Group (IBRD, IDA, MIGA and IFC) and regional International Financial Institutions (AfDB, ADB, EBRD, IADB, CAF, Islamic Development Bank and the new BRICS and China-led Asia Infrastructure Investment Banks) play a very large role in cities of Part-2 countries. The degree of influence varies by which cities the agencies work in, level of national income, e.g. IBRD or IDA lending, and city size and strategic value. Frequently, assistance overlaps, and is rarely coordinated, as it is often in the interest of the city or country to have more than one agency supporting activities in the city. This is further exacerbated when additional support is provided through bilateral (national) aid agencies and NGOs. For example, in the Dar es Salaam example, waste management support is provided through at least 10 different bilateral and international agencies.

As part of the GEF2020 programme, the Global Environment Facility (GEF) was tasked by its council to develop an Integrated Approach Platform (IAP) for sustainable cities. The sustainable cities IAP will help cities (urban areas) prepare, implement, monitor and refine integrated strategies for sustainable development (including reducing environmental impacts and increasing resilience and quality of life).

UN-Habitat and other city agencies

An important cities-focused agency is UN-Habitat, commonly considered the United Nation's 'cities-arm'. On 1 January 1975, the UN General Assembly established the United Nations Habitat and Human Settlements Foundation (UNHHSF), the first official UN body dedicated to urbanization (then under the umbrella of the UN Environment Programme, UNEP).

The Habitat I conference in 1976 in Vancouver resulted in the creation of the precursors of UN-Habitat: the United Nations Commission on Human Settlements – an intergovernmental body – and the United Nations Centre for Human Settlements (commonly referred to as 'Habitat'), which served as the executive secretariat of the Commission.

In 1996, the United Nations held a second conference on cities – Habitat II – in Istanbul, Turkey, to assess two decades of progress since Habitat I in Vancouver and to set fresh goals for the new millennium. Adopted by 171 countries, the political document contained over 100 commitments and 600 recommendations. On January 1, 2002, Habitat's mandate was strengthened, and its status elevated to a fully fledged programme in the UN system.

Stretching back to at least 1976 and the first UN-Habitat conference in Vancouver (followed by Istanbul in 1996),[12] national governments have attempted, through their own agencies, to work with cities in enhancing their local economies and environments while supporting global environmental objectives. National governments and their agencies appreciate the scale of assistance possible from cities in meeting sustainability objectives, the inherent pragmatism of cities, and the enormous and still growing city demands for new infrastructure and efficient service delivery.

From its outset, as highlighted on its own website, UN-Habitat complained of inadequate funding. Overlapping funding requests and mandates, especially with UNEP, were common. UN-Habitat and UNEP play critical roles in planning and focusing international support to cities, especially those in low- and middle-income countries. A challenge for both organizations is the non-permanence of mandate (and by extension, funding). This 'relevance of mandate' (and funding stability) plagues the UN overall and more intensely in individual agencies (and theoretically more readily discontinued). Traditionally, this instability was not part of the IFIs, largely as their core funding did not come through national contributions but rather through ongoing investment revenue. Recent re-organization challenges, however, at the World Bank, and the establishment of the BRICS Bank, raise questions about the long-term stability of these organizations.

The influence of cities is intensifying markedly: through their own agencies like C40, UCLG and ICLEI; international organizations like the GEF and World Bank; international agencies like WBCSD and WEF; local and global corporations; local and global NGOs; professionals and their agencies; and the financial and insurance communities. Cities through a host of mechanisms are playing a greater direct role in geopolitics. The influence is likely to intensify as cities establish more international offices[13] and embed their representatives more into the process.

Some argue that periodic events like Rio, Rio+10 and Rio+20 are unhelpful and distract and allow policy makers to regard green growth (or sustainability) as peripheral (Barbier, 2012). While Rio+20 was taking place, for example, the G20 met in Mexico, more concerned about immediate economic challenges than long-term sustainable development.

The complexity of international affairs is high, with some 560 international environmental agreements alone, of which 350 came into existence between 1972 and the early 2000s (Jabbour, 2012). These all have a direct impact on cities (Harrison and Hoyler, 2014; Grimm 2008).

Ruckelshaus (1989), the US representative author of *Our Common Future* and former head of the US EPA, writing in the *Scientific American* special edition 'Toward a Sustainable World', called for three things to improve institutions as they support sustainable development: (1) money especially for UNEP; (2) information – agencies to research and public information; and (3) integration of efforts. The example of Africa being served by 82 different international donors (in 1988) and 1,700 private organizations was highlighted. In 1980 Burkina Faso, with a population of 8 million, had 340 independent aid projects underway.

Examples of city agencies include C40, ICLEI, UCLG (and Metropolis) and Cities Alliance, in addition to the plethora of regional and national city associations. These agencies are likely to multiply and grow in importance and budgetary security (as cities grow).

The role of transnational municipal networks in climate mitigation activities is considerable; this will likely be replicated (and strengthened) for adaptation to climate change (Funfgeld, 2015). A city focus suggests that sustainability and resilience in the 'new urban world' from this point forward will largely be based on the sustainability of cities (Ahern, 2011). A system of connected cities for implementation of sustainable development presents considerable promise (focusing on city responsibility) (Seitzinger, 2012).

Some suggest a global parliament of mayors (Barber, 2013; Barber, Florida and Tapscott, 2014). This idea has been around for some time, e.g. Hoornweg (2011). New institutions, like a parliament of mayors, and strengthened and re-purposed existing institutions (from the perspective of cities) are likely to emerge in the next several decades.

Adaptation and resiliency, key aspects of sustainability, are likely to emerge as priorities for cities. More capable cities will respond with multi-functionality, greater redundancy and modularization, bio- and social-diversity, multi-scale networks and connectivity, and more adaptive planning and design (Ahern, 2013). Cities and their societies (i.e. institutions) need to enhance adaptive capacity, as they will be increasingly required to respond to rapidly changing conditions. Urban adaptation is emerging as a critical priority for cities.

The role of institutions

As early as Hardin's (1968) article 'Tragedy of the Commons' and his contention that the 'population problem' has no technical solution but rather requires a 'fundamental extension of morality', the role of institutions in achieving sustainable development has been promoted. The comparative analysis of sustainable development varies by institution (Mebratu, 1998). For example, the WCED through *Our Common Future* sought a nation-state solution platform with sustainable growth. IIED primarily sought rural development, while WBCSD sought eco-efficiency. Others call for a plurality of approaches (Sneddon, Howarth and Norgaard, 2006) and note that the institutional design affects public support for sustainable development (as observed in France, Germany, the UK and USA) (Bechtel and Scheve, 2013).

Good urban governance requires effective relations between various levels of government (Bulkeley and Betsill, 2005). The focus on inter-governmental relationship should not look for certainty in adapting to climate change, but rather plan for uncertainty (Hallegatte, 2009).

Putnam (1993), using north and south Italy as test-cases, highlighted how social capital and institutions are instrumental in determining the quality of governance, and by extension well-being. Building on this work, his two-level game theory suggests that international agreements will only be successfully brokered if they also result in domestic benefits (Putnam, 1988).

In 2009 Elinor Ostrom received the Nobel Prize in Economics, recognizing her 'analysis of economic governance, especially the commons'. Ostrom persuasively argued in her article 'Green from the Grassroots' that cities are critical to the challenge of protecting the global commons:

> This grassroots diversity in 'green policy making' makes economic sense. 'Sustainable cities' attract the creative, educated people who want to live in pollution-free, modern urban environment that suits their lifestyles. This is where future growth lies ... Of course, true sustainability goes further than pollution control. City planners must look beyond municipal limits and analyze flows and resources – energy, food, water and people – into and out of their cities.
>
> (Ostrom, 2012)

Leading up to this work, Ostrom (1996) called for input from citizens and synergy across disciplines. She discussed a general framework for analysing sustainability of social ecological ecosystems (Ostrom, 2009) and provided a framework for institutional analysis and development:

> (i) Clearly define boundaries; (ii) proportional equivalencies between benefits and costs; (iii) collective choice arrangements; (iv) effective monitoring; (v) graduated sanctions; (vi) conflict resolution mechanisms; (vii) recognition of rights to organize; and (viii) nested enterprises.
>
> (Ostrom, 2011)

The importance and efficacy of diverse institutions in human ecology and resource sustainability is well documented (Becker and Ostrom, 1995). Polycentric approaches, especially to climate change, are preferred, although two important challenges to polycentric governance remain – asymmetry and heterogeneity of risk perception (Ostrom, 2014; Tavoni, 2013). Local sanctioning institutions outperform global ones.

Challenges for planetary boundaries and global environmental governance include: (1) differing risk perceptions; (2) capacity of international institutions to deal with boundaries and interplay between stakeholders; (3) role of international organizations; and (4) global governance in framing social-ecological innovations (Galaz et al., 2012). A 'bottom-up institutional approach' to cooperative governance of the commons and its associated risks is recommended (Vasconcelos, Santos and Pacheco, 2013). Support to local institutional development through a self-organizational bottom-up poly-centric approach is warranted.

In providing a retrospective, 'The Tragedy of the Commons: Twenty-Two Years Later' Feeny et al. (1990) provide a more optimistic view than Garret Hardin's (1968) prediction of eventual overexploitation of common resources. They cite a number of cases of sustainable use of shared resources, suggest that private, state and communal property are all potentially viable resource management options and claim that Hardin's 'Tragedy of the Commons' argument overlooks the important potential role of institutional arrangements and cultural factors. Hardin, who apparently committed suicide with his wife in

2003,[14] might have issued a rejoinder to the optimism of Feeny et al. that based on current stresses on the global commons, e.g. atmosphere and biodiversity, certainty of success in sharing the commons is not yet evident.

Work by Ostrom, and others, on the governance of the commons and critical importance of competent institutions and agencies is an important contribution for implementing sustainable development in cities. Typically international agencies have focused on the commons such as oceans and shared ecosystems. However, as Ostrom opined in her last column, city planners need to look at the flow of resources and energy into and out of cities, as collectively this determines quality of life and local and global sustainability. In the next decade, as cities and researchers who work with them better understand their material flows and institutional dynamics relating to sustainability, cities will likely emerge as the 'new commons' despite the intense parochial protection cities enjoy.

Perhaps the most salient comment on institutions is that of Thomas Jefferson:

> I am not an advocate for frequent changes in laws and constitutions, but laws and institutions must go hand in hand with the progress of the human mind. As that becomes more developed, more enlightened, as new discoveries are made, new truths discovered and manners and opinions change, with the change of circumstances, institutions must advance also to keep pace with the times. We might as well require a man to wear still the coat which fitted him when a boy as a civilized society to remain ever under the regimen of their barbarous ancestors.[15]

Engineers and sustainable development

Engineering is the practical application of knowledge. Public policies and urban infrastructure prove themselves in the long run. Between the plans and eventual operation, fall the shadows and shades of grey. Just as the world's major civil works provide shelter, increased life expectancy (e.g. water and sewerage) and greater wealth (e.g. transportation systems), they also drive the majority of the world's environmental degradation.

'Knowledge is power', commented Sir Francis Bacon (1597). Applied knowledge as practised in engineering is particularly powerful, as impacts – positive and negative – are significant. With great power comes great responsibility, said Voltaire (1832). As engineers wrestle with the impacts of the cities they help build, they must also address how cities together now need to build sustainable development. 'Whatever you can do or dream you can, begin it. Boldness has genius, power, and magic in it. Begin it now' (attributed to Goethe).

The practice of engineering needs to be transformed in order to meet global health needs – more people have access to cell phones than basic sanitation (Niemeier, Gombachika and Richards-Kortum, 2014). Key suggestions: design for scarcity, scalability, simplicity and frugal design.

The Royal Academy of Engineering (2005) issued the report 'Engineering and Sustainability: a Comprehensive Assessment of Current Engineering Practices snd Recommendations for Future Standards'. Building on this, the World Federation of Engineering Organizations published its Model Code of Practice for Sustainable Development in 2013. Progress so far is arguably limited.

Engineers need to learn more 'soft skills', especially in urban settings (Cruickshank and Fenner, 2007). Also required is 'engineering with a human face' and engineers to act as 'stewards of the global commons' (Clift and Morris, 2002).

The growing shortage of qualified engineers and how this is likely to impact civil works in Sub-Saharan African cities is of particular concern (Hoornweg et al., 2014). In addition to constraints on finance, civil works are likely to be limited in future by availability of technicians, engineers and skilled tradespeople. New technologies are likely to emerge, e.g. pre-fabricated buildings; however, prioritizing major civil works in future is likely to have a greater consideration of staffing availability, in addition to economic concerns.

Institutional parallels?

Several organizations provide useful parallels for a possible city-based association-assigned oversight of city negotiations on sustainable development. Experience from the International Air Transport Association (IATA), the World Association of Nuclear Operators (WANO) and the Universal Postal Union (UPU) are informative.

The Universal Postal Union, founded in 1874 and headquartered in Bern, Switzerland, is the world's second-oldest international organization (to the Rhine Commission, founded in 1815). The agency, charged with facilitating global mail delivery, now exists within the United Nations framework. With about 250 employees, UPU focuses on global cooperation, standards, common fees and financial services. The 192 represented members annually deliver some 350 billion letters and 6 billion international parcels.

The International Air Transport Association (IATA) was founded 1945 in Havana, Cuba. IATA is mainly a trade association of the world's 250 airlines. Safety is the association's main priority. All members agree to undergo mandatory IATA Operational Safety Audits. Every year IATA members facilitate air travel of some 3.5 billion passengers, 50 million tonnes of cargo, and billing settlement transactions of $300 billion. The industry has a commendable safety record with the equivalent of one accident every five million flights. IATA has a staff of about 1,300 and is headquartered in Montreal.

Following the Chernobyl nuclear accident in 1986 nuclear operators reflected that an event at one plant impacted every plant and that nuclear safety was everyone's business. Leaders of every commercial nuclear reactor in the world set aside their competitive and regional differences and came together in 1989 to create World Association of Nuclear Operators (WANO). Much of the impetus for this came from the US, where preservation of the social licence to operate was critical; however, today, more than 130 worldwide members are represented, with 517 civil nuclear power reactors.

WANO is an autonomous organization with about 350 staff (many seconded from member organizations). Most activities are conducted through peer-to-peer processes. There are five regional offices – Atlanta, Moscow, Paris and Tokyo, plus headquarters in London, plus an affiliated office in Hong Kong.

One of the most powerful drivers of safety in a civil nuclear power plant is WANO's biennial safety rating. The metric is particularly important to operators as it is peer assessed and relatively free from political influence.

WANO is different from the International Atomic Energy Agency (IAEA) created in 1957 to help allay fears in nuclear technology and differentiate between the peaceful uses of atomic energy. IAEA's genesis was US President Eisenhower's 'Atoms for Peace' address to the UN General Assembly December 1953. The IAEA now has more than 2,500 staff working in some 100 countries. Funding mainly comes through the UN system (2014 operating budget €345 million) with about one third of the budget allocated to verification.

In 2008 the World Institute for Nuclear Security (WINS) was established, with representation from nuclear operators, industry and academia. The vision of WINS is 'to help improve security of nuclear and high hazard radioactive materials so that they are secure from unauthorized access, theft, sabotage and diversion and cannot be utilised for terrorist or other nefarious purposes'. WINS is closely affiliated with IAEA; both are headquartered in Vienna.

IAEA represents mainly nations and therefore takes on a geopolitical flavour of oversight and regulation – 'trust but verify'. The organization as part of the overall UN system is also subject to similar staffing practices (appointments by country and overall UN hiring practices). Countries attempt to exert influence through the organization.

WANO has a different mandate, with arguably greater pragmatism and professionalism. The operating budget – as mainly contributed by operating entities – is much more modest with a greater reliance on secondments. WANO has participation of every civil nuclear power plant operator (133 members with 517 reactors). Membership is voluntary, and degree of support and adherence to the organization's mandate obviously varies; however, the strength of peer influence, potential increases in professionalism and an understanding that safety is a shared responsibility is sufficiently compelling that no organization opts out. Participation in WANO is a key ingredient in many community-based social licences permitting facility operation (or, perhaps more likely, the failure to participate in WANO could degrade an operator's social licence).

WANO is 'engineer heavy': key staff and board members are predominantly engineers. This is both a strength and weakness. The peer-to-peer approach provides significant support, largely as plant operators typically share a common background and vernacular. Where this can become a weakness is when cultural norms and business practices play a significant role in plant safety. Peer-to-peer reviews that focus on cultural practices are more difficult to undertake. Recognizing this challenge, WANO's review of events at Fukushima Daiichi calls for a greater emphasis on mandatory reviews and an assessment of emergency preparedness 'outside the fence', and no more than the four-year interval between peer reviews of operations for all members.

Suggestions on a city association to oversee sustainable development negotiations

In reviewing IATA and UPU, and observing the different approaches taken by WANO and IAEA in overseeing the nuclear power industry, the following criteria for any new (or expansion to existing) city agency are suggested: (i) the bulk of funding should be from own (member) sources; (ii) heavy reliance on secondments; (iii) regional offices with as 'light management oversight' as possible; (iv) limit the focus, e.g. IATA and WANO focus on safety could be a city focus on sustainability (that includes resilience); (v) ideally no opting-out by member cities; (vi) self-management; and (vii) designate one representative from each city (urban area), e.g. an 'urban ambassador'.

Geoengineering – emergence of a 'wicked solution'?

When contemplating a cities approach to sustainable development, geoengineering emerges as a useful case study of how 'wicked problems'[16] and their solutions may evolve. Globally, cities will likely have as large a role in application of any planet-wide atmospheric solution, as will countries and corporations. Geoengineering includes a spectrum of actions ranging from painting roofs white and addition of iron to seawater to more aggressive methods, such as release of atmospheric sulphur.

Many important cities are particularly vulnerable to climate change and sea level rise due to their coastal proximity. Some will likely agitate more forcefully for 'solutions' than even their national counterparts. An example of this was provided in the 2012 US Presidential election when Mayor Bloomberg (notionally a Republican) argued loudly for candidate Obama to address climate change in his campaign platform (providing conditional support).

'Geoengineering' is already a difficult term to define clearly (Cairns and Stirling, 2014), a similarity shared with sustainable development. Geoengineering, like sustainable development, is about maintaining planetary systems versus concentrating global power. With regard to planetary boundaries and earth system governance, social tipping points are likely to trump technological step-changes (Biermann, 2012). The need for a safe and just regional approach is a key strategy in building local urban resilience (Dearing et al., 2014).

As climate perturbations grow, (some) cities are likely to experience impacts disproportionately greater than other cities, corporations and countries. Cities are home to the majority of infrastructure and therefore will experience the greatest financial impact. More developed cities (typically 'richer') with more infrastructure will experience greater financial loss, while less-developed cities, with more informal poor, will experience disproportionately high social costs.

Host countries may not be able to average costs and impacts. Individual cities will seek recourse, especially coastal and water-stressed cities.

Geoengineering is already well underway. For example, more than 145 million tonnes of nitrogen is produced annually, mostly as fertilizer (to grow food for people in cities). This nitrogen is already impacting global bio-systems. Many geoengineering options are relatively low cost to implement. Within the next 35 years it is possible that a city may be goaded by local citizens and businesses to implement climate action, either on its own, or collectively with similarly impacted cities.

The Future Fives cities proposed in this book to enter into negotiations toward collective sustainable development may well enter into a cooperative 'shadow agreement' on the use and oversight of geoengineering. Similarly, in protecting biodiversity, individual cities will likely be tasked with varying roles of habitat protection based on their location (and purchasing practices).

Shifting cities

In 1800 only one city, Beijing, had a population with over 1 million residents. The world's 10 largest cities each had an average population of about 614,000. China, reflecting its economic might at the time, had three of the top ten largest cities. Japan also had three, and the UK, France, Turkey and Italy each had one.

In 1900 the locus of economy and global stature shifted significantly. London was the world's largest city, with 6.5 million people. Manchester was also one of the top ten. The US, moving up quickly in economic heft, had three cities in the top ten (New York, Chicago and Philadelphia). Japan dropped from three cities in the top ten a century earlier to just one – Tokyo. China had none. France, Germany and Austria each had one, and Russia, gaining in prominence, had St. Petersburg and Moscow emerging. The average size of a top-ten city had increased more than fourfold from 1800, with a 2.6 million population in 1900.

Shift forward another 100 years to 2000 and the average top-ten city size grew more than sevenfold to 20 million residents each. The largest city, Tokyo, had 34.5 million. Shanghai and Beijing re-emerged. Mexico City and São Paulo also entered the top ten. Mumbai, Delhi and Kolkata highlight India's (re)emergence. Of cities with an Anglo-European origin, only New York remains in the top ten. Contrast this to 1900, when nine were in the US and Europe.

Shift forward yet another 100 years to 2100 and the average city size is again anticipated to triple from today. The average size of the top ten cities – Lagos, Kinshasa, Dar es Salaam, Mumbai, Delhi, Khartoum, Niamey, Dhaka, Kolkata, Kabul – is projected to be around 64 million. Lagos will likely be the largest city ever, reaching 88 million people. By the end of this century half of the top ten cities will likely be in Africa and half in South Asia (Hoornweg and Pope, 2014).

The year 2050 provides a useful waypoint. The top ten cities will likely have shifted to (i) Mumbai, India; (ii) Delhi, India; (iii) Dhaka, Bangladesh; (iv)

63 Cities in 2010 with Population > 5 Million

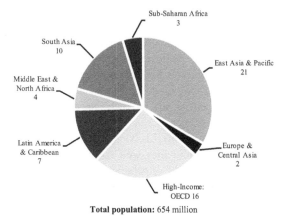

Total population: 654 million

122 Cities in 2050 with Population > 5 Million

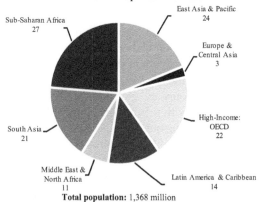

Total population: 1,368 million

181 Cities in 2100 with Populations > 5 Million

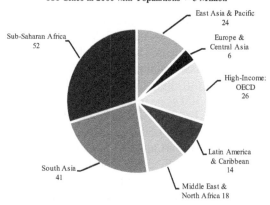

Total population: 2,787 million

Figure 3.3 The world's shifting cities – by region; cities with populations above five million in 2010, 2050, 2100.

Source: adapted from Hoornweg and Pope, 2014; 2010 values from WUP: The 2014 Revision.

Kinshasa, Democratic Republic of the Congo; (v) Kolkata, India; (vi) Lagos, Nigeria; (vii) Tokyo, Japan; (viii) Karachi, Pakistan; (ix) New York City–Newark, USA; and (x) Mexico City, Mexico.

A pattern of waves of urbanization emerges, beginning in 1800 when only Beijing was larger than 1 million. From 1800 to 1900, growth of cities concentrated in Europe and the US (as did the growth of wealth). From 1900 to 2000, large cities became more widespread. Urbanization spread to Latin America and grew in East Asia and South Asia. Going forward, the next wave of urbanization is South Asia (India, Pakistan, Bangladesh and Afghanistan). The last and largest wave of city growth will be in Sub-Saharan Africa.

Most geopolitics is assessed from the perspective of countries. Institutions like the United Nations and the World Bank, along with agencies like International Organization of Standards, plus projection of power through national militaries, is viewed from the objectives of countries. A country's objectives typically reflect the aggregate influence of citizens (with varying influence per capita, regionally, ethnically, etc.). When viewing likely future events from the perspective of cities for the remainder of this century, several massive trends emerge. These include:

The influence of East Asia, especially China, declines (2020–60).

By the end of the century, the world's top ten largest cities are all in countries that are currently low income.

Sub-Saharan Africa's cities will grow the most in size and number (and likely relative geopolitical influence) of all regions.

South Asia is the region second only to Africa likely to undergo major growth.

Indicative projections of energy demand and municipal solid waste generation illustrate the scale of the challenge facing humanity. Resource provisioning and assimilative capacities of ecosystems are well beyond sustainable levels.

Notes

1 Alfred Sauvy, in an article published in *L'Observateur*, August 14, 1952, is believed to have first coined the term Third World.

2 L. Lucas and P. Clark, 'Tesco Steps Back on Carbon Footprint Labelling', *The Financial Times*, January 31, 2012.

3 The author was a member of the first technical advisory board (for the EcoCoice designation on recycled paper content, 1988).

4 EPI ranks countries based on 20 indicators for human health (protection from environmental harm) and ecosystem protection.

5 www.sustainableinfrastructure.org/rating/.

6 From Global Footprint Network, http://footprintnetwork.org.

7 Launched by UN Secretary General Ban Ki-moon in August 2012, the Sustainable Development Solutions Network (SDSN) mobilizes scientific and technical expertise from academia, civil society and the private sector in support of sustainable development problem solving at local, national, and global scales. The SDSN works closely with United Nations agencies, multilateral financing institutions, the private sector and civil society.

The organization and governance of the SDSN aims to enable a large number of leaders from all regions and a diverse set of backgrounds to participate in the running of the network while at the same time ensuring effective structures for decision making and accountability. Twelve Thematic Groups involving experts from around the world lead the technical work of the SDSN. The SDSN Secretariat is hosted by Columbia University with staff in Paris, New York and New Delhi (http://unsdsn.org/, accessed December 8, 2014).

8 ISO 37120 – Sustainable Development' of Communities: Indicators for City Services and Quality Of Life is the first ISO 37120 international standard on city indicators. The first ISO standard was developed using the Global City Indicators Facility (GCIF) framework and input from the ISO Technical Committee on Sustainable Development of Communities (ISO/TC 268).

9 WBCSD in partnership with WRI also produced a GHG emissions inventory protocol (with Scopes 1, 2 and 3 sources) that was, with input from ICLEI and C40, later adapted as the Global Protocol for Community-Scale Greenhouse Gas Emission Inventories (launched December 8, 2014 in Lima, Peru).

10 Members of WEF's 2014 Foundation Board: Klaus Schwab, Chairman; Patrick Aebischer, Swiss Institute of Technology; H.M. Queen Rania Al Abdulla, Jordan; Mukesh Ambani, Reliance Industries, India; Peter Brabeck-Letmathe, CEO, Nestlé; Mark Carney, Bank of England; Victor Chu, CEO, First Eastern Investment Group, Hong Kong, Orit Gadiesh, Chairman, Bain & Company; Carlos Ghosn, CEO, Renault-Nissan Alliance; Herman Gref, CEO, Sberbank, Russia; Angel Gurria, Secretary-General, OECD, Susan Hockfield, Professor of Neuroscience, MIT, Donald Kaberuka President, African Development Bank; Klaus Kleinfeld, CEO, Alcoa Inc.; Christine Lagarde, Managing Director, IMF; Jack Ma, Chairman, Alibaba Group; Luis Moreno, President, Inter-American Development Bank; Indra Nooyi, CEO, PepsiCo; Peter Sands, CEO, Standard Chartered, United Kingdom; Joseph Schoendorf, Partner, Accel; Jim Hagemann Snabe, Member of the Board, SAP AG, Siemens AG, Allianz SE; Heizo Takenaka, Keio University, Japan; George Yeo Yong-Boon, Minister of Foreign Affairs of Singapore (2004–11); Min Zhu, Deputy Managing Director, IMF.

11 Personal field review and communications.

12 Barbara Crosette, Hope, and Pragmatism, for UN Cities Conference, by *New York Times*, June 3, 1996. 'Twenty years ago [in 1976] the United Nations held a conference in Vancouver to talk about a worrying world trend toward urbanization, especially the uncontrolled growth of cities in some of the poorest countries.

'That conference, held during the height of the cold war, swiftly descended into ideological bickering between industrialized nations and the third world, backed by the Soviet bloc. It ended with a statement of grandiose demands, almost none of which were fulfilled.

'Today [in 1996], the second United Nations Conference on Human Settlements opens in Istanbul. In the 20 years since the first conference, the problems – and size – of cities have grown enormously. But the atmosphere surrounding this meeting is markedly different, and delegates sound more pragmatic, businesslike and sober in their hopes of what can be achieved.

'For the first time, experienced city mayors may play a more prominent role in discussions than national government officials. Business leaders, scientists and hundreds of private organizations will be represented on national delegations or will hold their own meetings in the shadow of the conference, which runs to June 14. There will be a World Business Forum, a World Cities Assembly for mayors and a symposium of scientists from 72 national academies to discuss ways to use advanced technologies to make cities more livable and efficient.' (Habitat III is scheduled for October 2016.)

13 For example, around 1987, at the publication of *Our Common Future*, only a handful of the world's larger cities had 'Offices of International Affairs'. Today most larger cities devote staff and budget resources to International Affairs, and almost all cities have 'sister city' partnerships.

14 Scott Steepleton, 'Pioneering professor, wife die in apparent double suicide'. *Santa Barbara News-Press*, September 19, 2003, retrieved September 28, 2007. (Source: Wikipedia, December 7, 2014.)

15 Southeast Portico of Jefferson Monument, Washington, DC. Excerpted from a letter to Samuel Kercheval, July 12, 1816.

16 A wicked problem has no clear solution and is characterized by incomplete, contradictory, inter-dependent and dynamic requirements. Climate change is considered a wicked problem.

References

Ahern, J., 2011. From Fail-Safe to Safe-to-Fail: Sustainability and Resilience in the New Urban World. *Landscape and Urban Planning*, 100(4), pp.341–3.

Ahern, J., 2013. Urban Landscape Sustainability and Resilience: The Promise and Challenges of Integrating Ecology With Urban Planning and Design. *Landscape Ecology* 28(6), pp.1203–12.

Angel, S., 2011. *Making Room for a Planet of Cities*. Cambridge, MA: Lincoln Institute of Land Policy.

Barber, B., 2013. *If Mayors Ruled the World: Dysfunctional Nations, Rising Cities*. New Haven, CT: Yale University Press.

Barber, B., Florida, R. and Tapscott, D., 2014. *A 'Global Parliament of Mayors' Governance Network*. Toronto: Global Solutions Network.

Barbier, E., 2012. The Green Economy Post Rio+20. *Science*, 338, pp.887–8.

Baum, S. and Handoh, I., 2014. Integrating the Planetary Boundaries and Global Catastrophic Risk Paradigms. *Ecological Economics*, 107, pp.13–21.

Bechtel, M. and Scheve, K., 2013. Mass Support for Global Climate Agreements Depends on Institutional Design. *Proceedings of the National Academy of Sciences*, 110(34), pp.13763–8.

Becker, C. and Ostrom, E., 1995. Human Ecology and Resource Sustainability: The Importance of Institutional Diversity. *Annual Review of Ecology and Systematics*, 26, pp.113–33.

Best, A., Giljum, S., Simmons, C., Blobel, D., Lewis, K., Hammer, M., Cavalieri, S., Lutter, S. and Maguire, C., 2008. *Potential of the Ecological Footprint for Monitoring Environmental Impacts from Natural Resource Use: Analysis of the Potential of the Ecological Footprint and Related Assessment Tools for Use in the EU's Thematic Strategy on the Sustainable Use of Natural Resources*. Brussels: European Commission, DG Environment.

Biermann, F., 2012. Planetary Boundaries and Earth System Governance: Exploring the Links. *Ecological Economics*, 81, pp.4–9.

Bourguignon, F., Bénassy-Quéré, A., Dercon, S., Estache, A., Willem Gunning, J., Kanbur, R., Klasen, S., Maxwell, S., Platteau, J.-P. and Spadaro, A., 2009. The Millennium Development Goals: An Assessment. In: Kanbur, R. and Spence, M., eds, 2010. *Equity and Growth in a Globalizing World*. Washington, DC: The International Bank for Reconstruction and Development / The World Bank on behalf of the Commission on Growth and Development, ch. 2.

Bulkeley, H. and Betsill, M., 2005. Rethinking Sustainable Cities: Multilevel Governance and the 'Urban' Politics of Climate Change. *Environmental Politics*, 14(1), pp.42–63.

Cairns, R. and Stirling, A., 2014. 'Maintaining Planetary Systems' or 'Concentrating Global Power?' High Stakes in Contending Framings of Climate Geoengineering. *Global Environmental Change*, 28(1), pp.25–38.

Clift, R. and Morris, N., 2002. Engineering With a Human Face. *Engineering Management Journal*, 12(5), pp.226–30.

Costanza, R., d'Arge, R., de Groot, R., Farber, S., Grasso, M., Hannon, B., Limburg, K., Naeem, S., O'Neill, R., Paruelo, J., Raskin, R., Sutton, P. and van den Belt, M., 1997. The Value of the World's Ecosystem Services and Natural Capital. *Nature*, 387, pp.253–60.

Cruickshank, H. and Fenner, R., 2007. The Evolving Role of Engineers: Towards Sustainable Development of the Built Environment. *Journal of International Development*, 19, pp.111–21.

Dahl, A., 2012. Achievements and Gaps in Indicators for Sustainability. *Ecological Indicators*, 17, pp.14–19.

Dearing, J., Wang, R., Zhang, K., Dyke, J., Haberl, H., Hossain, S., Langdon, P., Lenton, T., Raworth, K., Brown, S., Carstensen, J., Cole, M., Cornell, S., Dawson, T., Doncaster, P., Eigenbrod, F., Florke, M., Jeffers, E., Mackay, A., Nykvist, B. and Poppy, G., 2014. Safe and Just Operating Spaces for Regional Social–Ecological Systems. *Global Environmental Change*, 28, pp.227–38.

Dietz, T., Ostrom, E., and Stern, P., 2003. The Struggle to Govern the Commons. *Science*, 302, pp.1907–11,

Dupuit, J., 1844. De la mesure de l'utilité des travaux publics. *Annales des Ponts et Chaussées*, 2nd series, 8(116). Translation by Barback, R.H., 1952. On the Measurement of the Utility of Public Works. *International Economic Papers*, 2, pp.83–110. London: Macmillan.

Feeny, D., Berkes, F., McCay, B. and Acheson, J., 1990. The Tragedy of the Commons: Twenty-Two Years Later. *Human Ecology*, 18(1), pp.1–19.

Folke, C., Carpenter, S., Elmqvist, T., Gunderson, L., Holling, C.S. and Walker, B., 2002. Resilience and Sustainable Development: Building Adaptive Capacity in a World of Transformations. *AMBIO*, 31(5), pp.437–40.

Fukuyama, F., 1992. *The End of History and the Last Man*. New York: The Free Press.

Fukuyama, F., 1995. *Trust: The Social Virtues and the Creation of Prosperity*. New York: The Free Press.

Funfgeld, H., 2015. Facilitating Local Climate Change Adaptation Through Transnational Municipal Networks. *Current Opinion in Environmental Sustainability*, 12, pp.67–73.

Galaz, V., Biermann, F., Crona, B., Loorbach, D., Folke, C., Olsson, P., Nilsson, M., Allouche, J., Persson, Å. and Reischl, G., 2012. Planetary Boundaries: Exploring the Challenges for Global Environmental Governance. *Current Opinion in Environmental Sustainability*, 4(1), pp.80–87.

Grimm, N., Faeth, S., Golubiewski, N., Redman, C., Wu, J., Bai, X. and Briggs, J., 2008. Global Change and the Ecology of Cities. *Science*, 319, pp.756–60.

Hallegatte, S., 2009. Strategies to Adapt to an Uncertain Climate Change. *Global Environmental Change*, 19(2), pp.240–47.

Hardin, G., The Tragedy of the Commons, 1968. *Science*, 162(3859), pp.1243–8.

Harrison, J. and Hoyler, M., 2014. Governing the New Metropolis. *Urban Studies*, 5(11), pp.2249–66.

Hoornweg, D., 2011. A League of Their Own: Cities Working Together for a Better World. *Sustainable Cities*, [blog] September 9. Available at: http://blogs.worldbank.org/sustainablecities/a-league-of-their-own-cities-working-together-for-a-better-world-0

Hoornweg, D. and Pope, K., 2014. *Population Predictions of the 101 Largest Cities in the 21st Century*. Toronto: Global Cities Institute.

Hoornweg, D., Sierra, K., Sanio, M. and Pressnail, K., 2014. Meeting the Infrastructure Challenges of African Cities. In: Crittenden, J., Hendrickson, C. and Wallace, B., eds, 2014. *Creating Infrastructure for a Sustainable World*. Reston, VA: American Society of Civil Engineers, pp. 471–81.

Hsu, A., Emerson, J., Levy, M., de Sherbinin, A., Johnson, L., Malik, O., Schwartz, J. and Jaiteh, M., 2016. *The 2016 Environmental Performance Index*. New Haven, CT: Yale Center for Environmental Law and Policy.

International Organization for Standardization, 2014. *Sustainable Development of Communities – Indicators for City Services and Quality of Life (ISO 37120:2014)*. Geneva: International Organization for Standardization.

Jabbour, J., Keita-Ouane, F., Hunsberger, C., Sanchez-Rodriguez, R., Gilruth, P., Patel, N., Sing, A., Levy, M. and Schwarzer, S., 2012. Internationally Agreed Environmental Goals: A Critical Evaluation of Progress. *Environmental Development*, 3(1), pp.5–24.

James, P., 2012. *Circles of Sustainability* [online image]. Available at: https://commons.wikimedia.org/wiki/File:Circles_of_Sustainability_image_%28assessment_-_Melbourne_2011%29.jpg

Klauer, B., Manstetten, R., Petersen, T. and Schiller, J., 2013. The Art of Long-Term Thinking: A Bridge Between Sustainability Science and Politics. *Ecological Economics*, 93(C), pp.79–84.

Kunreuther1, H., Heal, G., Allen, M., Edenhofer, O., Field, C. and Yohe, G., 2013. Risk Management and Climate Change. *Nature Climate Change*, 3, pp.447–50.

Mebratu, D., 1998. Sustainability and Sustainable Development: Historical and Conceptual Review. *Environ Impact Assessment Review*, 18, pp.493–520.

Niemeier, D., Gombachika, H. and Richards-Kortum, R., 2014. How to Transform the Practice of Engineering to Meet Global Health Needs. *Science*, 345(6202), pp.1287–90.

Ostrom, E., 1996. Incentives, Rules of the Game, and Development. In: The International Bank for Reconstruction and Development / The World Bank. 1995. *Proceedings of the Annual World Bank Conference on Development Economics 1995*. Washington, DC: The World Bank, pp.207–34.

Ostrom, E., 1996. Crossing the Great Divide: Coproduction, Synergy and Development. *World Development*, 24(6), pp.1073–87.

Ostrom, E., 2009. A General Framework for Analyzing Sustainability of Social–Ecological Systems. *Science*, 325(5939), pp.419–22.

Ostrom, E., 2011. Background on the Institutional Analysis and Development Framework. *Policy Studies Journal*, 39(1), pp.7–27.

Ostrom, E., 2012. Green from the Grassroots. *Project Syndicate*, [online] June 12. Available at: www.project-syndicate.org/commentary/green-from-the-grassroots.

Ostrom, E., 2014. A Polycentric Approach for Coping with Climate Change. *Annals of Economics and Finance*, 15(1), pp.97–134.

Poveda, C. and Lipsett, M., 2014. An Integrated Approach for Sustainability Assessment: The Wa-Pa-Su Project Sustainability Rating System. *International Journal of Sustainable Development and World Ecology*, 21(1), pp.85–98.

Poveda, C. and Lipsett, M., 2014. The Wa-Pa-Su Project Sustainability Rating System: A Simulated Case Study of Implementation Assessment. *Environment Management and Sustainable Development*, 3(1), pp.1–24.

Putnam, R., 1988. Diplomacy and Domestic Politics: The Logic of Two-Level Games. *International Organization*, 42(3), pp.427–60.

Putnam, R., 1993. *Making Democracy Work, Civic Traditions in Modern Italy*. Princeton, NJ: Princeton University Press.

Rees, W. and Wackernagel, M., 1996. Urban Ecological Footprints: Why Cities Cannot be Sustainable – and Why They are a Key to Sustainability. *Environmental Impact Assessment Review*, 16(4), pp.223–48.

Robinson, J., 2004. Squaring the Circle? Some Thoughts on the Idea of Sustainable Development. *Ecological Economics*, 48, pp.369–84.

The Royal Academy of Engineering, 2005. *Engineering for Sustainable Development: Guiding Principles*. London: The Royal Academy of Engineering.

Ruckelshaus, W., 1989. Toward a Sustainable World. *Scientific American*, 261(3), pp.166–75.

Seitzinger, S.P., Svedin, U., Crumley, C.L., Steffen, W., Arif Abdullah, S., Alfsen, C., Broadgate, W.J., Biermann, F., Bondre, N.R., Dearing, J.A., Deutsch, L., Dhakal, S., Elmqvist, T., Farahbakhshazad, N., Gaffney, O., Haberl, H., Lavorel, S., Mbow, C., McMichael, A.J., deMorais, J.M.F., Olsson, P., Fernanda Pinho, P., Seto, K.C., Sinclair, P., Stafford Smith, M. and Sugar, L., 2012. Planetary Stewardship in an Urbanizing World: Beyond City Limits. *AMBIO*, 41, pp.787–94.

Schlager, J., 1956. Systems Engineering: Key to Modern Development. *IRE Transactions on Engineering Management*, EM-3(3), pp.64–6.

Sneddon, C., Howarth, R. and Norgaard, R., 2006. Sustainable Development in a Post-Brundtland World. *Ecological Economics*, 57, pp.253–68.

Tavoni, A. Building Up Cooperation. *Nature Climate Change*, 3, pp.782–3.

Van den Bergh, J. and Grazi, F., 2013. Ecological Footprint Policy? Land Use and an Environmental Indicator. *Journal of Industrial Ecology*, 18(1), pp.10–19.

Vasconcelos, V., Santos, F. and Pacheco, J., 2013. A Bottom-Up Institutional Approach to Cooperative Governance of Risky Commons. *Nature Climate Change*, 3, pp.797–801.

World Commission on Environment and Development, 1987. *Our Common Future*. London, Oxford University Press.

Zio, E. and Pedroni, N., 2012. *Overview of Risk-Informed Decision-Making Processes*. Toulouse, France: Foundation for an Industrial Safety Culture. Available at: www.icsi-eu.org/docsi/documents/24/csi1210-ridm.pdf

4 Cities defining sustainable development

Cities, as regional centres and as agglomerations of individuals, neighbourhoods and communities, need to define their own version of sustainable development. For this definition to be a meaningful guide, it needs to be both locally relevant and globally considerate. A possible deal between cities to define and move toward sustainable development requires a credible process and a few key tools.

Structuring 'the deal'

An applied science or engineering approach may provide the best opportunity for the world to reach sustainable development. An applied science approach would focus on systems and available knowledge (which could be regularly updated) and is based on regular iterations and enhancements. This process, or engineering approach, is readily apparent in automobiles (e.g. the updated models released every year) and software engineering (e.g. regular updates included as part of the service). Engineers are likely not able to define specifically sustainable development per se, but rather through the professional application of a factor of safety (or factor of sustainability) move society toward greater sustainability.

Cities are well positioned to lead an effort toward sustainable development. As a starting point larger, fast-growing cities should be brought into any possible global negotiations. A forward approach is proposed with the Future Five cities expected to have populations of 5 million or more by 2050. The population estimates of cities should be subject to regular updating. City populations are provided here as a starting point for the engineering profession as effectively commissioning key infrastructure in the absence of these estimates is not possible.

A key aspect of sustainability is the provision and use of resources and assimilation of by-products (Running, 2012). Cities, as connected but unique systems, provide a useful scale of analysis. A scientific or systems approach can be taken when investigating the sustainability aspects of cities. Scientists, engineers and public policy experts can use the flow of materials through cities – with credible metrics – as a powerful surrogate for sustainable development.

The proposed agreement would focus on how each of the Future Five cities could be *sustained*. As cities are immobile (they cannot get out of harm's way), and as this agreement is structured for at least 35 years, significant uncertainty exists. For example, in larger countries like China and the USA, populations and economic activity can shift between cities. Countries and barriers to mobility are expected to remain in place this century; however, the negotiations envisaged are for all cities to support each other in concert with (or not) national objectives.

As quoted earlier, 'If all men were angels, governments would not be needed' (James Madison), nor would negotiations be needed to achieve sustainable development, which is in every city's and country's long-term interest. Human frailties emerge in many ways – power struggles, contests over resources, tribalism, ego, greed, insecurities and too little thought for the future. Human frailties and limits of governance usually manifest differently at national or local levels. For example, cities rarely go to war with each other. They use country frameworks for this. Much of today's unrest, however, is not country-versus-country, but rather concerns civil strife, regional factions, local unrest and local manifestations of broader geopolitical interests.

A global agreement between cities may be seen as more pragmatic and catering to local priorities, albeit globally connected. New tensions with this approach are likely. For example, many citizens are initially excluded. There may be little support, for example, in the rest of Canada as Toronto on its own enters global agreements. 'Toronto', like most of the other large cities, will need to establish methods on how the entire urban region can be represented through a single voice.

The methods and process of negotiation will be critical, for Toronto, Ontario and the rest of Canada will need to be highly supportive (and insistent) of an agreement. The participating cities will need to feel as if they are representing their countries and the rest of the world (although they will obviously need to negotiate for what is best for them). Similar to shadow pricing, a 'shadow agreement' is envisaged. Initially, this is not anticipated to be a legally binding agreement.

Countries expend considerable effort ensuring access to global resources (and markets) while trying to keep national borders from contracting (if not expanding). Larger countries like Canada, Spain, Russia, China, Indonesia and many of the fractured Sub-Saharan African countries have areas agitating for independence, or seeking 'special consideration'. Much of the strength of the USA comes from the absence of vigorous independence movements in aggrieved regions (post-Civil War). However, even in the USA, there are factions – parts of Alaska, Hawaii and the South agitate for greater independence. Economists argue major benefits accrue from a larger, stronger European Union, and yet major forces push to separate.

Cities, especially urban agglomerations, on the other hand worry less about being divided and more about everyone 'getting along'. Social factions obviously exist in cities; however, the structure of negotiations envisaged in this approach is to work toward an agreement that optimizes utility for each participating city (whole urban agglomeration). Presumably this would also be good for their host countries and smaller national partner cities. The Future Five negotiating cites would be tasked to assume a leadership role for themselves within a global agreement, as well as developing and encouraging a global framework that facilitates a similar move toward sustainability by countries, corporations and other cities. This process largely places the onus of accountability, i.e. leadership, with the participating cities. However, this mantle of leadership will likely be diminished (somewhat) by efforts at political positioning, which most cities and their leaders would undertake.

Local governments usually have a degree of political tension with senior levels of government, vying for less constituent consternation with taxes and public policy requirements. Local governments are often of a different political party than provincial/state and national representatives. As these proposed negotiations are structured to be open and completely inclusive for all Future Five cities (with proxy negotiating teams if required), there should be less likelihood of outcomes being good for the city but not good for its respective state and national government. Inclusion of both political and technical (i.e. bureaucratic) representatives for each participating city will also temper (some) political posturing.

The C40, for example, is a 'leadership-heavy' agency. Mayors started the agency[1] and mayors still lead the board and oversee annual conferences. But unlike a head of state representing a country, a mayor rarely represents his or her entire urban agglomeration. In Toronto, for example, the mayor would be quickly reminded if speaking overseas, by one of the area's other 27 mayors and regional chairs, that most of 'Toronto' is outside Toronto's city limits. This is similar in cities like Buenos Aires, Paris and Delhi.

Partitioning and changing local borders challenge most urban areas. Power utilities, water supply (source and distribution), waste management (collection and disposal), food supply, transportation and fuel supplies – these systems usually operate at different scales from a specific city, or urban area (Folke, 2002). This complexity is exacerbated with national controls on currency, citizenship, military and legal frameworks. Also, with many of the larger cities, global trade and international organizations associated with globalization play a critical role, e.g. ISO, UN and IFIs. Any agreement developed between participating cities will need to reflect senior levels of government and international organizations; however, an iterative process is expected to emerge where the changes needed for sustainable development by 2050 as negotiated by participating cities would influence related changes in other governments, corporations and agencies.

Mayor La Guardia of New York City, when speaking of the pragmatic nature of cities, is attributed with saying: 'There is no Democrat or Republican way to pick up the garbage.' Perhaps cities can highlight that there is no Democrat–Republican, Conservative–Liberal or left–right way to bring about sustainable development.

Probably for the first decade or so, any 'negotiations' as envisaged here would be conducted by representatives of the cities (academic and municipal employees) rather than heads of state, or mayors. However, as the negotiations proposed here are underpinned by solid scientific assessments and open-source metrics, any future 'political' negotiations would need (eventually) to take into account the experience developed in this proposed process.

The scope of negotiations

A signed agreement between the Future Five cities is not likely. Significant funds would be required to implement any agreement and participating cities will need to negotiate in turn with their respective regional and national governments. A lasting agreement without some method of wealth transfer is unlikely; however, every city could have a publicly vetted and continuously monitored 'path to sustainability'. The engineering profession (among others) would be well positioned to work with all cities to help define the path toward sustainability. As the urban agglomeration is the unit of negotiation, and a systems approach is proposed, the agreement should be (slightly) less political.

In some cities, agreement may not be possible, depending on how the city is represented internationally (the urban area). In this case, surrogate representatives such as the dean (or equivalent) of local professional schools, or academic presidents, might be invited to represent the city. Negotiations boil down to the following: (i) agreeing on what the planetary boundaries are for the physical and socio-economic indicators proposed – or proposing new indicators; (ii) assigning a global share of this for the Future Five cities to 2050; (iii) outline local city limits; and (iv) develop preliminary sustainability cost curves for each city and agree to keep these updated and publicly available.

Negotiations are not expected to deliver a final product, but rather an ongoing process that is supported by respective professions, academia and others should emerge. Also, as many of the metrics (Chapter 5) are subjective, the process of peer review and ongoing professional inputs (broader than the single city or country) should provide a mechanism to encourage more evidence-based public policy development.

Another important aspect of the proposed negotiations is that they will encourage better coordination of national and international agencies working within participating cities. The sustainability cost curves and boundaries mappings outlined in Chapters 5 and 6 provide a powerful tool to coordinate activities in cities (and enhance efficiency). The negotiation process should facilitate greater availability and use of tools supporting better infrastructure planning and financing.

A negotiated agreement is less likely, and initially less important, than developing an ongoing process of monitoring sustainability at the city level. This first requires a simple yet comprehensive assessment of conditions in Future Five cities and notional outlines of key urban infrastructure (as represented through preliminary sustainability cost curves). Volunteer engineers through programmes such as Engineers Without Borders (EWB) could help define these initial city assessments.

A metropolitan approach

All of the world's larger cities (Future Fives) are urban agglomerations. Some are made up of more than 40 local governments. Metropolitan Lagos (eventually to be the world's largest city) is made up of 20 local governments.

The boundary of the metropolitan area is often ill defined. 'Toronto', for example, is an urban area with at least six unique boundaries.[2] Other examples include the City of Jakarta, with a population of 10.1 million *vs* metro 'Jabodetabek' with 24.1 million; Mexico City, 8.8 million *vs* metro area, 21.2 million; Mumbai city, 13.9 million *vs* metro, 21.2 million.

A metropolitan-scale approach is critical as most large energy and materials-intensive services, like transportation, need a metro-wide analysis. This often makes analysis more difficult, as each local government may have disparate interests; however, the broad efficiencies envisaged from sustainable cities will not materialize without comprehensive metro-wide planning and delivery.

The entity of research, and its respective area, is the metropolitan region or urban agglomeration. This could be likened to a commuter-shed or *pomerium*.[3] A modern, albeit incomplete, method of defining the larger cities and their urban agglomeration is the (urban) area served by respective international airport(s). In addition to density, the urban area can often be defined through the provision of basic services, e.g. those areas with piped water supply, waste collection and minimum standards of healthcare and education provision.

The areas proposed in this approach (metro cities) is consistent with the United Nations World Urbanization Projections and the urban database from Angel et al. (2011). Urban areas for the Future Five cities (as a start) would also be provided on common data sites.

Why cities?

Cities, as urban agglomerations, provide several different attributes not typically seen in their national government counterparts. These include relative permanence, pragmatism and a complex systems dynamic. Countries are usually a political construct whereas cities tend to be more organic and place-based. The concept of sovereignty is usually not applicable to a city. A larger city is often partitioned by several political borders, e.g., Sydney, Australia (metro area, or 'Sydneysiders'), is made up of 38 local governments.

Military analogies are useful. Niccolo Machiavelli (*The Prince*, 1532) and Sun Tzu (*The Art of War*, c.500 BCE) both saw war as a means of protecting stature and access to resources. They saw this war being waged on behalf of cities by the monarchy or nation. Sun Tzu perhaps saw war more as a 'necessary evil', while Machiavelli also saw it as an extension of politics. The two men argued for speed in dispatching battles and advised the need for deception (Sun Tzu) and distinction between public and private morality (Machiavelli). Historically, cities urged the creation of regional collections (countries), which in turn exerted power on behalf of constituent cities. Wars are likely to continue and civil strife increase.

These proposed negotiations would not stop wars; however, they would serve as a powerful indicator of what is the cost of those conflicts (cost to well-being and local and global ecosystem degradation in addition to finance). They would also make deception (of resource use) more difficult.

There is only one voter and one taxpayer, yet some of our most entrenched tensions are between governments tasked with representing us at different scales, e.g. municipal, provincial and national. Many cities and their local regions may be at political odds with their national government, e.g. Barcelona, Catalonia and Spain, or Montreal, Quebec and Canada. Often, as with countries like Mexico, Colombia, China and Argentina, the role of mayor serves as precursor to national politics.

Many cities may also be at odds internally across local jurisdictions. Often tensions exist within large cities between city-core and suburbs. This negotiation process is designed to first, develop a consensus and common voice for each of the Future Five participating cities. This in itself will provide powerful impetus to other levels of government and other cities and corporations.

Some researchers argue that 'sustainability is binary' and cities are 'the very idea of unsustainability, built in contradiction to nature, unlike rural living within nature' (Berger, 2014). The world is unlikely to de-urbanize, and, from an ecosystems-impact perspective, this would not be beneficial. An agreement *toward sustainability* by the world's largest cities may be sufficient to tilt the global scales to sustainability (Lyon Dahl, 2012).

Cities and the growth in global wealth and health

Table 4.1 shows the historic growth in wealth from 1500 to the present day, with a projection to 2100. Per capita wealth and health (as measured by life expectancy) were largely consistent from 1500 to late 1800s. However, from 1900 to 2000, the world underwent a fundamental transformation – in one century urban population and wealth increased more than tenfold. Life expectancy almost doubled, while in the previous 400 years it increased by less than 50 per cent.

Table 4.1 The world's growing wealth and health

Year	GDP (per person)	Population (000,000)		Life expectancy
		Global	Urban	
1500	130	461	<40	33
1600	150	554	<50	35
1700	170	603	<60	36
1800	200	990	<100	40
1900	680	1,650	320	48
2000	6,500	6,144	2,950	78
2100	40,000	10,853	8,686	83

Total global wealth about: $2 trillion – 1900; $117 trillion – 2000 and $263 trillion – 2014 (from Credit Suisse, 2014); $1,500 trillion – 2100 (author estimate, with Credit Suisse estimates 2019 global wealth of $369 trillion). All values in constant US$.

Source: Hoornweg (2015).

This growth in wealth and health is just getting started. In 1900, total global wealth was about $2 trillion. By 2000, this had increased 55 times to $117 trillion; from 2000 to 2014 global wealth more than doubled again, and is now about $263 trillion (Credit Suisse, 2014). For the rest of this century, as national governments, institutions, cultural norms and memes adapt to the unprecedented growth in wealth, the relative importance of cities will increase. This will occur alongside greater recognition of city vulnerabilities and inter-connectedness (Arrow et al., 1995).

Cities are the drivers of this massive wealth increase. So too are cities, or, better stated, the lifestyles that cities make possible, the main drivers of the ecosystem degradation. This ecosystem impact is a by-product of material consumption, e.g. energy, water, food. Cities will need to be built in a way that reduces local and global ecosystem degradation. Much of the newly created wealth will be spent on building better cities.

City builders, e.g. planners, civil engineers, community advisers, have not been able to keep up with growing demands. The infrastructure backlog for today's three billion urban residents is severe – add to this shortfall the fact that by the end of the century cities will almost triple in size. An 85-year planning horizon is not uncommon in civil engineering, e.g. infrastructure now being commissioned, such as the Niagara Tunnel, can have a 100-year design operating lifespan. New tools are needed to prioritize and monitor these larger civil works as finance, materials and professional services will continue to lag demand (increasingly more so).

If Machiavelli and Sun Tzu were advising today, they would still likely focus on resource scarcity. However, with the growing inter-connectedness of cities and their importance as wealth generators (and ecosystem degraders), the whispered advice might be how to get cities to cooperate across different countries, despite what distractions might be taking place at the national level. For the last 100 years the world has nurtured a few hundred 'geese' as they lay 'golden eggs'. The geese consume significant resources and generate much waste, and their proclivity is increasing fast. The best way to protect the geese and maximize the benefits of their mammon is to make clear what they need and what their impact is, and to share clearly benefits and responsibilities (with codified progress accounts).

As highlighted in *The End of Power*, initial growth of humanity's wealth was much about size (Naim, 2014). Big countries and big companies with large sources of capital and military might were able to dictate agendas and provide the platform for urban growth and wealth generation. Efforts were exerted to protect borders and access to resources. Oil and the Middle East's geopolitical turmoil, canals, large power stations and Ford's Model T are examples of large-scale attributes. A similar dispersion of network power in global internet-based communications is evident (Castells, 2011).

The next phase of wealth creation is less about size and more about connection and 'rights [and obligations] of participation'. Borders and resources will still be important, but this will decline relative to the ability to participate in the global economy (with shared culture and knowledge). Cities, as the engines of economy and crucibles of culture and education, will be the main conduits of participation (as they already are) (Moreno Pires, Fidelis and Ramos, 2014).

Uber, the mobile phone taxi application that was launched in 2010, provides an excellent example of 'secondary' wealth creation. By early 2015, Uber was available in more than 200 cities in 50 countries (stock valuation around $40 billion). The service is almost exclusively a city-based application, and, even though it is banned in Spain and India, variants can readily develop. Regulators and existing taxi operators are scrambling to adapt and likely will be fundamentally changed. Global cities want to both help their local innovators come up with the next Uber while also hoping social norms in their city are not unduly disrupted.

Many of the Future Five cities are now scrambling to introduce programming and infrastructure provision that meets both locally specific requirements and global (or regional) network needs. City services need to provide the 'bones' as well the inter-connective tissue that are most commonly administered through institutions. Initiatives such as data management (e.g. 'smart cities'), procurement practices and local governance mechanisms are equally impactful for local quality of life as large scale infrastructure; however, common metrics for this service provision are less developed. Tools for public safety, risk management and simple economic analyses will likely evolve quickly as cities develop more urban infrastructure and local service provision (Haines et al., 2009).

The 'Future Fives'

Eventually, every city with a population over, say, 100,000 should have its 'urban DNA' publicly available, ideally with much of it in real time. Simple metrics akin to ISO (International Organization for Standardization) 37120 should be published annually by every first-order government (by the city or 'primary government' and third-party audited, e.g. WCCD). These data could be aggregated across metropolitan areas comprised of two or more local governments. Despite the fact that cities are humanity's most important creation, an agreed-to list of cities with boundaries and population estimates is not yet available.

In determining which cities to analyse first, a degree of arbitrariness is needed. Anywhere between perhaps 15 cities (the original C15 for example) and 150 would likely provide sufficient numbers to develop a comprehensive global agreement. Fewer than 15 would likely not be sufficient to generate enough global interest, and even the largest 15 cities represent less than 5 per cent of the global economy and only involve 10 countries. More than 150 would likely initially be too unwieldy and the disparities between largest and smallest would be exacerbated. Also, the more participants that are initially included the more likely entrenched and unhelpful factions might emerge. Megacities (the 27 cities with populations in excess of 10 million) are a possible starting point, but only 6 are in high-income countries, thereby possibly limiting the cross equity approach a larger number of cities can provide.

Today, there are about 75 cities over 5 million population and another 400 between 1 million and 5 million. This research effort could reasonably start with the cities over 5 million; however, as the key aspect of this proposed approach is to focus on long-lived, large-scale urban infrastructure, a futures scenario approach warrants consideration. The 'future' is loosely defined here as 35 years, this being about the optimum timeframe for analysis of major civil works like transportation systems, water supply, waste management infrastructure and energy generation and distribution. In dealing with long-lived urban infrastructure a key constituency is obviously the fastest-growing (larger) cities. Therefore the cities selected for inclusion are all cities (urban areas) expected to have 5 million or more residents by 2050. This introduces about 50 new cities to the current list of 75 (and 105 if the time frame to 2100 is selected).

The 'Future Fives' are expected to have a combined population of about 1.368 billion by 2050 (a 395 million increase from today).[4] A valid argument can be made that smaller but even faster-growing cities should take priority. Eventually, the list could grow, but initially 125 cities is about the maximum (optimum) number to select, as this includes sufficient African cities that will be more critical in the latter half of this century, but for the next few decades are still 'small' relative to Asian cities. The expected 122 cities likely maintains enough cities that are in OECD member countries now to anchor negotiations that are likely to see a major shift from OCED-member countries to non-member countries like China, India and, later, those in Sub-Saharan Africa. One impact of analysing cities of 5 million or more is that a relatively large number of Chinese cities are then included, particularly from 2010 to 2050.

The C40 provides an important lesson for city associations. The organization started as the C5, wanting to represent some of the world's largest and 'most important' cities, but reflecting an absence of cities from middle- and low-income countries. The list quickly grew to the C15, then the C40, with different membership standings (core and affiliate, with political pressure for smaller city participation), and now it is in flux with some 77 member cities of various sizes. The C40 emerged as a 'club' with the ability to expel members and closing the club to new members. This is similar to formation of the G7, then G8, then the more unwieldy G20, and emergence of the parallel G77.

Metropolis of UCLG is a possible model to follow, where any city with a population of over 1 million can be a member. However, this was somewhat diluted in that smaller national capitals could join as well, and membership is voluntary, with about 40 per cent of the world's cities with a population of over 1 million now participating in Metropolis.[5] Metropolis is likely the best-positioned city organization to serve as a catalyst for these efforts (if there is a desire to use an existing organization).

Starting with larger cities

There are about 340 cities with populations larger than 1 million, more than half in middle- and low-income countries; these are all strong contenders to act as crucial pilot sites. By 2050, about 122 cities are expected to have 5 million or more residents. These larger cities can be argued to be the priority, as they are home to the majority of the world's wealth, resource consumption, associated pollution and impacts to biodiversity.

Secondary cities, those with populations of under 500,000, contain the bulk of the world's urban population, and in most countries are the fastest-growing communities. Arguably, these cities could also be the priority for any sustainable cities initiative. Similar arguments can be made for cities of 500,000 to 1,000,000 residents. In fact, all cities will benefit from inclusion in the sustainable cities process outlined in this book; however, only a handful of cities may be selected for inclusion in phase one of the pilot project. Therefore the following considerations are suggested, with a recommendation to focus initially on larger cities, i.e., those projected to have 5 million or more residents in 2050.

- From the perspective of global sustainability and ecosystem impacts, large cities have a disproportionately large impact. Therefore, sustainable development will only be possible if the majority of large cities adhere to the tenets of sustainability.
- Large cities are usually made up of several contiguous local governments. By virtue of their size, they often appear threatening to national and regional governments. The politics of larger cities are often disproportionately difficult. Large cities should receive more international assistance and scrutiny.
- All larger cities have at least one academic institution in their urban area. Local academic institutions should be nurtured and treated as a critical ingredient of local sustainability.
- Large cities are traditionally more challenged by coordination issues, and should seek out objective external partnerships, especially with regard to metropolitan issues, which are emerging as one of the twenty-first century's most intractable challenges.
- Large cities over the next few decades will drive the largest-ever creation of wealth. As these cities grow, and local real estate values increase along with the growth in population and density, they should seek out opportunities to enhance and share this new wealth.

With respect to the global goal of sustainability, larger cities should be encouraged, as they can more efficiently use resources. Larger cities can also grow regional and national economies quicker, thereby providing more timely overall poverty reduction. Perhaps counter-intuitively, growing larger cities faster between 2015 and 2050 will enhance sustainability this century.

Preparing city-based sustainability limits and assessing the local hierarchy of urban management is somewhat onerous, especially during the first iterations as cities, and their partners, gain experience. Larger cities with greater capacity are logical first adopters. Their experience will help shape the methodology for the second group of pilot cities. Larger cities can then emerge as regional coordination and support nodes for other cities.

Table 4.2 World's largest cities (urban areas) by population (millions)

1800	1900	1950	2000	2050	2100
Beijing, 1.1	London, 6.5	New York, 12.4	Tokyo, 34.5	Mumbai, 42.4	Lagos, 88.3
London, 0.9	New York, 4.2	London, 8.9	Osaka, 18.7	Delhi, 36.2	Kinshasa, 83.5
Guangzhon, 0.8	Paris, 3.3	Tokyo, 7.0	Mexico City, 18.5	Dhaka, 35.2	Dar es Salaam, 73.7
Tokyo, 0.7	Berlin, 2.7	Paris, 5.9	New York, 17.8	Kinshasa, 35.0	Mumbai, 67.2
Istanbul, 0.6	Chicago, 1.7	Shanghai, 5.4	São Paulo, 17.0	Kolkata, 33.0	Delhi, 57.3
Paris, 0.5	Vienna, 1.7	Moscow, 5.1	Mumbai, 16.4	Lagos, 32.6	Khartoum, 56.6
Naples, 0.4	Tokyo, 1.5	Buenos Aires, 5.0	Delhi, 15.7	Tokyo, 32.6	Niamey, 56.1
Hangzhou, 0.4	St Petersburg, 1.4	Chicago, 4.9	Shanghai, 14.0	Karachi, 31.7	Dhaka 54.3
Osaka, 0.4	Manchester, 1.4	Ruhr, 4.9	Cairo, 13.6	New York, 24.8	Kolkata, 52.4
Kyoto, 0.4	Philadelphia, 1.4	Kolkata, 4.8	Kolkata, 13.1	Mexico City, 24.3	Kabul, 50.3

Source: Modified from Hoornweg (2015).

Why 2050?

Sustainable development is a long-term prospect. The WBCSD proposes a Vision 2050, as supported by many scenario-planning exercises. Cities in particular try to plan within a consistent and complimentary short- and long-term planning horizon (Kriegler, 2012; Moss, 2010).

Cities are usually built around large-scale 'civil works'. For example, much of today's major urban infrastructure was built more than 50 years ago. The US Interstate Highway system, Rome's aqueducts, Jakarta's port area, Niagara Falls Hydroelectric Power Plants, the subway systems of London, Paris and Moscow, most of Europe's and the USA's railway alignments, key canals, bridges and airports – these major infrastructure works are well over 35 years old and are still providing considerable service today. Much of the underpinning of any city, and especially those aspiring to be sustainable cities, is infrastructure with 35 years' or more life expectancy (and possibly amortization). This timeframe is likely the minimum when considering large-scale investments such as transportation (subways and new rail/road alignments), and power generation (power plants – hydro, solar, fossil fuel, tidal, geothermal, nuclear, etc.) usually have as a minimum a 35-year operating horizon.

To provide a credible assessment of potential key infrastructure proposed for pilot cities, a sufficiently long-term horizon is needed. Thirty-five years is a logical timeframe: sufficiently lengthy, yet not too far away. This facilitates a more fulsome comparison of existing technologies to new options, e.g. solar and wind generation options versus hydro. The proposed 35-year timeframe

(2015–2050) also coincides with the average career spans of today's graduates (Hansen, 2013).

Identifying 2050 as the 'target year' for sustainability meets the objectives and aspirations of the Sustainable Development Goals, facilitates credible and comparable cost curves, and provides sufficient time to cover potential political transitions, technological advances and personnel changes.

In order to prepare cost curves (as discussed in Chapter 6), the investigated intervention needs to be time bound: when will the project start, and to what date in the future can benefits be considered? This is somewhat problematic in that much large-scale infrastructure is long-lived. Many interventions also have considerable lead times for commissioning. All costs and benefits accrued by the project over the studied timeframe need to somehow be measured. A degree of arbitrariness is again needed.

Most national agencies and municipal planning authorities have long-term plans, e.g. land use plans, and shorter five-year plans. China, for example, is on the seventh five-year plan for major infrastructure. These sustainability cost curves are designed to harmonize (eventually) across national and local government master plans. All large-scale civil works and public policy interventions (in excess of $10 million) should be anchored in a relevant sustainability cost curve. For larger-scale interventions that extend beyond a single city (urban area) the costs and benefits should be apportioned to at least the relevant larger urban areas. Eventually, this would be similar to an environmental assessment, or cost-benefit analysis, typically applied to all civil works and updated at five-year intervals.

An inclusive list of cities

> *I don't care to belong to any club that will have me as a member.*
>
> Groucho Marx

Similarly to how cities behave like natural ecosystems, so too do they often exhibit traits of human nature. Pride, joy, insecurity and concern – cities behave as a collective of people. Cities are fractious. In large urban areas, the main city may overshadow the more dynamic neighbouring community. City leaders, often of different political parties or different appointment/election cycles, may be at odds with regional and national leaders.

Membership in the C40 or determination of 'global cities' provides valuable insight in city organizations. The C40 has wrestled with membership from its outset (personal communication, Mayor Bloomberg). Only for a short time were there 40 member cities, and these were of disparate population sizes, e.g. Basel with 165,000 to Tokyo of 30-plus million. Challenges also arose as some cities (e.g. Beijing and Shanghai) failed to provide information or were dissuaded to participate fully by national government.

New York, London and Tokyo were suggested as the first global cities (Sassen, 1991). This was further refined through the Globalization and World Cities

Research Network (GaWC) that ranked cities as Alpha++, Alpha+, Alpha and Alpha-, Beta and Gamma, based on economy and global connectivity. In 2008 *Foreign Policy* published a ranking of global cities (this was updated in 2010, 2012, and 2014).

Much effort, and often consternation, goes into rankings of cities. The work of Kennedy et al. (2015) on megacities provides an alternative approach. All 27 megacities are included in this review, despite varying ability to engage local researchers and data availability. This is a similar approach to the World Bank's annual WDR, which includes all of the world's 190+ countries.

The politics of cities differs from the science of cities, yet both are critical in bringing about sustainable development. The proposed approach to the envisaged 'negotiations' is that all cities (over 5 million population) would be included. Every year or two, representatives from the world's largest cities would negotiate and update a sustainability accord. The accord would be based on public, 'open source' sustainability cost curves. The negotiations *per se* would be indicative, and in theory could be negotiated by anyone representing the city. The broad context is sufficiently well defined to allow anyone representing the city to negotiate on the city's behalf. Data necessary for development of sustainability cost curves would be publicly available. When not available from local governments or senior levels of government, values could be estimated by respective engineering faculties or EWB volunteers (all the data needed to develop sustainability cost curves is likely known today for all cities, +/- 10 per cent, which is sufficient for planning and negotiation purposes).

The approach proposed here is that the initiative is not voluntary for the world's largest cities. Cities experience the impacts of unsustainable development; they are also in the best position to introduce the changes necessary to bring about more sustainable human behaviour. Arguably, the world's largest cities are best positioned to identify and implement these changes, and arguably starting with about 122 of the world's larger cities provides a sufficiently large critical mass to bring along the rest of the world (these cities generate about 25 per cent of the global economy and provide a disproportionately large share of patents and new technologies and organizational systems – they are also home to more than half the world's universities).

Unlike the G8, C40 or even Metropolis, this proposed negotiating strategy is fully inclusive. All cities over 5 million population would be included. An agreement would be developed that optimizes results for all of the world's larger cities. A 'win-win' some 122 times over is envisaged, rather than a win–lose binary approach. Those cities that do not send representatives to negotiations would still be included in allocations of resource flows and wealth generation projections. As much as possible, the final agreement would represent the optimum approach for the world's larger cities. Negotiations initially would likely be seen as an 'academic exercise' between urban planners, civil engineers and community representatives.

Developing within global limits

A key aspect of the proposed strategy for international negotiations is that cities need to operate within some level of bio-physical and social limits. These limits are largely defined by the assimilative capacities of critical ecosystems (e.g. climate change, ozone layer, food supply) and threshold levels of conflict and social tension, beyond which economic development (and personal safety and quality of life) declines. These limits are not rigid and are open to interpretation. They are transient, based on the individual, city and country's perspective at the time of analysis. Public safety, for example, becomes more important as a community's affluence increases.

Most global negotiations try to work with aggregate average perceived physical and social limits (with a national value for the time horizon, i.e. collective discount rate). Challenges arise in that an aggregate limit for negotiations is extremely difficult to derive, and costs to adhere to these limits are nebulous. Individual limits are also fraught with problems as individually, by country, city or corporation (shareholders), values are too disparate and difficult to define adequately. What emerges are minimum thresholds, e.g. human rights, which are not sufficient to design basic service delivery programmes around.

Cities (urban agglomerations) probably offer the best scale to define more meaningful limits (over any desired timeframe). Cities are charged with provision of basic services, i.e. transportation, water supply, order and (ideally) good governance. Education, healthcare and economic development are built upon these basic services. Local governments are also the most critical in emergency response.

Enormous disparities exist within cities (just like countries). However, a greater sense of shared purpose is possible because local slums and poverty directly impact the quality of life of other (more affluent) city residents. Cities (local governments) largely came into formal existence through Britain's 1848 Public Health Act (Table 2.1) as a means of mandating waste regulation (initially solid waste and then expanded to wastewater and potable water provision). Today, local governments are poised to tackle a similar challenge in providing sustainability (aggregated politically to sustainable development).

The world's largest cities have sufficient impact on the planet (locally and globally) that reductions in pollution and vicarious impacts, e.g. purchase of ivory and Bluefin tuna, are now needed and maximum levels of impact negotiated if individual and collective economies and quality of life are to be maintained and enhanced. An agreement to define and then operate within prescribed boundaries for the larger cities should be sufficiently detailed and robust to foster similar agreements between countries and smaller cities. Corporations would adhere to these negotiated limits as well as more than 20 per cent of their combined global sales are to these larger cities.

Much has been written on the 'limits *to* growth', with much criticism. A well-known 1980 wager between Paul Ehrlich and Julian Simon over the future price of five metals (copper, chromium nickel, tin and tungsten), expected to become scarce as populations grew, is often touted as evidence that limits are artificial and substitution quickly renders them obsolete. Ehrlich was advocating caution and adherence to limits, while Simon argued long-term costs of materials would not increase. The price of all five metals fell from 1980 to 1990. Substitution may be possible, e.g. if one country was rendered uninhabitable people could move to another; however, experience shows that limits do emerge although they tend to impact people differently, largely based on affluence.[6]

When looking at a collection of cities that are anchored and cannot move, i.e. limited substitutability, a 'system of systems' approach becomes necessary. Negotiating a contextual framework (time and space) for participating cities is then necessary (with sufficiently clear and present needs that the major tensions to emerge may be between city and host country rather than between cities or between countries) (Woodcock et al., 2009). Negotiations subtly change, hopefully with more pragmatism. Rather than negotiating for the preservation of global ecosystems and allocations within defined, agreed-to (i.e. negotiated) and monitored limits, participating cities agree to operate within a unique and collective limit (that could be changed as conditions warrant). Factors of safety and factors of sustainability (Chapter 6) are also likely to emerge naturally as an exact agreement would not be possible, but rather a 'good enough' negotiated settlement would emerge.

Estimates are order-of-magnitude approximations. Similar to engineering approaches for major infrastructure that use a 'factor of safety' against failure (e.g. a factor of safety of two implies that the assessed component is two times as strong as the expected failure limit), a factor of sustainability provides indicative sustainability levels. 'Sustainability' is not as easy to define as the specific failure of a concrete span or bolt; however, using an approach outlined in Chapter 5 (some 44 metrics in 14 categories) with regular public input (open-sourced peer review), a durable consensus on sustainability can be maintained (and variance from that level measured).

Negotiating sustainable development between cities is not a 'limits to growth' approach, but rather a 'limits *for* growth'. This is not a semantic distinction, but rather an engineering approach focusing on growth (aka development) within clearly defined 'factors of sustainability'. The factor of sustainability is defined and included in investment and policy initiatives for both the individual city as well as the collective larger cities (and presumably all other cities and countries). Less sustainable projects will still go ahead in richer cities, but their relative impact compared to other possible initiatives would be known by all cities.

Setting the starting point for negotiations on the limits for growth is difficult, yet sufficient work exists to provide credible proposals. Planetary bio-physical boundaries are relatively well defined and provide an excellent starting point. Global socio-economic limits have slightly more interpretation and global variability; however, sufficient work also exists to provide good starting points. The key input for global social limits is the Sustainable Development Goals.

Much of the negotiation with these goals is complicated by the underlying tensions associated with wealth and technological sharing between countries.

Negotiating between cities instead of countries will not eliminate this, but it should be significantly reduced as clear growth (population) trajectories exist for all participating cities. The impact of unsustainable growth in the larger, poorer cities is much more evident to other cities. Negotiations need to be convened within the system-of-systems approach. Problems in any of the larger cities quickly manifest in other cities. Negotiations would develop a platform of how best to achieve growth and enhancement/maintenance of quality of life.

Negotiating an agreement that uses 2050 as the target year provides an important benefit. By focusing on the future, and focusing only on long-lived urban infrastructure, the aspects of wealth transfer will be less paramount. A rough estimate is that the wealth of just the Future Fives cities (as measured by per capita GDP) will increase from today's $14.6 trillion to $30.5 trillion in 2050. Negotiations then take more of a flavour of how to nurture and encourage this growth, and what key infrastructure and actions are needed to foster it. Growing and sharing future wealth should be easier than re-distributing existing wealth.

One important aspect not fully reflected in the proposed negotiation approach is the uneven impacts meted to individual cities from a changing climate. Coastal cities, for example, are likely to face more severe impacts of climate change (sea level rise, increased storm intensity). In larger countries, such as the US and China, internal migration is likely, e.g. Miami and New York to Chicago; however, cities such as Dhaka and Lagos are likely to face growing strife and governance challenges, as viable options for residents and growth projections are limited.

The hierarchy of sustainable cities

Solid waste managers the world over often support the hierarchy of waste management: reduce, reuse, recycle and recover. Variations exist, but the concept remains consistent – follow a staged approach to waste management that first improves waste collection and simple disposal before bringing in more complicated (and expensive) waste processing systems. A similar hierarchy can be adopted for urban management and related efforts toward developing sustainable cities (Figure 4.1).

A hierarchy of sustainable cities[7] would follow the continuum: (i) basic service provision; (ii) service coverage and reliability; (iii) connectivity, resilience, integrated finance; and (iv)sustainability (environmental security, economic competiveness, social inclusion and equity). A city's progress on the management hierarchy can be readily observed. A measure of receptivity of pilot cities would be their willingness to be measured by independent observers (say a score of 1 to 5 for each attribute, perhaps through a peer-review process).

UNEP, through the Melbourne Principles of Urban Sustainability, suggests 10 key principles of urban sustainability: (i) vision; (ii) economy and society; (iii) biodiversity; (iv) ecological footprints; (v) modelling cities on ecosystems; (vi) sense of place; (vii) empowerment; (viii) partnerships; (ix) sustainable production and consumption; (x) governance and hope (UNEP 2002; Newman and Jennings,

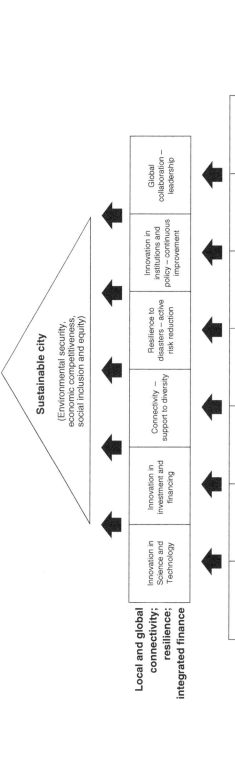

Figure 4.1 Hierarchy model for building a sustainable city.
Source: Hoornweg, (2015).

2008). These principles are laudable, although measuring something like 'sense of place' and 'governance and hope' is a challenge.

As a city (urban area) moves toward sustainability, a minimum 'level 1' of basic service provision must first be achieved. Basic services include: a credible legal and regulatory framework (especially as it pertains to land and labour rights); master planning documents (and adherence to them); water, wastewater, electricity and solid waste management; specific consideration of the poor; and credible involvement of the private sector. 'Level 2' enhancements toward sustainability are mostly about strengthened service provisions, e.g. coverage, reliability, monitoring and continuous improvement.

'Level 3' sustainability attainment is largely about integrated service supply, development and application of innovations, global connectivity and active risk reduction. Many cities are well focused on urban resilience. This is likely to emerge as an even more pressing prerequisite for sustainability.

As discussed earlier, an association made up of and managed by cities (similar to IATA and WANO) would provide valuable service to participating cities. A key mandate of the association could be to determine objectively the level of sustainability within the city, and provide suggestions for moving up the hierarchy. The main challenges to this approach are twofold. The crucial barrier will be cities continuously funding this organization. This is particularly challenging, as the urban area, usually made up of many local governments, needs to be the focus of attention, rather than a single city. Also, unlike with airlines and nuclear power plants, there is no single point of contact (responsibility). Existing city agencies such as C40 and ICLEI may see a new organization as duplicative or competitive. An initial approach may be first to develop boundaries assessments of the Future Fives (probably through local engineering schools) and order sustainability cost curves (Chapter 6). This should provide sufficient information to provide a preliminary assessment of a city's urban sustainability level. Metropolis may also be a credible existing agency to add this peer-to-peer evaluation service.

Agencies such as the World Bank, OECD, Cities Alliance and possibly GEF are also well versed in broad assessments of the key aspects of urban sustainability. These can be adapted to specific assessments of a city's progress on the hierarchy of sustainability. Eventually, progress, similar to WANO, should be conveyed in two forms: a clear web-based provision of key metrics and progress, and a confidential city assessment provided to heads of each local government.

Notes

1   C40 was largely started by the cities of London (Mayor Ken Livingston and his assistant Nicky Gavron) and New York (Mayor Bloomberg). The organization initially started as C5, then became C15, then C40 (now has about 70+ members).
2   Toronto's six urban boundaries include: (i) the City of Toronto (population of 2.62 million); (ii) the Census Metropolitan Area (5.71 million); (iii) the Greater Toronto Area (6.13 million); (iv) the Greater Toronto and Hamilton Area (6.65 million); the Toronto Urban Region (8.05 million); and (v) the Golden Horseshoe (9.09 million).

3 The *pomerium* was originally the scared area adjacent to the city walls and fortifications of Rome. The term was later broadened to refer to the religious extent, or hinterland, to which a city traditionally exerted influence.
4 The Future Fives (cities with more than 5 million residents) are expected to have 122 cities in 2050 with a total population of 1.368 million, and 181 cities in 2100 with a total of 2.787 billion (Fig. 3.1).
5 Metropolis has 138 members (website accessed July 4, 2014). There are about 475 cities with above 1 million population.
6 If the Simon–Ehrlich wager had been extended from 10 to 30 years, four of the five metals would have increased in cost.
7 The World Bank's Urban Resilience Management Unit defined sustainable cities as 'urban communities committed to improving the well-being of their current and future residents, while integrating economic, environmental, and social considerations'.

References

Angel, S., Parent, J., Civco, D., Blei, A. and Potere, D., 2011. The Dimensions of Global Urban Expansion: Estimates andProjections for all Countries, 2000–2050. *Progress in Planning*, 75, pp.53–107.

Arrow, K., Bolin, B., Costanza, R., Dasgupta, P., Folke, C., Holling, C., Jansson, B., Levin, S., Maler, K., Perrings, C. and Pimentel, D., 1995. Economic Growth, Carrying Capacity, and the Environment. *Science*, 268(28), pp.520–52.

Berger, M. The Unsustainable City. *Sustainability*, 6, pp.365–74.

Castells, M., 2011. A Network Theory of Power. *International Journal of Communication*, 5, pp.773–87.

Folke, C., Carpenter, S., Elmqvist, T., Gunderson, L., Holling, C.-S. and Walker, B. Resilience and Sustainable Development: Building Adaptive Capacity in a World of Transformations. *AMBIO*, 31(5), pp.437–40.

Haines, A., McMichael, A., Smith, K., Roberts, I., Woodcock, J., Markandya, A., Armstrong, B., Campbell-Lendrum, D., Dangour, A., Davies, M., Bruce, N., Tonne, C., Barrett, M. and Wilkinson, P., 2009. Public Health Benefits of Strategies to Reduce Greenhouse-Gas Emissions: Overview and Implications for Policy Makers. *The Lancet*, 374, pp.2104–14.

Hansen, J., Kharecha, P., Sato, M., Masson-Delemotte, V., Ackerman, F., Beerling, D., Hearty, P., Hoegh-Guldberg, O., Hsu, S., Parmesan, C., Rockstrom, J., Rohling, E., Sachs, J., Smith, P., Steffen, K., Van Susteren, L., von Schuckmann, K. and Zachos, J., 2013. Assessing 'Dangerous Climate Change': Required Reduction of Carbon Emissions to Protect Young People, Future Generations and Nature. *PLoS ONE*, 8(12), pp.1–26.

Hoornweg, D. and Pope, K., 2014. *Population Predictions of the 101 Largest Cities in the 21st Century*. Toronto: Global Cities Institute.

Hoornweg, D., 2015 (updated 2016). A Cities Approach to Sustainability. PhD. University of Toronto.

Kennedy, C., Stewart, I., Facchini, A., Cersosimo, I., Mele, R., Chen, B., Uda, M., Kansal, A. Chiu, A., Kim, K., Dubeux, C., La Rovere, E., Cunha, B., Pincetl, S., Keirstead, J., Barles, S. Pusaka, S., Gunawan, J., Adegbile, M. Nazariha, M., Hoque, S., Marcotullio, P., Otharán, F., Genena, T., Ibrahim, N., Farooqui, R., Cervantes, G. and Sahin, A., 2015. Energy and Material Flows of Megacities. *Proceedings of the National Academy of Sciences*, 112(19), pp.5985–90.

Kriegler, E., O'Neill, B., Hallegatte, S., Kram, T., Lempert, R., Moss, R. and Wilbanks, T., 2012. The Need For and Use of Socio-Economic Scenarios for Climate Change Analysis: A New Approach Based on Shared Socio-Economic Pathways. *Global Environmental Change*, 22, pp.807–22.

Lyon Dahl, A., 2012. Achievements and Gaps in Indicators for Sustainability. *Ecological Indicators*, 17, pp.14–19.

Moreno Pires, S., Fidelis, T. and Ramos, T. Measuring and Comparing Local Sustainable Development Through Common Indicators: Constraints and Achievements in Practice. *Cities*, 39, pp.1–9.

Moss, R., Edmonds, J., Hibbard, K., Manning, M., Rose, S., van Vuuren, D., Carter, T., Emori, S., Kainuma, M., Kram, T., Meehl, G., Mitchell, J., Nakicenovic, N., Riahi, K., Smith, S., Stouffer, R., Thomson, A., Weyant, J. and Wilbanks, T., 2010. The Next Generation of Scenarios for Climate Change Research and Assessment. *Nature*, 463, 747–56.

Naim, M., 2014. *The End of Power: From Boardrooms to Battlefields and Churches to States, Why Being in Charge Isn't What it Used to Be*. New York: Basic Books.

Running, S., 2012. A Measureable Planetary Boundary for the Biosphere. *Science*, 337, pp.1458–9.

Sassen, S., 1991. *The Global City: New York, London, Tokyo*. Princeton, NJ: Princeton University Press.

Woodcock, J., Edwards, P., Tonne, C., Armstrong, B., Ashiru, O., Banister, D., Beevers, S., Chalabi, Z., Chowdhury, Z., Cohen, A., Franco, O., Haines, A., Hickman, R., Lindsay, G., Mittal, I., Mohan, D., Tiwari, G., Woodward, A. and Roberts, I., 2009. Public Health Benefits of Strategies to Reduce Greenhouse-Gas Emissions: Urban Land Transport. *The Lancet*, 374, pp.1930–44.

5 Widening concepts
A cities approach to planetary boundaries

Following efforts to define and quantify safe planetary biophysical operating limits in areas such as climate change, biodiversity and water use, this chapter develops an approach to monitor boundaries from a city's perspective. Biophysical boundaries are largely a local presentation of Rockstrom et al.'s (2009) proposed planetary systems boundaries (updated in 2015 by Steffen et al.). Socio-economic boundaries or targets are largely derived from the Sustainable Development Goals (SDGs; previously the Millennium Development Goals). The approach is trialled for Dakar, Mumbai, São Paulo, Shanghai and Toronto.

Cities, or, better-stated, the residents of cities, are the main contributors to planetary challenges. Mobilizing cities to respond effectively to these challenges while meeting their own local imperatives is likely the most critical aspect for sustainable development over the next 35 years.

In order for broad objectives like planetary boundaries and Sustainable Development Goals (SDGs) to yield meaningful movement toward sustainable development, a mechanism to enable their application at an individual city scale is needed. The majority of ecosystem impacts are delivered through the lifestyles of urban residents. So too will the majority of sustainability initiatives be delivered through cities and their residents. This work provides a suite of metrics that can help cities apply sustainable development objectives locally and broadly as part of a global network of urban systems.

Introduction

Rockstrom et al. (2009) proposed a suite of planetary systems boundaries, namely, climate change, ocean acidification, ozone depletion, nitrogen and phosphorous cycles, freshwater use, changes in land use and biodiversity. Loss of biodiversity, the nitrogen cycle and climate change were estimated to be beyond the planet's sustainable carrying capacity. Atmospheric aerosol loading and chemical pollution were included, but not yet quantified. Steffen et al. (2015) updated the estimate, replacing chemical pollution with 'novel entities' (e.g. new substances such as heavy metals and modified life forms not yet quantified), and sub-dividing biodiversity loss into genetic diversity and functional diversity. Four planetary systems – biochemical flows (phosphorous and nitrogen), land-system change, loss of genetic diversity and climate change – are beyond the safe operating space (Figure 5.1).

Building on Rockstrom et al., Dearing et al. (2014) and Raworth (2012) stated that ensuring a safe and just operating space for human well-being requires that both biophysical and social boundaries be defined. They proposed a framework that integrated these operating spaces at regional scales. The 'social-ecological' system is demonstrated for two rural regions in China. Environmental ceilings are defined for water, soil and air quality, and social foundations are explored for food, health, education, energy and jobs. While these indicators provide insights into a region's social-ecological state, for cities, other important aspects of basic urban services, such as transportation, security and safety, geophysical risks and biodiversity may also be needed. The initial physical boundaries assessment were extended with the addition of hunger, inequity and water stress (Gerst, Raskin

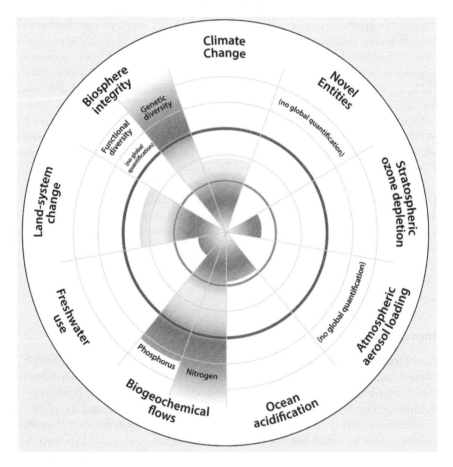

Figure 5.1 Bio-physical planetary boundaries.

Source: International Geosphere-Biosphere Programme (2015) (adapted from: Stockholm Resilience Centre/Globaïa and Steffen et al., 2015).

and Rockstrom, 2014). The proposed 'contours of a resilient global future' remain at a global scale and support long-term scenario planning.

Many have refined ways to apportion contributions to ecosystem degradation and potential impacts to cities, relative to countries (Galaz et al., 2012). Cities are acutely impacted by global trends, e.g. the price of commodities and climate change, and similarly cities are significant drivers of environmental degradation, e.g. GHG emissions, and city-residents purchase the bulk of threatened and endangered species. Many international treaties negotiated by national governments are by and large undertaken on behalf of their respective cities, or potential customers in international cities. Greenhouse gas emissions and international climate negotiations provide a useful precedent.

Recognizing the need for a corporate down-scaled GHG emissions inventory able to reflect vicarious or embodied emissions (generated on behalf of the entity but done so through a third party or in another geographic area), the World Business Council for Sustainable Development and World Resources Institute began, in 1997, to work together to develop a standard methodology consistent with national GHG inventories as proposed under UN requirements. Scopes 1, 2 and 3 were defined to account where the emissions were generated while ensuring globally consistent national, local and corporate emissions inventories. This ensured consistent regional corporate and national inventories of GHG emissions. In 2006, the International Organization for Standardization (ISO) adopted the WRI-WBCSD corporate standard as the basis for ISO 14064-I: Specification with Guidance at the Organization Level for Quantification and Reporting of Greenhouse Gas Emissions and Removals.

The initial work by WRI-WBCSD (and ISO 14064; WBCSD, 2011), efforts by researchers (Kennedy et al., 2011), the World Bank (2010) and a common global protocol by C40-ICLEI-WRI led to a city-wide GHG emissions inventory now widely accepted and included within the recent ISO 37120. Cities are now able to measure their GHG emissions credibly, relative to each other and linked to national inventories.

Objective and methodology

A key objective now is to develop a methodology that enables cities to measure their degree of sustainability and monitor this locally and within a global context. Cities need to understand better their individual and collective contribution to biophysical boundaries and socio-economic progress.

The methodology here builds on the planetary boundaries approach and proposes socio-economic limits, based largely on the Sustainable Development Goals (that follow the Millennium Development Goals).[1] The additional target areas include youth opportunity, economy, access to energy access and energy intensity, mobility and connectivity, institutions, basic services, and security and public safety.

Sustainable development will only emerge through an integrated and holistic approach. Therefore a suite of 14 indicators are presented, some with multiple inputs and some that include estimated indices. The boundaries (or limits) are roughly half bio-physical and half socio-economic. Larger cities are trialled first, as they generally possess greater data availability, staff and local research capacity, and have greater ecosystem impacts. A metropolitan-wide scale is used as a city's overall ecosystem and economic impact is driven by the entire urban agglomeration, i.e. the actions of all residents. Metropolitan-scale programmes in areas such as energy and transportation also offer the greatest opportunity to reduce system impacts (Sovacool, 2012).

In taking a cities systems approach to planetary limits, both local and global impacts should be considered for individual cities as well as aggregated for global impacts. The aggregate base level is provided for bio-physical and socio-economic limits of the largest cities (Tables 5.1 and 5.2), as well as specific assessments for Dakar in Senegal (metro region), Mumbai in India (Mumbai Metropolitan Region, MMR), São Paulo in Brazil (São Paulo Metropolitan Region, SPMR), Shanghai in China (metro region) and Toronto in Canada (Greater Toronto Area, GTA).

These initial efforts should be refined and applied to all larger cities across the world. Regular updating and consultations with residents will improve data estimates.

The approach used for city-based GHG emissions and consumption is similarly proposed for other physical limits such as total water consumption (local and embodied), total nitrogen use and land use – local and embodied. For example, the total land use metric needs to reflect land converted locally as well as an estimate for land-use changes driven on behalf of the urban customer regardless of location.

A similar approach proposed here is to estimate a city's impact on biodiversity. The impact on local species is estimated as is the city's estimated impact around the world. Therefore cities whose citizens buy an inordinate amount of endangered animal parts, or purchase products grown on land cleared in sensitive habitats, would trend higher on the biodiversity metric. Similarly, cities that have a disproportionate negative, or positive, impact on species habitat or migration are denoted. Initially, these values are only estimated indicatively; however, support from groups like WWF and the World Bank, plus local engineering faculties, is anticipated as the indices are further refined.

Socio-economic limits similar to bio-physical limits are derived here from targets suggested through programmes such as the Sustainable Development Goals. These are mostly service level targets, e.g. per cent of population with solid waste collection and electrical service, that influence quality of life globally or specifically within the analysed city. Some researchers suggest upper limits for several of these targets, e.g. caloric intake, energy consumption and GDP. The methodology presented here uses limits (existing, aggregate and targets) without upper-bounds to facilitate comparison across cities and over time, and is consistent with several engineering approaches.

Table 5.1 Biophysical science indicators, global average

Physical science indicators	Unit	Global (current)	Global (Targets/limits)	Source
Carbon dioxide emission				
GHG emissions per capita	(tCO$_2$/cap. year)	4.71	2	adapted from Comm. on Cl. Change
Rate of biodiversity loss				
Ecological footprint	global hectares demanded per capita	2.6	1.7	WWF Living Planet Report (downscaled national values)
Index of biodiversity impact	low–very high	Very High	Low	estimated
Fresh water use				
Total per capita water consumption[1]	L/cap/day	1148	1546	Rockstrom et al. (2009)
updated value	L/cap/day	989	1522	Steffen et al. (2015)
Per cent of city with potable water supply	%	81	95*	adapted from WHO, *estimated value
Index of embodied water consumption (litres)	low–very high	Low	Low	estimated
Change In Land Use				
Local land use change (Ha)	% of land converted for cropland	11.7	15	Rockstrom et al. (2009)
updated value	area of forested land as % of original forest cover	65	75	Steffen et al. (2015)
Population density	person/km^2	3500	TBD	Demographia 2006
Index of global land use impact (Ha)	low–very high	Low	Low	estimated
Nitrogen cycle				
Per capita values as per cent of global values based on estimated consumption patterns	kg-N$_2$/cap/year	18	5.5	Rockstrom et al. (2009)
updated value	kg-N$_2$/cap/year	21	9	Steffen et al. (2015)

Physical science indicators	Unit	Global (current)	Global (Targets/limits)	Source
Pollution				
Percentage of city population with regular solid waste collection	%	50	80*	municipality waste management, *estimated data
Percentage of city population served by wastewater collection	%	76	80*	http://www.worldwaterweek.org/, *estimated data
PM 2.5; PM 10; O3	µg/m³	20	10	WHO
Geophysical risk				
Number of natural disaster-related deaths	per 100,000 population	0.134	0.09*	adapted from Guha-Sapir, *estimated
Percentage of GDP loss due to natural disasters	%	0.2	0.1	b$ 143 in 2012/UCL_WHO
Resilience of city	low–very high	medium	high	estimated

1 This represents cumulative fresh water withdrawal from all sources. Cities usually report only their domestic water consumption; eventually, embodied water consumption would be included, similar to GHG emissions inventories.

Table 5.2 Global social science indicators (global average values compared to target/limit)

Indicators	Unit	Current	Target	Comment/source
Youth opportunity				
Under 5 mortality	deaths per 1,000 live births	51	17	Development Goals (UN 2013, 2015)
Gender equity				
Percentage of female in schools	%	85	95	Development Goals (UN 2013, 2015) 495.9 m illiterate woman in 2007 (UN)
Youth unemployment rate	%	12.4	12.8	2012 rate and 2018 estimate by UN-ILO
Average life expectancy	years	70	70	70 is 2015 target/United Nations
Economy				
Unemployment rate	%	6	6*	ILO-UN, 2013, *estimated
Gini coefficient		0.52	0.2*	The Conference Board of Canada, *estimated
Percentage of population living in slums	%	25	18	Development Goals (UN 2013, 2015)
GDP	$/cap	10,496	20,000*	b$74910, 7.13 million pop, 2013 (WB), *estimated
Energy access and intensity				
Percentage of city with authorized electrical service	%	94	100	0.21 million urban residents w/o access (IEA)
Percentage of city with access to clean energy for cooking	%	88	100	0.43 million urban residents w/o access (IEA)
Energy intensity	MJ/$	8.9	8.9	Wikipedia: List of countries by energy intensity, 2003
Mobility and Connectivity				
Number of personal automobiles per capita	vehicle/cap	0.15	0.2	1.02 billion in 2010, 1.58 billion in 2020
Daily number of public transport trips per capita	trips/cap/day	0.35	0.35*	*estimated
Number of internet connections	% population	40	50	Internet Live Stats
Percentage of commuters using a travel mode other than a personal vehicle to work	%	30	50*	*estimated
Transportation fatalities	per 100,000 population	17.2	8.6*	World Health Organization, *estimated
Commercial air connectivity	# of destinations			
Institutions				

Indicators	Unit	Current	Target	Comment/source
Ease of doing business – World Bank (downscaled from country to city level)		95	95	International Finance Corporation
Number of convictions for corruption by city officials	per 100,000 population	42.7	50	Index average/transparency international
Tax collected as a per cent of tax billed	%			TBD from GCI (WCCD)
Debt service ratio				TBD from GCI (WCCD)
Basic Services				
Percentage of population with regular solid waste collection	%	50	80*	Urban solid waste management, *estimated
Percentage of city population served by wastewater collection	%	76	80*	2008, urban regions, www.worldwaterweek.org, *estimated
Percentage of population served with potable water supply	%	81	95*	United Nations, *estimated
Security and Public Safety				
Number of fire related deaths	per 100,000 population	3.6	0.5*	265,000 deaths/y/WHO, *estimated
Number of homicides	per 100,000 population	6.1	3.05*	437,000 cases in 2013/UNODC, *estimated
Violent crime rate	per 100,000 population			TBD from GCI (WCCD)

Accessing city data

The approach presented here requires more than 44 data points for each evaluated city. Where necessary, the data are estimated for the urban agglomeration (metro area) either by aggregating all local government information or down-scaling national data (Tables 5.1 and 5.2). The quality of data varies, with some expected to be third-party verified, i.e. ISO 37120, and some initially estimated. Some are down-scaled national values.

As illustrated with GHG emissions values, city-data needs to include what the city and its residents are directly responsible for, and what residents are responsible for outside city-limits, possibly half a world away. City-values also need to coincide with regional and national estimates. Four new indices are established for biophysical science indicators: index of biodiversity impact; index of embodied water consumption; index of global land use; and urban resilience. Similar to GHG emissions and Scope 3, the indices for biodiversity impact, embodied water consumption and global land use are mainly the embodied, or vicarious impact, associated with a product or service consumed by residents in the evaluated city. The index of urban resilience is estimated through the risks affecting the assessed city added to the city's presumed adaptive capacity.

Data associated with evaluated cities are expected to be regularly updated; a global effort is needed to collect this information. Two key sources of data input and support are envisaged. Data for the indices will be provided by peer experts and possibly 'crowd sourced' until more exact values can be obtained. An urban electronics market needs to be developed, similar to the Iowa Electronics Markets. Comparable indices are Transparency International's Country Index and the World Bank's 'Ease of Doing Business' country index.

Larger cities have one or more schools of engineering located within them. Faculties of civil engineering could be canvassed to establish an ad hoc global network for data collection, compilation and regular updating. The World Federation of Engineering Organizations could loosely coordinate the effort (costs expected to be borne by schools of engineering through several partnerships).

Global biophysical boundaries

Building on the planetary boundaries (or limits), Figure 5.2 and Table 5.1 present a global aggregate for proposed boundaries of the world's largest cities. The boundaries are applicable to all cities; however, larger cities are prioritized, i.e. those cities (urban agglomerations) with a population of over 5 million by 2050. Values are presented as per capita (average for all city residents). The analysis includes an additional boundary for geophysical risk. This reflects seismic and weather-related risk the city faces, e.g. sea level rise, earthquake, volcanoes, landslides, storms and flooding. The value is an aggregate estimate of risk to life and property. Geophysical risk includes rapid onset events such as typhoons and earthquakes: long-term climate-related events, such as drought, pestilence and changes to growing seasons, are considered elsewhere. The values are presented as urban resilience (a function of risk and adaptive capacity).

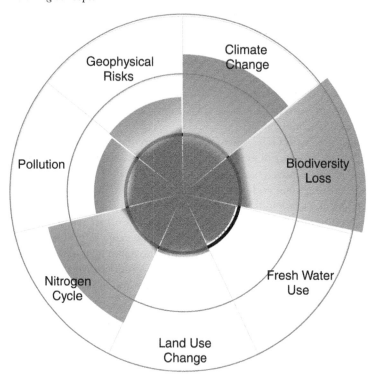

Figure 5.2 Biophysical boundaries for cities in a global context (aggregate estimates).

'Pollution' is added to the biophysical boundaries to estimate local (and cumulative) values for air pollution (smog and indoor/outdoor particulate matter), water pollution (COD, BOD, flotsam and heavy metals) and land pollution (solid waste and brownfields). These wastes lead to pollution and tend to be locally generated and experienced. The values for pollution are expected to vary markedly for assessed cities. An eventual refinement of the methodology will include global aggregation for (local) pollution that impacts at the local and global scale, e.g. smog, trace organics, black carbon. The boundaries are presented as an average for the overall urban area, even though pollution levels can vary significantly within a city. Pollution could equally be presented as socio-economic boundary as it has a major impact on local quality of life and health (Shaw et al., 2014); however, to reflect best the link between local pollution and global impacts – smog in cities and global GHG emissions, for example – the boundary is presented in the biophysical suite.

The limits for climate change are common with Rockstrom et al. and Steffen et al. (a total city-wide per capita GHG emissions value is provided using Scopes 1, 2 and, where available, 3). So too nitrogen limits – absolute per capita values are provided. Biodiversity, fresh water use and land use change are common with current planetary boundaries and estimated for individual cities. Values are derived from local and global impacts, each given equal weighting. For activities like biodiversity loss, an index is provided (see Table 5.1). Rockstrom et al.'s values were recently updated (Steffen et al., 2015) for total per capita water consumption, land-use change and nitrogen consumption (Table 5.1). Two additional boundaries are now said to be surpassed: land-use and biogeochemical flows (nitrogen and phosphorus). These are in addition to climate change and biodiversity (surpassed in the original 2009 assessment).

Moving from a global boundaries approach to a cities perspective

Modifications to the global planetary boundaries approach to a cities perspective are shown in Figure 5.2. Changes include: atmospheric aerosol loading is omitted (atmospheric limits included in 'pollution' indicator); ocean acidification is omitted (included in climate change indicator); climate change is presented as aggregate GHG emissions by city, i.e. Scopes 1, 2 and, where available, 3; biodiversity impact is estimated for local and global activities deriving from city residents – two metrics are used, one capturing local impacts on neighbouring ecosystems and species, and another estimating global index of biodiversity impact; fresh water use is similar to GHG emissions, estimated as a local and global aggregate usage; change in land use includes local and global activities; 'pollution' is intended to capture particulate matter, smog, BOD, COD, solid waste and heavy metal contamination generated inside and outside the urban boundary, but directly impacting the city; nitrogen is estimated from consumption of food and horticultural products, plus relevant industrial activities (phosphorous to be added later – nitrogen considered first priority, although phosphorous loading of local water courses severe near some cities); geophysical risks are estimated for each urban area – risk is residual (geophysical and climate risk) and aggregate (estimated against life and property for entire urban area).

Data sources for the seven proposed cities-based physical indicators are:

Climate change: GHG emissions per capita (Scopes 1, 2 and [eventually] 3; C40-ICLEI-WRI GPC, GCI-C and SDG)[2]

Rate of biodiversity loss: ecological footprint (WWF Living Planet Report); index of biodiversity impact (SDG – TBD)

Fresh water use: percentage of city with potable water supply (GCI-C); total per capita water consumption (GCI-S, SDG); index of embodied water consumption (SDG – TBD)

Change in land use: local land use change in Ha (SDG – TBD); index of global land use impact (embodied; SDG – TBD)

Nitrogen cycle: per capita values as percentage of global values based on estimated consumption patterns

Pollution: PM 2.5 (GCI-C); PM 10 (GCI-C); O3 (ozone – GCI-S); percentage of city population with regular solid waste collection (GCI-C); percentage of city's wastewater receiving no treatment (GCI-C)

Geophysical risk: number of natural disaster related deaths per 100,000 population (GCI-C); resilience of city (SDG – Index); life and property casualty (by insurance payment – TBD)

Global socio-economic limits

The socio-economic limits, or boundaries, of sustainability also include seven metrics. Where definitive values are not available, values are estimated (and denoted). The boundaries align with the Sustainable Development Goals (SDG) and previous Millennium Development Goals (MDG).

In an attempt to develop 'contours of a resilient global future', researchers combine scenario analysis (to 2100) with planetary boundaries and targets for human development (Gerst, Raskin and Rockstrom, 2014). The methodology is sufficiently robust to accommodate dramatic social and technological change. The approach presented here provides planetary and local objectives as human development targets that would facilitate a similar application of 'contours of a resilient global future', but from a metropolitan city perspective. No upper-bounds are suggested, as in Raworth (Figure 5.6), although in many cases, such as unemployment rate, mortality in under 5s and percentage of population with regular solid waste coverage, the values would approach asymptotically 0 or 100 per cent.

Figure 5.4 provides approximate global social boundaries (i.e. socio-economic) estimated in relation to existing targets and global limits. These targets are mainly a reflection of the SDGs. Most of the data is regularly available through data sets such as the Global City Indicators Facility (and partner World Council on City Data); however, approximations are needed as values are required for the entire urban area rather than the individual city alone.

The proposed socio-economic limits are: (i) youth opportunity; (ii) economy; (iii) energy access and intensity; (iv) mobility and connectivity; (v) institutions; (vi) basic services; and (vii) security and public safety. These limits are consistent with a hierarchy of sustainable cities (Chapter 4) and reflect the foundations of urban service delivery. Three to five indicative measures are used for each limit. Youth opportunity includes metrics targeted to girls to reflect the critical nature of gender in economic growth. In addition to per capita GDP (city-based), the economy limit includes Gini coefficient and population in slums to capture general equity, as well as the overall city unemployment rate.

Access to energy and energy intensity measure service provision, especially for the poor, and overall efficiency of energy use as measured through energy intensity (energy used per unit GDP). Mobility and connectivity are considered critical, as urban economies are facilitated through personal interactions. The limits of institutions and security and public safety are particularly broad and challenging to capture across all cities. Indicative and readily available indicators are used initially, with possible augmentation as more data becomes available. Comprehensive education and health limits are not used as these are often not the remit of the city and are predicated on minimum quality of life and basic service delivery levels. Table 5.2 gives the current values of the global bio-physical science indicators compared with the target values or limits.

Data sources for the seven proposed cities-based socio-economic indicators are:

Youth opportunity: under 5 mortality (SDG, GCI-C); gender equity (SDG); female percentage in schools (GCI-C); youth unemployment rate (GCI-S); average life expectancy (GCI-C)

Economy: unemployment rate (GCI-C); Gini coefficient (SDG); percentage of population living in slums (GCI-C, SDG); local GDP (TBD)

Energy access and intensity: percentage of city with authorized electrical service (SDG-C); energy intensity (SDG and partial GCI-S)

Mobility and connectivity: annual number of public transport trips per capita (GCI-C); number of personal automobiles per capita (GCI-C); percentage of commuters using a travel mode other than a personal vehicle to work (GCI-S); commercial air connectivity (GCI-S); transportation fatalities per 100,000 population (GCI-S); number of internet connections per 100,000 population (GCI-C); Index of Connectivity (TBD)

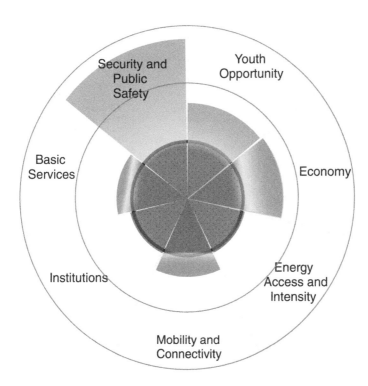

Figure 5.3 Socio-economic limits: global situation compared to targets.

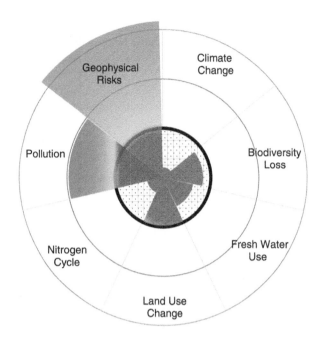

Figure 5.4a Biophysical science: Dakar vs global condition.

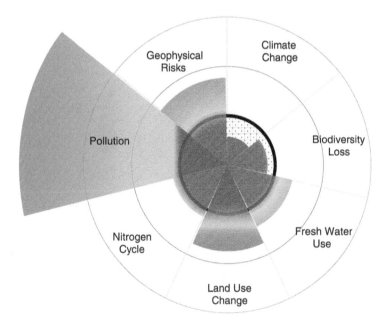

Figure 5.4b Biophysical science: Mumbai vs global condition.

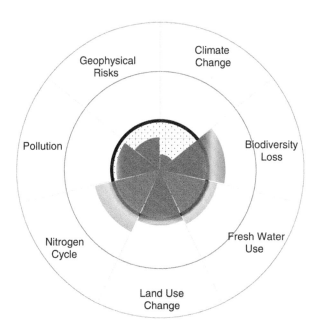

Figure 5.4c Biophysical science: São Paulo vs global condition.

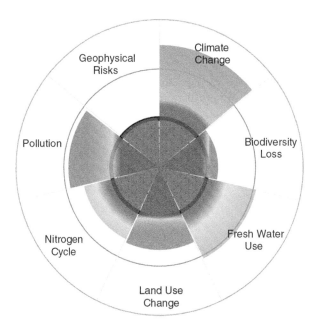

Figure 5.4d Biophysical science: Shanghai vs global condition.

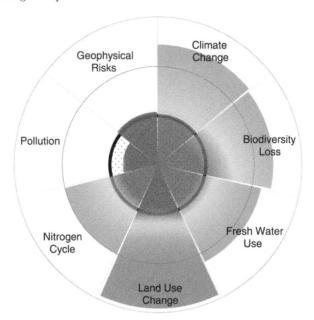

Figure 5.4e Biophysical science: Toronto vs global condition.

Institutions: 'ease of doing business' – World Bank (downscaled from country to city level); number of convictions for corruption by city officials per 100,000 population (GCI-S); tax collected as a per cent of tax billed (GCI-S); debt service ratio (GCI-C)

Basic services: percentage of population with regular solid waste collection (GCI-C); percentage of city population served by wastewater collection (GCI-C); percentage of population served with potable water supply (GCI-C); percentage of houses flooded, per year (SDG – TBD)

Security and public safety: number of fire-related deaths per 100,000 population (GCI-C); number of homicides per 100,000 population (GCI-C); violent crime rate per 100,000 population (GCI-C)

Results

Socio-economic limits are closely linked to biophysical limits, e.g. access to energy and GHG emissions, GDP and biodiversity impact. Analysing limits from a city's perspective requires an integrated perspective at both the local and global scale. Figures 5.5a–5.5e illustrate the 14 limits of 5 example cities, relative to each other. These comparisons and targets enable a city-assessment of sustainable development locally and globally.

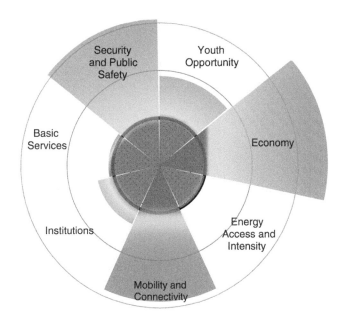

Figure 5.5a   Socio-economic: Dakar vs global condition.

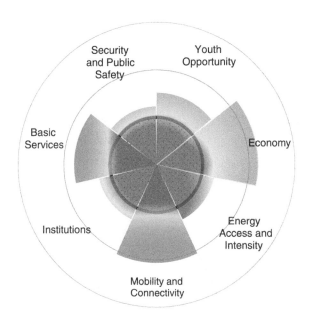

Figure 5.5b   Socio-economic: Mumbai vs global condition.

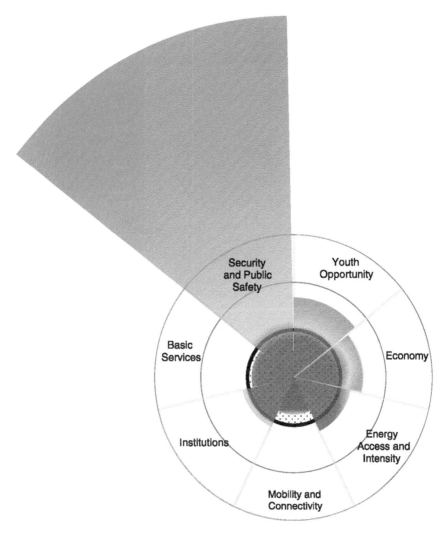

Figure 5.5c   Socio-economic: São Paulo vs global condition.

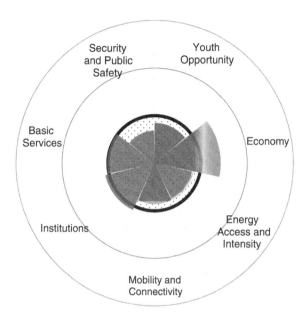

Figure 5.5d Socio-economic: Shanghai vs global condition.

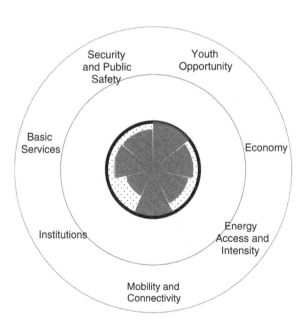

Figure 5.5e Socio-economic: Toronto vs global condition.

Biophysical science indicators of five world cities

The biophysical science (and later socio-economic) indicators discussed above are evaluated for five of the world's largest cities. The cities and their populations are[3]:

- Dakar (Metropolitan Area, DMA): 2.8 million (2012); 9.9 million (2050)
- Mumbai (Metropolitan Region, MMR): 18.8 million (2012); 47.4 million (2050)
- São Paulo (Metropolitan Region, SPMR): 21.0 million (2012); 25.3 million (2050)
- Shanghai (Metropolitan Area, SMA): 18.4 million (2012); 25.3 million (2050)
- Toronto (Greater Toronto Area, GTA): 6.3 million (2012); 7.9 million (2050)

The seven biophysical boundaries are scaled according to current global conditions; four results are provided in Table 5.3. Toronto and Shanghai are notable for their relatively high greenhouse gas emissions and fresh water use. The nitrogen values are estimated against global averages and a specific estimate of the city's energy and food consumption compared to the global average (and the corresponding increase/decrease in N_2). Mumbai has the highest levels of chemical pollution compared to the other four cities.

Table 5.1 provides detailed information on the cities' current data for biophysical science indicators. The cities are also compared with current global averages and the average of the five pilot cities. Transportation modes in Dakar are mainly public transit, walking and biking, rather than personal automobiles, which have the greatest share in Toronto and Shanghai. Nearly 88 per cent of Dakar's commuters use a travel mode other than personal vehicles.

Measuring the rate of biodiversity loss at a city level is challenging, as both local and global impacts need to be quantified. Biodiversity is affected by many parameters and phenomena such as greenhouse gas emissions, land use, water consumption and nitrogen phosphorous cycles. Table 5.4 provides a preliminary assessment of biodiversity indices for the five cities. These are an initial starting

Table 5.3 Biophysical science indicators for the five example cities, scaled according to the global average

Physical Science Indicators	Dakar	Mumbai	São Paulo	Shanghai	Toronto
Carbon dioxide emission	0.2	0.6	0.3	2.5	2.4
Rate of biodiversity loss	0.8	0.8	1.4	1.2	2.4
Fresh water use	0.7	1.4	1.2	2.1	2.2
Change in land use	1.0	1.8	1.5	1.7	2.9
Nitrogen cycle	0.3	1.2	1.4	1.6	2.0
Chemical pollution	2.0	4.5	0.9	1.9	0.7
Geophysical risk	3.2	1.8	0.7	1.0	1.0

Table 5.4 Biodiversity index (aggregate local and global impacts)

	Local Impact	Global Impact	Average
Dakar	3	1.5	2.3
Mumbai	3.5	2.5	3
São Paulo	2.5	3	2.8
Shanghai	3	4	3.5
Toronto	3.5	2	2.8

point and would need to be refined as a more comprehensive methodology emerges (WWF, personal discussions). Aside from Mumbai and Dakar, the other three cities have higher than (global) average biodiversity impacts.

The following is an approximation of bio-physical indicators for the Greater Toronto Area. In Table 5.5, the highlighted cells represent estimated values based on current available data. The values are approximations intended to start an open-source iterative process. Ideally, the values would be regularly updated, with a broader consensus, perhaps with support of local engineering faculties and city officials. Figure 5.4e (Biophysical limits) highlights that the Toronto Area follows common traits of most affluent cities with a disproportionate contribution to climate change, nitrogen cycle, change in land use and fresh water consumption. Of the 44,838 species assessed in the IUCN 'Red List' (2014), 16,928 are listed as threatened, of which 180 are local to Ontario. Canada's ecological footprint is used to estimate biodiversity loss in Toronto, as these numbers are reported at country scale in the WWF's 2014 Living Planet Report. The same approach is also used for the other four major cities. Values are expected to be further refined with additional consideration for activities such as migratory bird loss in Toronto (high-rise tower strikes at night).

São Paulo is prone to landslides, lightening and floods. From 2005 to 2011, 35 casualties were reported in the City of São Paulo due to natural disasters, and 37 people died annually due to the disasters between 2005 and 2011 in the state of São Paulo, leading to 0.09 deaths per 100,000 inhabitants. This is less than the global annual average of 9,655 natural disaster-related deaths between the years 2002 and 2011, according to a joint study by Université Catholique de Louvain and the World Health Organization (WHO) in 2012. Figure 5.4c compares São Paulo with global averages on the biophysical science indicators.

With a population of 18.4 million (2012 data), Shanghai is China's largest metropolitan, and, like São Paulo, is susceptible to flooding. Greenhouse gas emissions and air quality are relatively higher than global averages (Figure 5.5d). The levels of CO_2 equivalent emissions and particulate matter (PM2.5) are reported as 11.7 tCO_2e/cap/year and 81 ug/m^3 respectively. The average domestic fresh water use in Shanghai Metropolitan Area is 411 L/cap/day, which is four times the global 'water right level' proposed by the United Nations.

Mumbai is India's largest metro area. Air quality is as poor as Shanghai's. Mumbai also has disproportionately high impacts on biodiversity loss, fresh water use and land use change. Figure 5.5b shows the city's status compared to the global average.

Table 5.5 Status of the world's major cities – socio-economic indicators compared to a global average scale of 1

Indicators	Dakar	Mumbai	São Paulo	Shanghai	Toronto
Youth opportunity	1.9	1.5	1.7	0.8	1.0
Economy	3.6	2.2	1.5	1.4	0.9
Energy access and intensity	1.0	1.2	1.2	0.8	0.8
Mobility and connectivity	2.9	2.1	0.8	0.9	1.0
Institutions	1.4	1.3	1.1	1.1	0.6
Basic services	1.1	1.8	0.9	1.0	0.9
Security and public safety	3.1	1.2	7.7	0.7	0.8

Dakar Metropolitan Area covers 1 per cent of Senegal's land area; however, it is home to nearly 50 per cent of the country's urban population. Much of the city's population reside in the 'pre-urban' part of the metropolitan, vulnerable to natural disasters, especially flooding and coastal erosion, which is exacerbated by weak local governance and rising sea levels.

The city is the economic and political hub of the country, and any impact to Dakar affects Senegal overall. For example, more than 5 per cent of Dakar Metropolitan Area is exposed to high-risk natural hazards. The city's population has grown an average 1 per cent per year since 1988; current predictions estimate the city reaching 9.2 million by 2050. The city also suffers from high ambient air pollution with 80 ug/m^3, compared to the WHO targets of 10 ug/m^3. Access to clean water is not provided to 3 per cent of the population; the figure for solid waste collection is nearly 25 per cent. Figure 5.5a shows the city's status compared to the global average.

Socio-economic indicators of world's major cities

The socio-economic limits for the five major cities given in Table 5.4 are compared to a global average scale of 1. Compared to the global average, only Shanghai has a better level of youth opportunity; Toronto's youth unemployment is highest of the five pilot cities, yet it has the lowest Gini coefficient. Dakar's economic challenges are manifest, reflected by relatively low youth opportunity and low economic performance (Table 5.5).

Toronto has the highest Gross Domestic Product (GDP) per capita among the five pilot cities ($51,000), and Dakar the lowest at $3,700. Nearly 20 per cent of Shanghai's residents do not have access to solid waste and wastewater collection, while this number is more than 60 per cent for residents in Mumbai Metropolitan Region. Mumbai also has the second highest fire-related deaths rates among the five cities, after Dakar.

Figure 5.6e highlights Toronto's relative strength in social limits. On average, compared with the global values, Toronto has higher opportunities for youth, a larger per capita economy, full energy access, and higher public safety and security indicators. São Paulo, on the other hand, has lower youth opportunity

Table 5.6 Biophysical indicators for Dakar, Mumbai, São Paulo, Shanghai and Toronto

Physical Science Indicators[1]	Unit	Global	Cities average[2]	Dakar	Mumbai	São Paulo	Shanghai	Toronto
Carbon dioxide emission								
GHG emissions per capita	(tCO$_2$/cap/year)	4.71	6	1[3]	2.7	1.5	11.7	11.5
Rate of Biodiversity Loss								
Ecological footprint (Global hectares demanded per capita)	ha	1.7	2.8	1.5	1.1	3	2.1	6.5
updated value	ha	1.9	3.6	1.4	1.1	4.4	3.9	7.4
Index of biodiversity impact			2.9	2.3	3	2.8	3.5	2.8
Fresh water use								
Total per capita water consumption	l/cap/day	100	267	69	250	175	411	431
Per cent of city with potable water supply	%	81	95	90	96	92	98	100
Index of embodied water consumption			2.4	1	2	2.5	3	3.5
Change in Land Use								
Local land use change	% of cropland area	11.7	31	19.5	42	24	30	39
updated value	Area of forested land - % of original cover	75	61	89	62	95	33	28
Population density	person/km^2	3500	2927	4122	4225	2503	2902	850
Index of global land use impact			2.4	1	2	2.5	3	3.5
Nitrogen cycle								
Per capita as % of global values based on estimated consumption patterns	kg-N$_2$/cap/year	18	23	6	21	25	29	36
updated value	kg-N$_2$/cap/year	9	12	3	11	13	15	18

Physical Science Indicators[1]	Unit	Global	Cities average[2]	Dakar	Mumbai	São Paulo	Shanghai	Toronto
Chemical pollution								
Percentage of city population with regular solid waste collection	%	50	76	75	32.8	90	82	100
Percentage of city population served by wastewater collection	%	76	76	64	42	99	73	100
PM 2.5; PM 10; O_3	µg/m³	20	82	81	202	28	81	18.7
Geophysical risk								
Number of natural disaster related deaths	per 100,000 pop.	0.134	0.2	0.4[6]	0.3[5]	0.05	0.06[4]	0.01
Percentage of GDP loss due to natural disasters	%	0.2	0.4	1		0.1	0.3[7]	0.5
Resilience of city		57	57	37	44	51	52	100

[1]Data highlighted in grey are estimates. [2]Average of the 5 major cities. [3]Based on Senegal's urban GHG emissions. [4]China, 2011. [5]State of Maharashtra, 2012. [6]Senegal, 52 deaths in 2012. [7]Country scale. Updated values from Steffen et al., 2015.

References in Hoornweg et al., Ambio, 2016 (ESM) and D. Hoornweg, A Cities Approach to Sustainability, University of Toronto, 2015.

and per capita economy, although the city has relatively high service levels in areas such as mobility and connectivity, and basic services, as shown in Figure 5.6c.

Shanghai is well served by its public transportation system, and, as shown in Figure 5.6d, provides relatively high level socio-economic boundaries. Compared with Toronto, Shanghai's higher Gini coefficient and lower per capita income are key economy indicators.

Comparing Toronto, Shanghai and São Paulo with Mumbai and Dakar, the significant need for improved economy, youth opportunity, and mobility and connectivity is evident. Mumbai also lags in providing basic services such as waste collection and improved sanitation. The socio-economic status of Mumbai and Dakar are shown in Figures 5.6b and 5.6a respectively.

Conclusion

Sustainable development and planetary boundaries are often presented as a global challenge, and rightly so, as broad issues such as climate change, loss of biodiversity and stratospheric ozone depletion are global manifestations of unsustainable actions. However, the vast majority of the actions leading to these impacts originate in cities. Cities, i.e. urban areas, are the nodes of the global economy. Residents of cities drive the world's material and energy flows. Cities by their nature, with fragile infrastructure, immobility and, in many cases, coastal settings, are particularly vulnerable to global trends such as climate change and food insecurity.

The challenges and integrated nature of sustainable development and associated threats to planetary boundaries is well presented (e.g. Figure 5.2). The eight quantified and two yet-to-be quantified physical limits capture well the requirements and magnitude of global impacts.

As shown in this chapter, applying global biophysical limits and socio-economic targets at a city level is possible. The city level is considered the critical unit for sustained action. The methodology presented in this chapter facilitates integration across limits and targets as well as integrating local and global impacts. Each city can develop its target to sustainability. Efforts can be readily monitored and compared with other cities.

The proposed methodology and city targets, if used by the majority of the world's larger cities, could support an international agreement on sustainable development facilitated through cities.

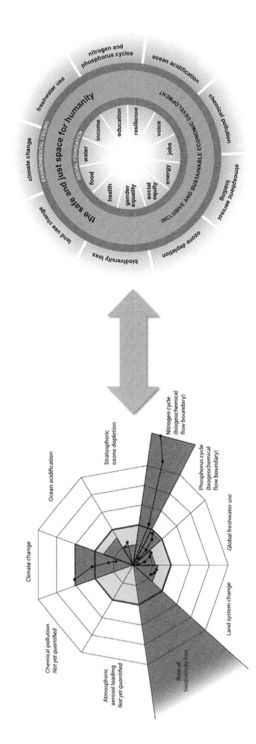

Figure 5.6 Safe and just operating spaces for regional social–ecological systems. Merging (a) the planetary boundary framework (Rockstrom et al., 2009a,b) and (b) the social 'doughnut' framework (Raworth, 2012) into a new framework and tool for defining safe and just operating spaces for sustainable development at regional scales.

Source: Global Environmental Change, 28 (2014).

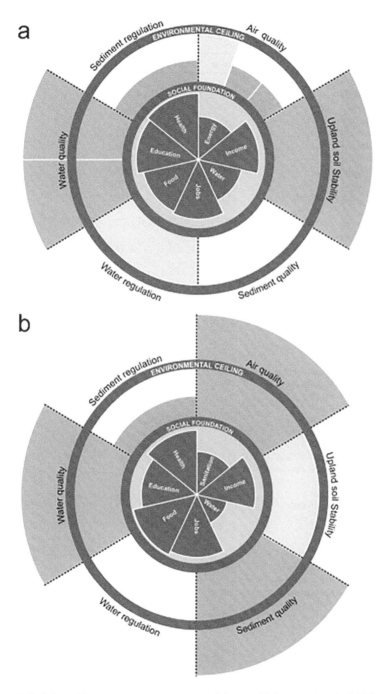

Figure 5.7 Safe and just operating spaces mapped for two Chinese regions in 2006.
(a) Erhai lake-catchment system, Yunnan Province; (b) Shucheng County, Anhui Province.
Source: Dearing et al., 2014.

Table 5.7 Socio-economic indicators for Dakar, Mumbai, São Paulo, Shanghai and Toronto

Indicators	Dakar	Mumbai	São Paulo	Shanghai	Toronto
Youth opportunity					
Under 5 mortality	53	40	22	1.1	6.4[i]
Gender equity	0.44	0.7	0.37	0.81	0.74
Percentage of female in schools	68	87.2	95	97.3	0.91
Youth unemployment rate	14.8	11	17.7	0.68	18.1
Average life expectancy	61	68	69	82	80
Economy					
Unemployment rate	30	11.7	5.2	4.2	8.6
Gini coefficient	0.39	0.35	0.61	0.45	0.33
Percentage of population living in slums	35	37.7	20	31	0
GDP	3700	6700	22700	19100	51300
Energy access and intensity					
Percentage of city with authorized electrical service	96	95	99.9	99	100
Percentage of city with access to clean energy for cooking	90	68.6	99	99	100
Energy intensity	10.2	6.5	5	14.8	24.6
Mobility and connectivity					
Number of personal automobiles per capita	0.017	0.036	0.31	0.13	0.61
Daily number of public transport trips per capita	0.5	0.63	0.9	0.83	0.25
Number of internet connections	53	65	50	63.1	83[b]
Percentage of commuters using a travel mode other than a personal vehicle to work	88	94	71	78	23
Transportation fatalities	17.2	34.2	7.8	6.3	2.5
Commercial air connectivity					
Institutions					
Ease of doing business – World Bank (downscaled from country to city level)[b]	178	134	116	96	19
Number of convictions for corruption by city officials[b]	41	36	42	40	81
Tax collected as a per cent of tax billed					
Debt service ratio					
Basic services					
Percentage of population with regular solid waste collection	75	32.8	90	82.3	100
Percentage of city population served by wastewater collection	64	42	99.1	72.5	100
Percentage of population served with potable water supply	97	96	92	98	100
Security and Public Safety					
Number of fire related deaths	3.2	1.65	0.5	0.3	0.44
Number of homicides	8.7	1.2	64.8	1.4	2
Violent crime rate					

[a]Infant mortality rate. [b]Country level.

References in Hoornweg et al., Ambio, 2016 (ESM) and D. Hoornweg, A Cities Approach to Sustainability, University of Toronto, 2015.

Notes

1 Sustainable Development Goals, United Nations [online]. Available at: http://sustain abledevelopment.un.org/?menu=1300
2 GCI-C and S, Global City Indicator core and supporting as defined in ISO 37120; SDG – Sustainable Development Goal, expected 2015; TBD – to be developed. Where values are not yet available through GCI (WCCD) estimates are made by authors (to be updated as data becomes available).
3 Population estimates from D. Hoornweg and K. Pope, 2014. *Population Predictions of the 101 Largest Cities in the 21st Century*. Toronto: Global Cities Institute.
4 Cities average if available, otherwise data assessed against the global average.

References

Dearing, J., Wang, R., Zhang, K., Dyke, J., Haberl, H., Hossain, S., Langdon, P., Lenton, T., Raworth, K., Brown, S., Carstensen, J., Cole, M., Cornell, S., Dawson, T., Doncaster, P., Eigenbrod, F., Florke, M., Jeffers, E., Mackay, A., Nykvist, B. and Poppy, G., 2014. Safe and Just Operating Spaces for Regional Social–Ecological Systems. *Global Environmental Change*, 28, pp.227–38.

Galaz, V., Biermann, F., Folke, C., Nilsson, M. and Olsson, P., 2012. Global Governance and Planetary Boundaries: An Introduction. *Ecological Economics*, 81, pp.1–3.

Gerst, M., Raskin, P. and Rockstrom, J., 2014. Contours of a Resilient Global Future. *Sustainability*, 6(1), pp.123–35.

International Geosphere–Biosphere Programme, 2015. *The Nine Planetary Boundaries, as Visualised by the Stockholm Resilience Centre/Globaïa (adapted from Steffen et al. (2015)* [online figure] Stockholm: IGBP Secretariat. Available at: www.igbp.net/download/18 .950c2fa1495db7081e1754b/1446110005354/NL84-reflections_ES_science.pdf

Raworth, K., 2012. Defining a Safe and Just Space for Humanity. In: The Worldwatch Institute, 2013. *State of the World 2013: Is Sustainability Still Possible?* Washington, DC: Island Press, ch. 3.

Rockström, J., Steffen, W., Noone, K., Persson, Å., Chapin, S., Lambin, E., Lenton, T., Scheffer, M., Folke, C., Schellnhuber, H., Nykvist, B., de Wit, C., Hughes, T., van der Leeuw, S., Rodhe, H., Sörlin, S., Snyder, P., Costanza, R., Svedin, U., Falkenmark, M., Karlberg, L., Corell, R., Fabry, V., Hansen, J., Walker, B., Liverman, D., Richardson, K., Crutzen, P. and Foley, J., 2009. A Safe Operating Space for Humanity. *Nature*, 461, pp.472–5.

Shaw, C., Hales, S., Howden-Chapman, P. and Edwards, R., 2014. Health Co-benefits of Climate Change Mitigation Policies in the Transport Sector. *Nature Climate Change*, 4, pp.427–33.

Sovacool, B., 2012. The Methodological Challenges of Creating a Comprehensive Energy Security Index. *Energy Policy*, 48, pp.835–40.

Steffen, W., Richardson, K., Rockström, J., Cornell, S., Fetzer, I., Bennett, E., Biggs, R., Carpenter, S., de Vries, W., de Wit, C., Folke, C., Gerten, D., Heinke, J., Mace, G., Persson, L., Ramanathan, V., Reyers, B. and Sörlin, S., 2015. Planetary Boundaries: Guiding Human Development on a Changing Planet. *Science*, 347(6223).

6 Market concepts

Sustainability cost curves

Introduction

Around the world the largest city-building effort in human history is underway. Many older civil works in the cities of Europe, North America and Japan are being replaced and retrofitted, and new construction is taking place in fast-growing cities. East and South Asia is now the world's fastest-growing region; Asia Pacific alone is approaching $5.4 trillion in annual infrastructure spending.[1] Cities of Sub-Saharan Africa are also ramping up growth as the region's urban population is expected to surpass East and South Asia's by mid-century. Cities and their agencies are expected to spend at least $100 trillion on infrastructure and urban service delivery by 2050.

While this enormous urban infrastructure rush is underway, as many as four planetary boundaries have been crossed. Climate change, the rate of biodiversity loss, the nitrogen cycle and land-use change are all believed to be beyond sustainable boundaries. The drivers of ecosystem degradation are mostly by-products of current urban lifestyles, e.g. greenhouse gas emissions, water use and land clearing associated with agriculture and forestry. This impact is bound to increase as urban populations and their wealth double. There is a need to adhere to planetary boundaries and strive to reduce environmental degradation and meet socio-economic targets as proposed through the sustainable development goals. These biophysical boundaries and socio-economic goals are critical considerations for all urban infrastructure.

Marginal abatement cost (MAC) curves present a set of available options for a longer-term and comprehensive programmes such as greenhouse gas abatement (Figure 6.1) and adaptation (Figure 6.2).

MAC curves rose in prominence after the 1997 Kyoto Protocol agreement as countries sought to optimize delivery of mandated greenhouse gas emission reductions. Various economists, research organizations and consultancies have produced MAC curves. Bloomberg New Energy Finance (2010) and McKinsey & Company (2010) have produced notable economy-wide analyses on greenhouse gas emissions reductions for the United States and globally (Creyts et al., 2007). MAC curves also provide powerful public policy tools for climate adaptation.

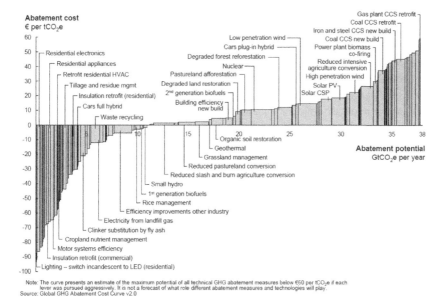

Figure 6.1　Marginal abatement cost curve – global greenhouse gas emission reduction measures.

Source: McKinsey & Company, 2009.

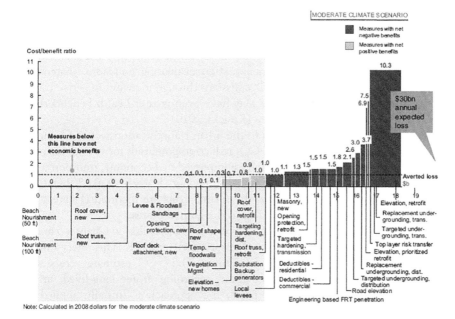

Figure 6.2　Adaptation cost curve – state of Florida.

Source: Economics of Climate Adaptation Working Group, 2009.

Salient features of MAC curves are shown in Figure 6.1, which displays a global suite of possible GHG mitigation options. Each bar represents a single carbon mitigation option; the width of the bar represents the abatement potential relative to business as usual; the height of the bar represents the abatement cost per tonne, relative to business as usual. The costs are expressed per tonne of emissions avoided.[2] The sum of the width of all the bars (x axis) represents the total carbon reduction potential; the area of each bar represents the marginal cost for that particular mitigation option.

Variations on the standard MAC curve were developed. For example, Figure 6.2 provides a similar assessment for enhanced adaptation and coastal protection in Florida, USA. A suite of activities and their cost–benefit ratio are presented for coastal protection in a moderate climate scenario. All measures below a cost–benefit ratio of 1 provide net positive benefits.

Advantages and disadvantages of MAC curves have been widely discussed. The advantages are a powerful visual display of results, which facilitates public sharing, with considerable information such as break-even lines. Discount rates can be customized by activity. Marginal costs (or benefits) are determined for any given project (or idea), and comparison can be made across sectors and entities (e.g. countries, cities, corporations). Disadvantages include: tendency to favour technological solutions over behavioural change (Ward, 2014); limitation of analysis to one point in time; path dependency not represented; and ancillary benefits not considered (Ekins, Kesicki and Smith, 2011; Kesicki and Ekins, 2012). Results are sensitive to assumptions, which are not always made transparent, so that the curves often convey unrealistic certainty (Ackerman and Bueno, 2011). Actual costs of activities may also vary from those presented due to time dependency (Avner, Rentschler and Hallegatte, 2014). There is a need to include health and social benefits when evaluating emissions abatement projects. For example, reducing CO_2 emissions through increases in active travel and reduced use of motor vehicles may have even greater health benefits than those attributed to GHG mitigation (Kesicki, 2010).

MAC curves have been applied to the urban transportation sector. Examples include, the cost-effectiveness and CO_2 reduction potentials for various changes in the US transportation sector, such as: improved fuel economy, transportation system improvements and shifts in travel behaviour (Hartgen et al., 2011). CO_2 emissions reduction potentials and the related costs are reported (Figure 6.3). The study covers 48 major urban areas in the United States.

The sustainability cost curve (SCC) presented here builds on Chapter 5 and is a modification of the abatement (and adaptation) approach. This offers a more comprehensive assessment of sustainability. The SCC estimates costs and opportunities of increased sustainability accruing from long-lived urban infrastructure. For illustrative purposes, the approach is initially applied to Toronto's transportation sector. The sustainability potential is derived from the project's impact on biophysical limits and socio-economic targets. Biophysical limits are a city-scale reflection of planetary boundaries and include climate change, biodiversity loss, fresh water use, change in land use, nitrogen cycle,

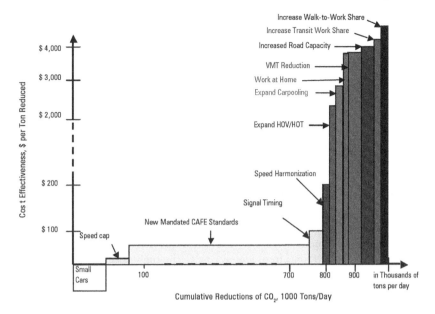

Figure 6.3 Summary of cost-effectiveness and CO_2 reduction potentials in US regions.
Source: Hartgen, et al., 2011.

pollution and geophysical risk. Socio-economic limits, largely derived from the Sustainable Development Goals, include youth opportunity, economy, energy access and intensity, mobility and connectivity, institutions, basic services, and security and public safety (see Chapter 5).

Developing a sustainability cost curve – methodology

Sustainability cost curves can help decision-makers select among a variety of long-term investment options. Policy-makers can apply sustainability cost curves as merit order curves to prioritize investments for greater sustainability, at lowest cost (Vogt-Schilb and Hallegatte, 2014).

Each activity, or wedge, along the curve represents an additional opportunity to increase sustainability. The width (x-axis) of each wedge represents the increase in 'sustainability potential' that the opportunity could deliver to 2050. Sustainability potential is derived from the aggregate contribution of the fourteen biophysical and socio-economic indicators (Tables 5.1 and 5.2). Sustainability potential, SP, is determined by:

$$SP = \sum_{i=1}^{14} w_i \Delta SI_i \tag{1}$$

where ΔSI_i denotes the estimated annual change in a sustainability indicator, weighted by w_i. Changes that help to improve sustainability have a positive value for the change in sustainability indicator. The fourteen sustainability indicators are discussed in Chapter 5. The area of the wedge represents the activity's total expenditure, which is the product of sustainability potential and unit cost of sustainability (UCS):

$$Total \ Expenditure_a = SP_a \times UCS_a \hspace{3cm} (2)$$

The height (y-axis) of each wedge represents the average net present cost of that activity, per unit of sustainability potential. Net present cost includes capital and operating costs less operating revenues (but not increased land value). Costs include expected expenditures to 2050 (benefits only start accruing from year of commissioning; on some longer-lived infrastructure a residual value at 2050 is estimated and discounted to today – a simple 50 per cent discount rate on capital cost is used; operating costs are not discounted). Cost estimates are based on expected government or utility financial outlays for the activity. The approach closely aligns with public expenditure in local governments and utilities. The curve is ordered left to right from lowest cost to the highest cost opportunities.

SCCs provide an overview of available development alternatives and offer a starting point to prioritize options. Sustainable development involves more than choosing between options with least cost or largest sustainability potential; however, SCCs provide a quick way to gauge the relative merits of activities, as well as enable comparisons between sectors and cities. For example, the degree of sustainability potential is consistent if derived for the transportation or energy sectors and uses a common metric for any evaluated city. SCCs can help identify where policy interventions could be particularly effective and can initiate dialogue among affected stakeholders.

Cost curves require a specific future date to evaluate costs and benefits against; 2050 is selected in this analysis. A relatively long planning horizon of 35 years is used, as this helps evaluate larger-scale long-lived civil works that may require 35 years or more to amortize investments. The longer time-frame also encourages a more comprehensive analysis of options, combining capital and operation costs. Long lead times are also necessary to bring about large-scale changes in sectors such as energy and transportation. Many of the options being evaluated, e.g. power plants and subway lines can take more than a decade to plan and build. Also, much of the critical infrastructure in today's cities is older than 35 years; roads, rail and ports typically can last more than a century.

Sustainability cost curves are proposed for the urban sectors of energy, transportation and connectivity, and basic service provision (water and sanitation). In this chapter, a model cost curve for the transportation sector of metropolitan Toronto is provided. Evaluated options are mostly seen as 'the bones' of a city, although policy initiatives can also be evaluated, e.g. the change to transfer pricing in the Toronto transportation analysis. Many of the investments are large scale and can be provided through private–public partnerships or directly by the city or its designated utility. In all cases the metropolitan area is evaluated since most large-scale infrastructure such as transportation and energy systems are developed to serve the overall urban agglomeration (and sometimes beyond).

Initially, larger cities are targeted for analysis, as they generally possess greater staff capacities and data availability, and local research capacity, and larger cities also have greater global ecosystem impacts. A metropolitan-wide scale is used, as ecosystem impacts are influenced by the overall effect of the city and the actions of all of its residents. Metropolitan-scale programmes in areas such as energy and transportation also offer the greatest opportunity to ameliorate system impacts.

Each city has a current value SI_i and target value SI_i^* in 2050 for each of its sustainability indicators. The target value is apportioned (based on population fraction) from global bio-physical boundaries and socio-economic goals. Fourteen sustainability indicators are presented, some with multiple inputs and estimated indices.

Developing sustainability cost curves requires a degree of subjectivity. A proposal within this work is to make these estimates public and eventually 'crowd sourced' by peer associations, municipal staff and academic representatives. Initially, this could be undertaken by respective (local) engineering faculties as many of the city-based values should emerge as public indicators and general 'rules of thumb' for the engineering community.

A key difference between marginal abatement cost curves such as McKinsey's carbon mitigation proposals and sustainability cost curves proposed here is the transparency of data assumptions. As outlined in Chapter 5, the boundaries (and objectives) that underpin sustainability cost curves are public estimates. These estimates would presumably be provided through the infrastructure planning process, similar to an environmental assessment. Retained professionals would be expected to estimate the sustainability costs and sustainability potential of every proposed long-lived urban infrastructure project. Continuous peer inputs on sustainability estimates associated with the city and the specific project would move estimates toward greater accuracy. This 'crowd sourced' accuracy is evident in 'guessing the weight of the ox' (Galton, 1907 – see Box 3.1), the point spread in Vegas-sanctioned sports bets and the Iowa Electronics Market.[3]

Applying the concept to Toronto's transportation system

Like any large city, and like most urban sectors, numerous planning reviews are available for transportation in metropolitan Toronto. The transportation planning authority Metrolinx published a comprehensive transportation Master Plan in 2008. Preliminary budgeting and planning assessments are often available for proposed key infrastructure projects. The Toronto Transit Commission and Province of Ontario (various agencies, including Ministry of Transportation) have proposed several significant initiatives. Several key activities are examined here to demonstrate the SCC method.

90-minute transfer

The Toronto Transit Commission (TTC) is considering a switch from its longstanding single-continuous-trip transfer system to time-based transfers between buses, streetcars and subway trains. The TTC currently issues paper transfers to riders who pay fares with cash, tickets or tokens and whose trip requires a change of vehicle. Transfers are purposely limited and must be used to transfer to the next available train or vehicle from a valid transfer point. Under a time-based transfer system, transfers would allow riders to potentially exit and re-enter the system within the prescribed time limit. TTC officials estimate an unrestricted-use time-based transfer valid for 2 hours would cost the TTC $20 million a year in lost revenues, while a 90-minute transfer would cost around $12 million a year.

Highway 407 extensions

Highway 407, known as the 407 ETR (Express Toll Route), is privately operated and tolled. The Highway 407 East extensions will be built in two phases, first, a 22 km extension to Harmony Road in Oshawa and the West Durham Link, scheduled to open in 2016; a further 43 km extension to Highway 35 and Highway 115, as well as the East Durham Link, is scheduled to open in 2020.

Union Pearson Express

The Union Pearson Express (UP Express) is a 23 km rail link between Canada's two busiest transportation hubs: Union Station in downtown Toronto and Toronto Pearson International Airport. The UP Express trip takes 25 minutes and departs every 15 minutes. Ridership is planned to carry 5,000 passengers per day, replacing approximately 1.2 million car trips per year. The initial use of diesel locomotives and relatively high ticket cots ($27.50 cost per passenger trip) was a source of opposition and legal challenges from the Clean Train Coalition (CTC).

Richmond Hill subway extension

The planned Yonge subway extension will extend 6.8 km north from the current Finch Station to the Richmond Hill/Langstaff Urban Growth Centre at Highway 7. It will include up to six additional stations. This urban centre will be a major transit hub where transit riders will be able to connect to GO Trains, GO Buses, TTC Subway, YRT/Viva buses, the future 407 transit way and other transit services.

Downtown Relief Line

The Downtown Relief Line (DRL) is a proposed additional subway line in Toronto. Fully built, the line would form a shallow U-shape, running east–west through downtown (parallel to but south of the current Bloor–Danforth subway line). The main rationale for the DRL is to reduce congestion on the existing Yonge Line, particularly at the main Bloor–Yonge Station. Four DRLs alignments are proposed:

- from Pape to St Andrew
- from Pape to Dundas West through St Andrew
- from Don Mills at Eglinton through Pape to St Andrew
- from Don Mills at Eglinton through Pape and St Andrew to Dundas West

The two most likely DRL lines are denoted as DRL Don Mills and DRL Pape in the following tables and graphs.

Pickering International Airport

Pickering Airport is a proposed additional international airport to be built north-east of Toronto in Pickering, Ontario, approximately 65 km east of the existing Toronto Pearson International Airport. Cost estimates of approximately $2 billion, anticipating up to 11.9 million passengers per year by 2032. A decision to proceed with airport planning and construction was announced June 11, 2013.

SmartTrack

The SmartTrack line is a Regional Express Rail 'surface subway' planned to connect major hubs in the GTA (Airport Corporate Centre in the west, southeast to Union Station and northeast to Markham in the east). The planed service year is 2021, and the line would have 22 stops at major interchanges. The SmartTrack is expected to help reduce congestion in both the current subway lines and road traffic. The 53 km surface subway line would use existing train rail alignments while being integrated with the overall TTC system. Part of the attraction of the SmartTrack is its use of existing alignments and tracking and potential speed of implementation compared to subways requiring extensive tunnelling. The estimated capital costs are $5.3 billion.

GO electrification

GO train is a major part of metropolitan Toronto's public transit system. Currently, the trains run on diesel fuel. Metrolinx began a review in 2009 on the feasibility of electrification of the entire GO rail system. Economic, environmental, social, health and technological considerations led to the final conclusion as the feasibility of the project. Metrolinx has started the project in phases, of which electrification of Union Station–Pearson Airport line is the first. The capital costs are estimated as $0.9 billion.

Rapid Transit Network Plan

Rapid Transit Network Plan is complimentary to the existing Viva services and aims to implement new services to expand York Region's transit network. The plan intends to decrease traffic congestion, increase transit ridership and increase schedule reliability, and will begin in 2017. Estimated costs are: capital – $132 million; annual operation and maintenance – $37.4 million.

Toronto–York Spadina Subway extension (Vaughan Subway)

Currently, Toronto's subway lines are only within the City's boundaries. Construction of an extension of the University–Spadina line started in 2010 and is planned to be in service in 2016. The Toronto–York Spadina Subway is an 8.6 km extension from Downsview Station northwest (last station on University–Spadina line) through York University within the City of Toronto and north to the Vaughan Metropolitan Centre, in the Regional Municipality of York. Six stations are being constructed, with 2,900 parking spaces. Estimated project costs are $2.6 billion.

Mississauga LRT projects

Metrolinx, along with the cities of Mississauga and Brampton, are expanding and improving public transit in the area with a light rapid transit line from the Port Credit GO Station in Mississauga to the GO Station in Downtown Brampton. This Hurontario–Main LRT will address congestion and improve traffic along the corridor.

GO relief projects

GO trains can serve some of the TTC subway riders during peak hours by increasing train frequency. For example, a GO train trip can be scheduled to move TTC riders on the Danforth Subway Line to downtown directly. An estimated 5,000–20,000 current TTC riders could use this service and get downtown in only 10 minutes. A considerable passenger load could be diverted from the TTC Yonge and Bloor lines. The cost to operate additional trips on the 10 km line between Union and Main Street every morning and evening peak would be about $1.4 million per year. Similar ideas can be applied from Kennedy (east of Toronto) and Kipling (west of Toronto) subway stations to Union Station. These projects are marked as 'GO Relief' in the following tables and figures.

Alternative transportation options for metropolitan Toronto

In addition to the current transportation projects proposed through Metrolinx 'The Big Move', the TTC and other government agencies, three additional options are evaluated here and placed within the region's sustainability cost curve (for transportation).

The three additional options assessed are:

1   Expansion by 30 per cent of current market penetration of electric and natural gas vehicles;
2   Introduction of a Highway 401/407 bus rapid transit (BRT) system. This would include stops at designated interchanges where associated electric vehicle parking lots would be located. Passengers would use privately owned EVs to drive to work and locally;

3 Expansion of the BRT system to Waterloo, Niagara Falls, Ottawa, Kingston and Montreal, along with publicly available (shared) EVs at key parking lots. Passengers could drive EVs (personal or shared) to home or work, and locally. Cars are recharged at parking lots and homes, mostly at night, thereby taking advantage of relative surplus electricity at night. Natural gas conversion of heavy-duty trucks, buses and conversion of some automobiles is also included (a separate truck transport bypass alignment is also proposed).

Option 1 is largely 'business as usual' with recognition of an emerging price for carbon and natural gas being a long-term cheaper and cleaner fuel source than gasoline and diesel (EV-NGV). Option 2 is the emergence of a more collective and integrated commuter approach (407 BRT). Option 3 is best characterized as a 'sharing economy' where most vehicles are shared rather than owned and connectivity is maximized in order to support greater productivity and economic development (as well as improved quality of life) in the region.

Data for each of the transportation options is used to estimate sustainability potential. Tables 6.1a–6.1c provide the changes made in the physical and socio-economic indicators of sustainability due to the implementation of each transportation option. The final sustainability cost curve is shown in Figure 6.4.

Launching a natural gas-powered bus rapid transit (BRT) system across the GTHA and initiating an EV car-sharing programme connected to the BRT lines (Option 3) has the highest sustainability potential compared to other options. SmartTrack surface-rail expansion has the next highest sustainability potential. Comparatively, the 90-minute transfer option provides high sustainability potential at the lowest unit cost. This highlights how operational changes can yield significant sustainability benefits with minimal cost or infrastructure requirements. The sustainability cost curves provide an important venue to explore comparable initiatives that may, or may not, require major infrastructure investment.

Within the sustainability cost curve calculations changes in 'carbon emissions intensity', 'population density' and 'percentage of commuters using a travel mode other than a personal vehicle to work' have more significant impacts on the sustainability potential of a transportation project. The 'number of new users' benefiting from a transportation project also affects the results. Therefore, changes made to any of the indicators are greater for projects with more 'new daily users'. Among the transportation projects in Toronto, the GTHA-BRT Line has the highest sustainability potential due to its relatively large number (1,143,000) of new daily users. Conversely, the relatively high 'cost per unit sustainability' (4.89) for the Highway 407 extension is driven by the relatively small number of 'new daily users' (6,000). (See Figure 6.4.)

The two relative extremes between the highest 'sustainability potential' (49.48) for the GTHA-BRT and the high 'cost per unit sustainability' (4.89) for the Highway 407 extension highlight why a systems approach is needed when interpreting sustainability cost curves. For example, when viewed in isolation, sustainability merits of the Highway 407 extension are moderate; however, when integrated as part of a broader programme with electric vehicles and development

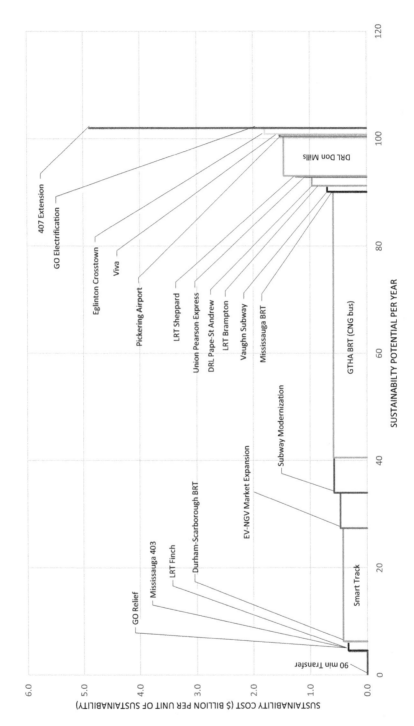

Figure 6.4 Sustainability cost curve (transportation – Toronto).

Table 6.1a Cost estimation and sustainability factors (1) – Toronto transportation

Cost estimation (US$ billion)	90-Min transfer	407 ext.	UP exp.	Subway Richmond Hill	DRL Pape	Pickering Airport	Viva	Go Electrification	Subway Modification	Subway Vaughn	Durham-Scarborough	Mississauga 403
Total cost	0.00	1.00	0.38	2.50	3.32	2.00	1.51	0.86	2.25	2.72	0.37	0.26
Operation cost	0.00	0.60	0.31	0.28	0.60	0.18	0.21	0.42	0.93	0.40	0.19	0.14
Residual value in 2050	0.00	0.00	0.19	1.25	1.66	1.00	0.75	0.43	1.13	1.36	0.18	0.13
Residual value with 50% discount factor	0.00	0.00	0.10	0.63	0.83	0.50	0.38	0.21	0.56	0.68	0.09	0.06
Revenues from new users	−0.49	−7.84	−1.51	−1.73	−0.74	−0.30	−0.07	−0.44	−2.07	−1.38	−0.03	−0.02
Users' benefit	−0.875	−0.25	−0.50	−2.76	−1.84	−0.60	−3.06	−0.48	−0.85	−0.37	−0.23	−0.16
New daily users	100,000	6,000	6,000	50,000	53,600	32,600	7,667	4,617	150,000	40,000	12,000	14,153
Net cost	0.00	1.60	0.59	2.16	3.09	1.68	1.34	1.06	2.62	2.44	0.47	0.33
Operation starting year	2015	2015	2023	2023	2023	2030	2018	2023	2023	2016	2021	2021
Sustainability												
Factor	5.97	0.33	0.54	3.04	3.21	1.10	0.87	0.56	4.51	3.52	1.19	1.03
Potential per year	4.43	0.01	0.03	1.46	1.66	0.47	0.05	0.02	6.52	1.08	0.13	0.13
Cost per unit of sustainability	0.00	4.89	1.09	0.71	0.96	1.53	1.54	1.91	0.58	0.69	0.39	0.32

Table 6.1b Cost estimation and sustainability factors (2) – Toronto transportation

Cost estimation (US$ billion)	Eglinton Cross	DRL Don Mills	Mississauga BRT	GO Relief Danforth	GO Relief Kennedy	GO Relief Kipling	Huronario LRT	Finch LRT	Brampton LRT	Scarborough LRT	Sheppard LRT	Smart Track
Total cost	5.24	8.62	0.37	0.10	0.05	0.01	1.02	1.08	0.52	1.13	1.15	5.30
Operation cost	1.05	1.08	0.25	0.03	0.05	0.05	0.38	0.30	0.11	0.25	0.39	1.00
Residual value in 2050	2.62	4.31	0.18	0.05	0.03	0.01	0.51	0.54	0.26	0.56	0.57	2.65
Residual value with 50% discount factor	1.31	2.16	0.09	0.03	0.01	0.00	0.26	0.27	0.13	0.28	0.29	1.33
Revenues from new users	−0.61	−2.03	−0.05	−0.07	−0.05	−0.03	−0.11	−0.19	−0.07	−0.21	−0.19	2.50
Users' benefit	−3.06	−1.93	−1.54	−0.17	−0.07	−0.02	−3.56	−0.66	−0.44	−0.98	−0.65	2.00
New daily users	44,000	147,400	11,340	5,000	1,250	250	25,560	54,700	6,600	15,000	13,750	200,000
Net cost	4.98	7.54	0.53	0.11	0.09	0.06	1.15	1.12	0.50	1.10	1.25	4.98
Operation starting year	2020	2023	2021	2023	2023	2023	2021	2020	2021	2023	2021	2021
Sustainability												
Factor	2.78	5.16	0.86	0.54	0.34	0.26	1.72	3.35	0.59	1.08	1.00	6.51
Potential per year	1.06	7.32	0.09	0.03	0.00	0.00	0.39	1.59	0.03	0.16	0.12	11.67
Cost per unit of sustainability	1.79	1.46	0.61	0.20	0.27	0.22	0.67	0.33	0.86	1.02	1.25	0.76

Table 6.1c Cost estimation and sustainability factors (3) – Toronto transportation

Cost estimation (US$ billion)	GTHA BRT	407 BRT	EV-NGV market expansion
Total cost	14.57	1.39	3.40
Operation cost	0.82	0.16	1.00
Residual value in 2050	7.29	0.70	1.70
Residual value with 50% discount factor	3.64	0.35	0.85
Revenues from new users	–1.00	–1.00	–0.20
Users' benefit	–1.00	–1.00	-0.20
New daily users	285,640	5,940	1,143,000
Net cost	11.75	1.21	3.55
Operation starting year	2020	2020	2016
Sustainability			
Factor	19.99	0.66	7.58
Potential per year	49.48	0.03	6.63
Cost per unit of sustainability	0.59	1.84	0.47

of a region-wide BRT, the extension emerges as a critical component. Details of project impacts on bio-physical and socio-economic indicators are available from Hoornweg (2015).

Applying sustainability cost curves across cities

As illustrated in Section 6.2, detailed sustainability cost curves can be developed for a sector, e.g. transportation and connectivity in Toronto. As use grows and cost curves emerge in various cities, their application across cities becomes useful. The investments are relative to each other in constant costs (US$), a common timeframe (to 2050) and local application of planetary boundaries and SDGs (consistent within the global framework for the world's larger cities). Potential infrastructure and related operational activities, e.g. 90-minute subway transfer in Toronto, can be compared within and across cities.

The cities of Dakar, Mumbai, São Paulo and Shanghai, largest cities of Senegal, India, Brazil and China respectively, along with Toronto, were selected as trial cities for application of the methodology. Mumbai, São Paulo and Shanghai exhibit well the rapid growth and infrastructure development in these countries and regions. All three metro-cities have populations in excess of 10 million, and are expected to continue to grow to 2050. Dakar is also the largest city in Senegal, but is smaller than Mumbai, São Paulo and Shanghai. Dakar is an important city to investigate, as it is typical of fast-growing African cities and population is expected to surpass São Paulo or Shanghai before 2100.

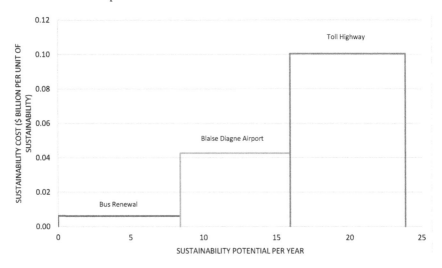

Figure 6.5   Sustainability cost curve (transportation – Dakar).

Dakar, Senegal

Three representative transportation projects are evaluated. The bus renewal project is already complete, and the international airport is being commissioned. Assessment of the toll highway is from the user's perspective (the main providers of toll revenues). Optics of the investment could differ if assessed from local government's perspective (who would provide minimal finance while recouping some benefit).

Blaise Diagne International Airport

The Blaise Diagne International Airport is under construction near the town of Diass, Senegal, about 40 km from Dakar. It will serve as the new main international airport for Dakar, as the old Léopold Sédar Senghor International Airport is too small for future operations. The airport will have an initial operating capacity of 3 million passengers per year, with a single runway. A second development phase could provide capacity for 10 million passengers a year with development of a second runway. Estimated capital cost is $0.38 billion.

Dakar Diamniadio Toll Highway

The Dakar Diamniadio Toll Highway (DDTH) will provide the Dakar peninsula with a 32 km, triple-lane carriageway to improve the flow of goods and people between the capital and the new airport with the Dakar Integrated Special Economic Zone (DISEZ). As part of a national plan to upgrade national infrastructure massively, the government hopes to facilitate the rapid movement of goods and people into and out of Dakar and provide a downtown-to-airport target transfer time of 30 minutes. The highway also encourages development outside main downtown congested areas, as well as establishing sub-regional corridors from Dakar to Bamako (Mali), Banjul (Gambia), Bissau (Guinea Bissau), Conakry (Guinea). The project's estimated capital cost is $531 million and it is expected to open in 2017.

Bus renewal

A leasing mechanism, supported by the International Development Association (IDA – World Bank) was launched to improve urban mobility improvement project in Dakar. The goal was to renew the ageing minibus fleet, which were mostly operated by independent drivers. In 2008, 505 new minibuses replaced one-fifth of the existing fleet. Due to the improved passenger comfort and lower maintenance costs of the new vehicles, revenue for owners increased. Fare increase was kept to a minimum. IDA funded 75 per cent of the programme ($16 million), and the remainder was paid by vehicle owners through a leasing scheme.

As illustrated in Figure 6.6, the bus renewal project in Dakar provides considerable sustainability potential for relatively low cost. This is largely driven by the large number (95,000) of daily users and low net cost ($0.09 billion). The project also increased use of public transit, thereby reducing greenhouse gas emissions (newer, more efficient minibuses were provided). Similarly to other transportation projects, the toll highway costs do not fully reflect increased land values. As information improves, subsequent iterations of the project may provide updated values.

Table 6.2 Cost estimation and sustainability factors of transportation projects in Dakar

Cost estimation (US$ billion)	Blaise Diagne Airport	Toll Highway	Bus Renewal
Total cost	0.376	0.531	0.02
Operation cost	1.30	1.75	0.07
Residual value in 2050	0.19	0.27	0.01
Residual value with 50% discount factor	0.09	0.13	0.01
Revenues from new users	–3.5	–1.5	–0.2
Users' benefit			
New daily users	27,400	50,000	95,000
Net cost	1.58	2.15	0.09
Operation starting year	2015	2015	2010
Sustainability			
Factor	37.04	21.37	13.60
Potential per year	7.54	7.94	8.40
Cost per unit of sustainability	0.04	0.10	0.01

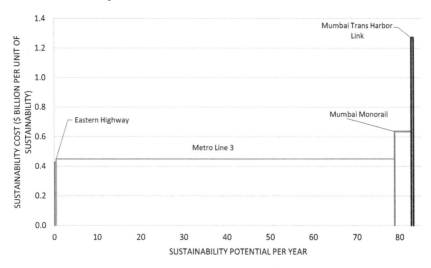

Figure 6.6   Sustainability cost curve (transportation – Mumbai).

Mumbai, India

Mumbai, with a population of 20 million, is India's largest city and is experiencing severe mobility challenges. Four representative projects are evaluated: a metro line, monorail, freeway and trans-harbour link.

Metro Line 3

The Mumbai Metro is a major infrastructure project under India's Mass Rapid Transit System (MRTS). Metro Line 3 (Colaba–Bandra–SEEPZ) is 32.50 km long and is fully underground, with 27 stations. It connects the major business districts of Nariman Point, Bandra Kurla Complex, the Domestic and International Airports, and industrial areas of MIDC and SEEPZ. The project is managed by Mumbai Metropolitan Region Development Authority (MMRDA) and is partially funded by Japan International Co-operation Agency (JICA). The trains will operate for 18.5 hours per day (5:30 am to midnight). Metro line 3 will cost around $3.7 billion and is expected to be completed by 2020.

Monorail

The monorail is a rail-based transportation system and the country's first monorail. Mumbai Metropolitan Region Development Authority is implementing the project in association with Larsen & Toubro (L&T) and the Malaysian firm Scomi Engineering. The monorail will have a top speed of 80 kilometres per hour and an overall scheduled speed of 31 kilometres per hour. The project, initiated in 2008, is 20 km long and will cost around $0.43 billion. Estimated operation and maintenance costs are $39 million a year. The monorail system is designed to carry 200,000 passengers per day (7,500 passengers at peak times).

Eastern Freeway

The Mumbai Eastern Freeway is a 16.9 km highway specially designed for high-speed vehicular traffic between the Fort area in South Mumbai and Eastern Express Highway in Ghatkopar. The Eastern Freeway will be completed in three phases: the first (9.3 km) runs from SV Patel junction on P D'Mello Road and meets Anik Panjarpol Link Road via Mumbai Port Trust (MbPT); the second (4.3 km) starts from Anik to Panjarpol, Panjarpol to Mankhurd and then to Ghatkopar on the Eastern Express Highway. The last phase is 3 km long. The elevated portion of the Eastern Freeway is equipped with seismic arresters that can tolerate an earthquake of 7.5 on the Richter scale. The project includes two 500 m-long tunnels at the Bhabha Atomic Research Centre (BARC) Mountain. The estimated capital costs are $0.2 billion.

Mumbai Trans Harbour Link

Mumbai Trans Harbour Link (MTHL) was proposed to reduce congestion in Mumbai by improving connectivity between Island city and the mainland (Navi Mumbai) and for development of the Navi Mumbai Region. The Link is 22 km in total length (16.5 km as a bridge) and will cost about $1.6 billion. Purported benefits of the project include:

- development of areas in Navi Mumbai and Raigad District;
- faster connectivity to the proposed International Airport in Navi Mumbai;
- savings in fuel and vehicle operating cost/travel time of commuters due to reduction in distance between Mumbai and Navi Mumbai, Raigad and Konkan;
- decongestion of traffic in Mumbai city.

Table 6.3 gives cost estimates for the four assessed transportation projects in Mumbai. Metro Line 3 is expected to have more than 860,000 new daily users, which is considerably higher than the other projects, and therefore has a high (78.39) annual sustainability potential. The relatively small number of daily users for the eastern highway and trans-harbour link (50,000 each) results in their low sustainability potential (0.44 and 0.52 respectively).

São Paulo, Brazil

São Paulo's congestion challenges are severe. The more affluent can resign themselves to using helicopters while single traffic jams can exceed 200 km. Much work is underway, although the task is enormous. Four representative projects are evaluated (Table 6.4, Figure 6.7).

Table 6.3 Cost estimation and sustainability factors for Mumbai projects

Cost estimation (US$ billion)	Metro Line 3	Mumbai Monorail	Eastern Highway	Mumbai Trans Harbor Link
Total cost	3.74	0.43	0.2	1.56
Operation cost	1.90	1.34	0.36	0.36
Residual value in 2050	1.87	0.22	0.10	0.78
Residual value with 50% discount factor	0.94	0.11	0.05	0.39
Revenues from new users	-1.5	-0.4	-0.5	-0.5
Users' benefit				
New daily users	864,000	200,000	50,000	50,000
Net cost	4.71	1.66	0.51	1.53
Operation starting year	2020	2015	2015	2020
Sustainability				
Factor	10.47	2.61	1.19	1.20
Potential per year	78.39	3.88	0.44	0.52
Cost per unit of sustainability	0.45	0.64	0.43	1.27

Table 6.4 Cost estimation and sustainability factors for transportation projects in São Paulo

Cost estimation (US$ billion)	Monorail Line 2	Line 5 Expansion	Monorail Line 17	Sustainable Transport Project
Total cost	1.6	2.516	1.22	0.429
Operation cost	7.50	8.80	4.30	0.60
Residual value in 2050	0.80	1.26	0.61	0.21
Residual value with 50% discount factor	0.40	0.63	0.31	0.11
Revenues from new users	−7.3	-4.9	-3.7	-0.36
Users' benefit				
New daily users	500,000	334,000	252,000	1,000,000
Net cost	8.70	10.69	5.22	0.92
Operation starting year	2015	2016	2010	2020
Sustainability				
Factor	5.28	3.42	2.75	6.13
Potential per year	19.60	8.72	4.50	53.10
Cost per unit of sustainability	1.65	3.13	1.90	0.15

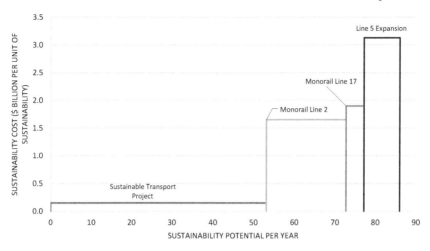

Figure 6.7 Sustainability cost curve (transportation – São Paulo).

Monorail

The São Paulo Monorail system is designed to connect Vila Prudent and Cidade Triadentes. The journey that now takes almost two hours by car will be reduced to approximately 50 minutes by the new monorail system, benefiting 500,000 users daily. The project is an extension of subway (metro) line 2. The line will be 24 km long with 17 stations. Estimated capital cost is $1.6 billion.

Subway Extension Line 5

The objective of the São Paulo Line 5 project for São Paulo is to improve public mobility in the Capao Redondo–Treze-Chacara Klabin corridor in a cost-effective and environmentally sound manner. The expansion encompasses the construction of 11.7 km of track, 11 new stations and purchase of 26 new trains. The project's capital cost is estimated at $2.5 billion and is expected to open December 2016.

Monorail Line 17

Line 17 is one of several new monorail lines planned to complement the city's existing rail network. The line is an 18 km driverless system designed to move 250,000 passengers a day, with trains travelling at 90-second intervals. The line has 18 stations and 24 trains. Line 17 connects Congonhas International Airport to the metro rail network, linking four metro lines and three bus corridors. Project implementation was completed in three phases; final completion was in 2014.

Sustainable Transport Project

The objective of the São Paulo Sustainable Transport Project is to improve the efficiency and safety of transport and logistics, while also enhancing capacity in disaster risk management. The project has three components. The first component provides support to the state's transport and logistics efficiency and safety through the following activities:

i   rehabilitating and upgrading the state's transport network;
ii   sustainable transport planning and management.

The second component is strengthening sustainable environmental and land use planning and territorial management capacity. This component provides support in land use planning and territorial and environmental management through:

a   improving environmental enforcement and environment quality monitoring;
b   supporting the modernization of the environmental licensing system.

The third component is increasing resilience to natural disasters. This component will provide support to enhance capacity to plan for and manage disasters through:

1   mainstreaming disaster risk management in the transport sector;
2   enhancing disaster risk management policy and institutional capacity.

São Paulo's sustainable transport project as an integrated multi-faceted initiative serves the highest number of daily users and therefore provides the highest sustainability potential among the four studied transportation projects (53.1). The cost per unit of sustainability for this project is also the lowest due to lower capital cost of a highway compared to a subway line.

Shanghai, China

Shanghai has China's longest subway network at 476 km, which is longer than New York's (370 km) and London's (439 km). The network is set to reach 877 km by 2020. Table 6.5 provides general information regarding Shanghai's subway network. The sustainability potential of the four studied projects is provided in Tables 6.5 and 6.6 and Figure 6.8.

Transport projects considered for Shanghai are subway extension lines 11, 8, 10 and 2. Average capital and operations and maintenance costs are $84 million/km and $1.9 million/km a year, respectively. For each project the biophysical and social science indicators are evaluated against estimates for costs and financial benefits of the project. The net cost of each activity (from published data) and the total sustainability factor obtained from the biophysical and socio-economic indicators are given. Activities are plotted relative to each other to yield a sustainability cost curve.

Table 6.5 Shanghai subway network data

O&M total metro lines cost, million-dollar/year	905
Shanghai total metro length, km	476
O&M cost million$/ km-year	1.90
Total subway annual ridership, million-passengers/year	2,276
Average ridership per one km subway line, passenger/km-day	13,100

Table 6.6 Cost estimation and sustainability factors for Shanghai transportation projects

Cost estimation (US$ billion)	Subway Line 11	Subway Line 8	Subway Line 10	Subway Line 2
Total cost	0.7	0.36	0.94	0.21
Operation cost	0.61	0.44	0.67	0.13
Residual value in 2050	0.35	0.18	0.47	0.11
Residual value with 50% discount factor	0.18	0.09	0.24	0.05
Revenues from new users Users' benefit	-2	-1.5	-0.2	-0.36
New daily users	120,520	86,460	131,000	26,200
Net cost	1.14	0.71	1.37	0.29
Operation starting year *Sustainability*	2015	2015	2015	2015
Factor	2.98	2.61	2.52	1.89
Potential per year	2.66	1.68	2.45	0.37
Cost per unit of sustainability	0.38	0.27	0.54	0.15

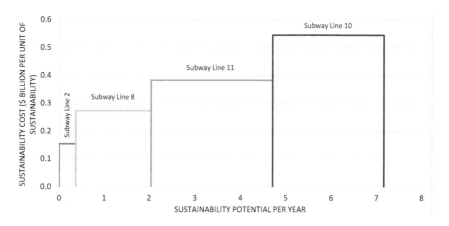

Figure 6.8 Sustainability cost curve (transportation – Shanghai).

Shanghai Subway – Line 11

Line 11 is a northwest–southeast line of the Shanghai subway network. The line is 72 km long and has 35 stations. Daily ridership for 2014 is estimated at 630,000. Metro Line 11 will be extended from its Luoshan Road to Disneyland, a 9.15 km stretch at a cost of $0.70 billion.

Shanghai Subway – Line 8

Line 8 is a north–south line of the Shanghai subway network. It is 37.4 km and has 30 stations with an estimated 935,000 daily ridership in 2014. Metro Line 8 will go beyond the Shanghai Aerospace Museum stop to Huizhen Road with a 6.6 km extension costing $0.36 billion.

Shanghai Subway – Line 10

Line 10 is a west-northeast line of the Shanghai subway network. The line is 29.6 km long and has 27 stations. Daily ridership for 2014 is estimated at 808,000. Metro Line 10 will be made 10 kilometers longer with a new route from New Jiangwan City to Gangchen Road at a cost of $0.94 billion.

Shanghai Subway – Line 2

Line 2 is an east–west line of Shanghai subway network. Its length is 60 km and it has 31 stations. Daily ridership for 2013 is estimated at 1,650,000. Metro Line 2 will extend 2 km eastward, from Xujingdong to Panlong Road, with an investment of $0.21 billion.

The transportation projects in Shanghai have relatively similar sustainability potential since they all advocate public transit. Slight differences in the results are linked to the number of new daily users and revenues from new users. Subway Line 2 has a relatively lower number of new users that leads it to having the lowest sustainability potential.

Figure 6.9 provides a consolidated cost curve for transportation projects in the five assessed cities. Three particularly 'sustainable' projects emerge: Sustainable Transport (São Paulo), Metro Line 3 (Mumbai), and Regional Rapid Transit (Toronto) with Sustainability Potentials above 50. The lowest cost per unit of sustainability is the Toronto 90-minute transfer, and highest is the Highway 407 Extension (Toronto). Reflecting the low level of current transportation infrastructure, all reviewed investments in Dakar provide low sustainability cost options.

The costs and assumed benefits are indicative (proof of concept) at this time. Through refined local estimates, a more accurate assessment will emerge. The method is not intended to have projects compete against each other, but rather provide indicative priorities and assist in the refining the questions of 'What are the priorities?'

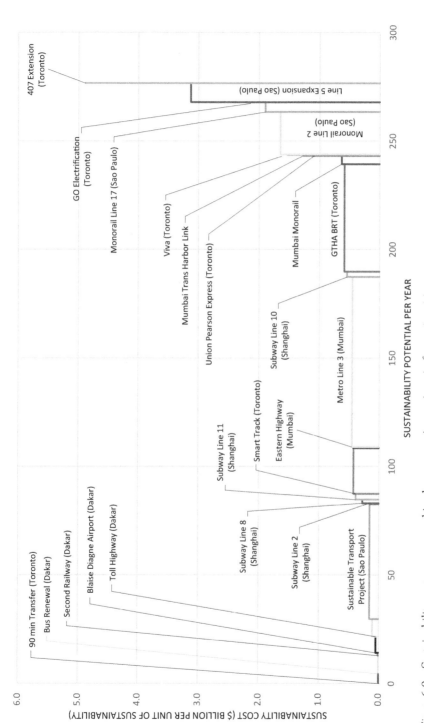

Figure 6.9 Sustainability cost curve – combined transportation projects in five major cities.

Applying sustainability cost curves in other sectors

Similarly to how sustainability cost curves can be applied across cities, so too can they be applied across sectors. The three key sectors envisaged for sustainability cost curves are: (i) transportation and connectivity; (ii) energy; and (iii) basic services. These are all inter-related, of course. For example, transportation projects like metrorail systems can not move forward if there is not sufficient electricity provision, and improved waste management relies on an adequate transportation system. For illustrative purposes, five projects in the Toronto region are assessed: the Niagara Tunnel hydroelectric project; refurbishment of Darlington and Bruce nuclear power plants; Durham York Energy Centre; and Green Lane Landfill (Figure 6.10). Some of these are already completed, but the methodoology is consistent with existing or proposed infrastructure.

Niagara Tunnel project

The Niagara Tunnel project was commissioned in 2013 with the purpose of generating more electricity through available hydropower. The project is expected to provide renewable hydropower for the next 100 years (tunnel design life 100 years). The tunnel directs water from the Niagara River to the Sir Adam Beck Generation Station, a hydropower plant 10.2 km downstream of the tunnel's intake. The tunnel delivers enough water to increase average annual energy output by 1.6 GWh (supply for about 160,000 Ontario homes). Total capital cost of the project was $1.6 billion.

Darlington nuclear power plant refurbishment

Darlington power plant began operating in 1990 and generates nearly 20 per cent of Ontario's overall electricity supply. After 25 years of operation, the facility requires a mid-life refurbishment, which began in 2016. The first phase of the project is budgeted at $8 billion over four years.

Bruce nuclear power plant refurbishment

Located in Tiverton (Ontario), Bruce Nuclear Facility is the largest power plant in North America, with a nominal power output of 6,600 MW. The facility has two nuclear stations, Bruce A and B, each with four CANDU nuclear reactors. Refurbishment of Bruce A was completed in 2012, and the government of Ontario authorized refurbishment of Bruce B, units 5–8, to secure their 6,300 MW baseload electricity supply. Project costs are estimated at $12 billion.

Durham York energy centre (incinerator)

The regions of Durham and York collaborated to develop ways to manage household solid waste. Based on recommendations in the Durham/York Residual Waste Study, the two regions approved construction of an energy from waste

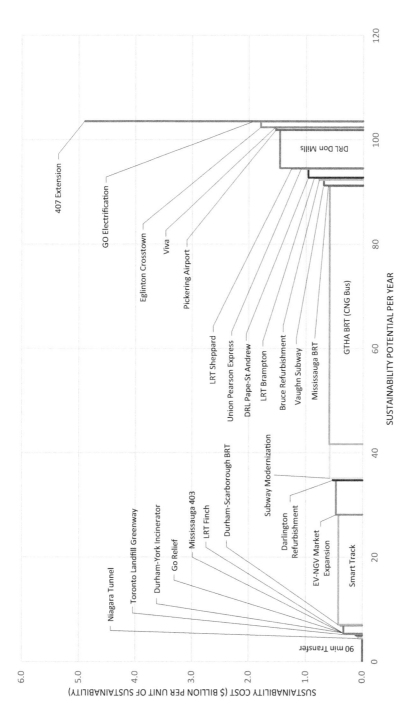

Figure 6.10 Sustainability cost curve – Toronto aggregated projects: transportation, energy, basic services.

(EFW) facility that will generate 17.5 MW electricity from 140,000 tonnes of residential waste annually. The facility is located in the Municipality of Clarington on 12 Ha, north of the Courtice Water Pollution Control Plant, in the Regional Municipality of Durham. Energy sold to the electricity grid will partially offset the annual operating costs of the facility. The capital cost of the project are approximately $0.272 billion. Waste tipping fees are up to $150/tonne for the Durham–York Incinerator.

Toronto Green Lane landfill

The city of Toronto acquired the Green Lane landfill located in London, Ontario to dispose of residential waste. Prior to Green Lane Landfill Toronto shipped its residential waste to Michigan. Toronto operations at Green Lane Landfill began in 2010. The estimated site capacity is 15 million cubic metres; approximate life expectancy is 28 years with a 70 per cent waste diversion level. Cost of waste disposal at the landfill is $67/tonne.

Conclusion

Sustainability cost curves provide an effective tool to compare projects within cities in the same sector (Figure 6.4), between cities (Figure 6.9) and across sectors (Figure 6.10). These curves can be readily communicated to the public, helping to better prioritize infrastructure investments. They are based on public assumptions on biophysical and socio-economic objectives (Chapter 5) and can quickly be updated as new information emerges. Every city can have a typical 'urbanscape' made up of its own unique sustainability cost curve. These curves can be readily aggregated regionally, nationally or globally.

The sustainability cost curves presented in this chapter are not constrained by limitations often found in marginal abatement cost curves, i.e. limited data availability and undisclosed assumptions. They are developed more as an 'engineering tool' than a finance or economic analysis of possible projects. Engineering analyses of a city's possible infrastructure development can apply a 'factor of sustainability' in a similar manner that today's engineering analyses now apply factors of safety.

Each participating city (urban area) can readily develop their own sustainability cost curves for transportation and connectivity, energy and basic services. As shown in Figure 6.10, a simple 'hierarchy of investment' is likely to emerge that tends to favour basic service provision (water and waste management), then energy supply, and finally transportation and connectivity projects. This reflects the relatively higher costs of transportation infrastructure and the need to first meet basic needs before investing in the urban infrastructure that drives the urban economy. The relative sustainability of transportation projects also varies considerably as it is largely dependent on numbers of users, and as presented in this chapter does not yet fully capture potential increases in land values.

Table 6.7 Cost estimation and sustainability factors for Toronto energy and basic services projects

Cost Estimation (US$ billion)	Niagara Tunnel	Darlington Refurb	Bruce Refurb	Durham York Incinerator	Toronto's Landfill Greenlane
Total cost	1.6	8	12	0.27	0.22
Operation cost				0.53	0.43
Residual value in 2050	0.8	4	6	0.14	0.11
Residual value with 50% discount factor	0.4	2	3	0.07	0.06
Revenue	1.48	38.88	51.84	0.31	0.61
Net Cost	1.2	6	9	0.73	0.60
Number of new users	416,000	2,500,000	1,900,000	1,500,000	5,900,000
Operation starting year	2013	2020	2020	2014	2010
Sustainability					
Factor	9.92	9.16	9.32	3.43	4.73
Potential per year	0.27	0.31	0.31	0.1	0.12
Cost per unit of sustainability	0.12	0.66	0.97	0.21	0.13

Sustainability cost curves could provide cities with an important tool to enter into discussions and negotiations globally, and with their national governments as a significant contribution to sustainable development.

Notes

1 PwC, August 2014.
2 Although CO_2 is the most common greenhouse gas, various other gases also contribute to the greenhouse effect. Methane, for example, is a very potent greenhouse gas, having a global warming potential around 25 times higher than CO_2. For comparison, low carbon impacts in a MACC are normalized to CO_2-equivalent.
3 The Iowa Electronics Market (http://tippie.uiowa.edu/iem/), established by the University of Iowa, College of Business, provides a forum for peer-sanctioned electronic estimates. The facility has an uncanny ability to project elections and other market opinions. A similar city-focused market system is proposed to be established as part of the city negotiations approach envisaged in this thesis.

References

Ackerman, F. and Bueno, R., 2011. *Use of McKinsey Abatement Cost Curves for Climate Economics Modeling (Working Paper WP-US-1102)*. Somerville, MA: Stockholm Environment Institute.

Avner, P., Rentschler, J. and Hallegatte, S., 2014. *Carbon Price Efficiency: Lock-in and Path Dependence in Urban Forms and Transport Infrastructure (Policy Research Working Paper 6941)*. Washington, DC: The World Bank.

Creyts, J., Berkach, A., Nyquist, S., Ostrowsky, K. and Stephenson, J., 2007. *Reducing US Greenhouse Gas Emissions: How Much at What Cost?* McKinsey & Company.

Economics of Climate Adaptation Working Group, 2009. *Shaping Climate Resilient Development: A Framework for Decision-Making*.

Ekins, P., Kesicki, F. and Smith, A., 2011. *Marginal Abatement Cost Curves: A Call for Caution*. London: UCL Energy Institute.

Hartgen, D., Fields, M., Scott, M. and San Jose, E., 2011. *Impacts of Transportation Policies on Greenhouse Gas Emissions in U.S. Regions (Report # 387)*. Los Angeles: Reason Foundation.

Hoornweg, D., 2015 (updated 2016). A Cities Approach to Sustainability. PhD. University of Toronto.

Kesicki, F., 2010. Marginal Abatement Cost Curves for Policy Making – Expert-Based vs Model-Derived Curves. In: UCL Energy Institute, *33rd IAEE Conference*. Rio de Janeiro, 6–9 June 2010. London: UCL Energy Institute.

Kesicki, F. and Ekins, P., 2012. Marginal Abatement Cost Curves: A Call for Caution. *Climate Policy*, 12, pp.219–36.

McKinsey & Company, 2009. *Pathways to a Low-Carbon Economy: Version 2 of the Global Greenhouse Gas Abatement Cost Curve*.

Vogt-Schilb, A. and Hallegatte, S., 2014. Marginal Abatement Cost Curves and the Optimal Timing of Mitigation Measures. *Energy Policy*, 66, pp.645–53.

Ward, D., 2014. The Failure of Marginal Abatement Cost Curves in Optimising a Transition to a Low Carbon Energy Supply. *Energy Policy*, 73, pp.820–22.

7 Towards effective agreements on sustainable development through cities

This book started with the intention of developing a methodology that could underpin sustainable development negotiations similar to UNCED (Rio–Rio+20), but led by cities. The proposed sustainability cost curves could accomplish much of this goal for financing and prioritization. Just as the curves, if developed and maintained in an open and professional manner, would encourage collective agreement (or at least awareness) in a targeted urban area, so too could they be aggregated across a sufficiently large collection of urban areas with the goal of a common approach to sustainability.

People, ideas, vision, finance and energy – these come together in most cities. As social unrest and impacts from local and global ecosystem perturbations grow, cities obviously need to increase their resilience and adaptive capacity. However, cities differ from countries and corporations in that their immobility forces them to develop 'shelter in place' coping mechanisms. These coping skills are likely to include more city-to-city partnerships (mutual support agreements), greater agitation in the national political discourse, publication of data and diagnostics, and greater adoption of multi-sector partnerships.

With possible economic (including demographic) decline and local disasters, such as earthquakes, flooding and storms, strategic retreats may be necessary in some cities, e.g. Detroit's 60 per cent population decline. However, all the Future Five cities presented in this thesis are very likely to have large urban populations in 2050 and 2100. They need help planning effective approaches to a century with much greater change than they have experienced so far.

The cities (urban areas) assessed through this work are sufficiently large that each is acting as an independent complex system, as well as being part of broader regional, national and global urban system. Urban centres need to determine their own local priorities, but they also need to determine their contribution to global issues. They also need to understand better global trends and how the trends will be impacted by them. Ideally, these metrics need to be sufficiently simple for lay people to understand the choices available (while also conveying meaningful information).

A critical role of central banks is signalling their government's long-range intentions and macroeconomic plans. Corporations, in particular, seek stability and certainty. The Future Five cities represent economies larger than many countries. As many as 30 cities are expected to join the ranks of those with 5 million or more residents by 2050. The world's megacities (populations above 10 million) will increase from today's 27 to 50 by 2050. This represents an enormous increase in real estate wealth as well as infrastructure needs. Signalling prioritization and location of this infrastructure will reduce corruption and increase efficiency while providing an important contribution to trust within and between cities.

Diamond (2005) illustrates how civilization on Easter Island (among other areas) collapsed largely from capture into a 'competitive spiral'. Arguably, current global trends and geopolitical actions indicate much of humanity is now in a similar competitive spiral, at least to some degree. And this trend is likely to accelerate with China and India's re-emergent role, and Sub Saharan Africa's impending entry, into the global economy (with corresponding material consumption and waste generation).

'Distant threats' to cities are increasingly less distant. Disruption in material supplies and energy, refugees and pandemics can quickly impact any city, anywhere in the world.

Cities and their agents may be less interested in a 'negotiated settlement' and more keen on an ongoing process of shared purpose. All cities are charged with delivering maximum sustainability as exhibited through local quality of life and well-being.

A cooperative agreement among at least the world's largest cities, as outlined in this book, could be sufficient to offset the especially debilitating aspects of a competitive spiral. Hopefully, these cooperative agreements will be inclusive, rather than following international geopolitical agreements between groups of countries, e.g. NATO and the Warsaw Pact. Cities will need to develop mechanisms to cooperate despite potential friction among their national counterparts. One of the best ways to do this will be to focus on the science and sustainability of cities, with the aspects of local service provision. Similarly to how every city supplies waste management services, so too should every city provide a sustainability framework.

Cities need professional champions to provide independent observations on quality of life and service provision. ISO37120 and the subsequent standard on urban resilience go a long way to providing this; however, these initially are provided only for individual local governments and an aggregated city-region summary is not yet available (a pilot initiative is underway in Toronto). Also, the values need to be applied against future infrastructure work to provide prioritization of sustainable development programming. Engineers and urban planners are well placed to opine collectively on city progress toward sustainable development.

By introducing a local 'cooperative ascent' along with a national competitive spiral, cities will better articulate the inherent inconsistencies with current economic systems. Human nature encourages formation of tribes, cliques and cultures (and countries), and these typically compete for resources and stature (Freud, 1930). However, with interconnected economies, power grids, globally dispersed manufacturing, international finance, air traffic control and linked healthcare systems, the world's cities are increasingly dependent on shared networks. Unless these global networks are sufficiently resilient, cities are particularly vulnerable to network breakdowns. Even if these system breakdowns are rare, their debilitation can be enormous. The most effective way to increase network resilience is to increase capacity (staff and citizenry), infrastructure strength and redundancy, and trust: trust between the community and service provider and within and across cities.

The science, and engineering, of cities needs to provide the foundation for high-quality decision making (e.g. financial prioritization). By providing comprehensive 'system diagnostics' for every participating city (with verified professional input), the foundation for a cooperative approach is available. The tools are designed to be applied initially with large cities, as these are likely the most important stratum within the world's current (and growing) hierarchy of economic and eco-systems.

The methodology suggested here encourages the emergence of an 'honest broker(s)' for participating cities. The likelihood of this focal point(s) emerging is enhanced through: (i) ongoing provision of key information that builds on existing programmes and benefits everyone (not necessarily linked to a specific project or agency); (ii) simplified data requirements (initial provision expected by recent graduates or international volunteers); (iii) publication of the sustainability baselines benefits participating cities in that 'more sustainable' projects emerge (e.g. preferred for 'green bonds'); (vi) within five years, the infrastructure development community should routinely provide and use the information in infrastructure assessments; (v) an informal and loose network is envisaged (with little management or funding requirement); (vi) key data is mostly secondary, provided by other agencies, thereby enhancing their stature and reducing costs (and perceived competition); (vii) no new oversight agency is proposed, therefore funding requirements are modest – cities may wish to encourage the development of a relatively modest organization such as IATA or WANO; (viii) methodology encourages duplication (non-exclusive) and is not subject to country or region capture as it is first applied to all cities over 10 million, then 5 million, and then, as interest and support warrants, smaller cities; (ix) is fully consistent with large-scale global initiatives such as the SDGs; (x) the concept is seeded at a 'grassroots level' and takes full advantage of the power of hierarchies; and (xi) takes advantage of the availability and enthusiasm of recent graduates in targeted cities.

The value of hierarchies – a fable

An analogy on the role of hierarchies is provided in Meadows' (2008) *Thinking in Systems: A Primer*. When assessing global financial and ecological systems, the role of cities as critical intermediate forms is apparent.

There once were two watchmakers, Dana and Dennis. Both made fine watches that were very popular. Their stores were always busy as customers stopped by, and the phones rang constantly with new orders. Over the years, however, Dana prospered, while Dennis's business fared poorly. That's because Dana applied the principle of hierarchy.

The watches made by both Dana and Dennis each consisted of about 1,000 pieces. Dennis assembled his in such a way that if he had one partly assembled and had to put it down to answer the phone or greet a customer in the store it fell to pieces. When he returned, Dennis would have to start the whole process over again. The more his customers contacted him, the harder it became to find enough uninterrupted time to finish a watch.

Dana's watches were no less complex than Dennis's, but she assembled stable parts of about 10 pieces each. Then she put 10 of these parts together into a larger assembly, and 10 of those together made the whole watch. Whenever Dana had to put down a partly completed watch to answer the phone or meet a customer, she lost only a small part of her work. So she assembled her watches much faster and more efficiently than Dennis.

Complex systems tend to evolve from simple systems through stable intermediate forms. The resulting complex form will naturally be hierarchic. Hierarchies are common in natural systems and, among all the possible complex forms, hierarchies are the only ones that have had the time to evolve.[1]

A 'global agreement on sustainable development' may be too large a task to undertake in its entirety. A strategic approach would encourage stability and sustainability within critical intermediate forms.[2] Working with cities to implement local sustainability, with a clear understanding on how efforts are linked globally and how impacts move up and down the hierarchy of the world's urban system, may be the fastest way to improve the overall system. By providing a specific target date along the way to sustainable development (say, 2050) and starting with a sufficiently large number of significant cities (say, the cities with populations of 5 million or more by 2050), a clear and measurable 'fast-tracked' path to sustainability is possible.

Shortcomings of the approach

Many countries and cities that eventually need to be part of any agreement will feel left out and may actively boycott the process. Countries, even if they have cities participating in the process, may try to sabotage the process, and may ignore any possible agreement. Would Canada, for example, back an agreement entered into by just one of its cities? Or the US with just a handful of cities with mayors often at political odds with Washington?

Naim in *The End of Power* argues that 'power' (the ability to directly influence behaviour) is dissipating – or dispersing – throughout the world. Large countries, corporations and agencies have less ability to determine outcomes. Arguably, power is shifting to cities (from countries and corporations), but it now often takes the form of collaborative loosely associated power. Therefore the initiative will likely need to succeed as an 'organic' approach (which implies slower start-up initially and much greater participation than just city councils or ministers of urban affairs).

At its roots, this proposed negotiation will imply transfers of wealth. The cost curves will show why that transfer is in all participant's best interest, and a *transfer of wealth is not as critical as focusing locally generated future wealth*; however, this will not make it any easier for those required to pay relatively more in the short term.

Transfer of funds and knowledge on the scale envisaged in this approach requires national support (and likely leadership). This is in no way guaranteed – national to urban fiscal transfers are not fully in place today within the same country. Attempting it across countries is a formidable challenge.

The process proposes to involve the world's larger cities (inhabited by five million people or more in 2050). Cultures are different. It may not be possible to propose, let alone maintain, common values for things like gender equality, walkability and 'clean' air across some 120 cities with such disparate cultures.

Cities are already dynamic, complex systems; a global network of urban systems is several orders more complex. Possible events like widespread viruses or climate impacts may overwhelm any negotiated agreement.

Similar to the concept of biodiversity metrics in Chapter 5, major activities and trends that have varied impacts across systems are ascribed a local and global value. For simplicity, this is now set at 50–50 (local–global). There may be a more dynamic and regionally specific value for each city. This will take time and effort to assess, and as a dynamic value may introduce instability into any ongoing negotiation process.

The city-scale (up to metro level) of this approach may be too large. 'Communities' or neighbourhoods within cities may be a more appropriate scale for action. Work at the community level would then need to be aggregated upward to a metropolitan level.

The proposal places significant responsibility with professionals. Civil engineers in particular need to be involved on an ongoing basis. The likely nexus of support would be through engineering faculties within participating cities. Mobilizing some 300 volunteer graduates to start the process is challenging and costly. Financing, managing and maintaining this ongoing support is a formidable challenge. In the cases where government representatives of the city would not join in the initiative, this would add a level of insecurity within participating engineering schools.

A significant challenge the approach will face is its ability to highlight the relative sustainability of projects across cities (and countries). As illustrated in Figure 6.10, a road in Dakar may have a significantly lower sustainability cost than a similar road in, say, Toronto. Project proponents in Toronto will likely criticize the overall findings and approach. Also the costs of land, expected financial rates of return and local urban systems are different across cities, therefore comparisons may not always be directly applicable.

Within individual cities (as well as across cities) many conflicting objectives are aggregated in order to prioritize investments. The World Bank, for example, may have a higher priority to invest in one city over another. Similarly, national governments may favour one city over another. Over time, this proposed system would help prioritize long-lived urban infrastructure, but the process will face challenges to existing practices.

The system envisaged with expert peer input (similar to the World Bank's annual Doing Business review) will take time to be established. Checks and balances need to be developed to prevent undue influence for some projects over others (outright or subtle). An initial trial start-up period will be needed for a few years.

Why try?

The proposed cost curves and a negotiated agreement between cities that they could facilitate is unprecedented. The potential impact is enormous. The agreement may not be enforceable. However, if negotiated and monitored in good faith, the trust it would engender may be sufficient upon which to base a global agreement. By 2075 the world will be about 75 per cent urban. The 500 largest cities will be home to more than half the world's population and probably three-quarters of the global economy. If countries are not able to negotiate a 'safe operating space' for the impact (and access) of these cities and the global commons, a fundamental rift in the nation-state concept is likely. Continued success for cities will at least require an implicit agreement similar to that proposed through these negotiations.

Cities (except in the case of Singapore) do not support their own armies. Rather, they empower countries to tax the urban economy so as to fund standing armies and enact fiscal (international) controls. So too, in most cases, are the legal and contractual underpinnings of societies overseen by countries. This is not likely to change during this century. Countries, however, will know the results of these negotiations and will be unlikely to dismiss them completely as large cities usually have a disproportionate influence on national economies.

By entering into these negotiations (or simply observing) participating cities are signalling that a parallel track to geopolitical negotiations warrants consideration. City cooperation undoubtedly has limits. Two formidable barriers to this plan exist: (i) getting a coordinated (metro) voice for each of the Future Five cities and (ii) introducing 'surrogate negotiators' for cities not able to field their own negotiators. Yet with city representatives such as urban ambassadors, professional associations such as the engineering community and urban planners, plus key international agencies like the GEF, a comprehensive 'shadow agreement' could be negotiated.

Even if this approach does not enable a global agreement on sustainable development, individual urban areas critically need the tool. Toronto, for example, has struggled for several decades to engender sufficient agreement to move forward with critical large-scale transportation infrastructure. Having an open, publicly understood, independently (and professionally) maintained baseline of sustainability is a valuable contribution for all cities (urban areas).

Few professions are given the honour to help the world on the scale envisaged here. The opportunity to launch a public service at a similar scale to the public health provisioning through potable water and wastewater treatment again presents itself to the engineering profession (among others). Hopefully the profession will grasp the opportunity.

Engineers do not need to lead the negotiations or broker the agreement; however, they are well placed to develop this new language of urban decision-making. Evidence-based urban planning is critical. Engineers developing a new cost curve of sustainability will provide an invaluable service. The methodology is sufficiently simple and robust to be initially launched through volunteers and interns (mentor-supported), and later supported at individual cities by peer reviews and open- or crowd-sourced assessments.

Cities are the most visceral, anchored level of government. Along with the military they are a country's 'doing-arm'. Cities usually try to exercise the politics of pragmatism – or delay if consensus is not available. Cities copy cities. Many cities, for example, have a Santiago Calatrava-like bridge. Or witness the speed at which Paris's bike-share programme was replicated worldwide. This potential 'speed of city pragmatism' gives many urban practitioners hope.

Proposed negotiations could enhance optimism and provide a durable methodology for sustainability efforts through the world's cities. Efforts to enhance public trust in government should also follow this negotiation.

A recent MIT Sloan Management Review (Joining Forces: Collaboration and Leadership for Sustainability, 2015) outlines how the world's corporations are concluding that 'The path to success is travelled with others.' In 2012, the world's 1,000 largest corporations generated $34 trillion in revenue (about one-third the global economy). Many of these corporations recognize the impetus to collaborate. Examples abound: Walmart's support of the sustainability consortium; the Higgs Index for textiles and apparel; Forest Stewardship Council.

Similar to corporations, cities need tools to enhance collaboration and better articulate their needs and planned paths forward. Cities also need to work with trusted professional partners, e.g. engineers, planners and development workers.

Sustainability targets will vary by city and over time. A robust blend of accuracy, pragmatism, flexibility and consistency is needed to influence action at the community and personal level. The mechanism suggested here should enable targeted and effective impacts within participating cities.

Why cities are acting more like countries

Generally, a city is not a country, and they exhibit unique local attributes. However, more cities are assuming greater international involvement. For example, in July 2009, Italy hosted the annual G8[3] meeting. During that time, cities were rising in stature, especially with regard to climate change activities. Cities and their representatives were planning a strong showing at the upcoming December 2009 COP15 meeting in Copenhagen. Rome was a member of the C40,[4] but Milan was not. Milan was gearing up to host Expo 2015.

Letizia Moratti, mayor of Milan in 2009, proposed a parallel 'C8' meeting for cities alongside the G8 meeting (personal communication). She shared political parties with Prime Minister Berlusconi, and there was receptivity from several cities. The C8 meeting did not happen, but the G8 meeting in Italy included city representatives, and served as a harbinger for the rise of the C40, and more active participation of cities at COP15. The event is indicative of cities searching for new and enhanced international roles.

Cities are cautious in their involvement with international events such as UNFCCC's Conference of the Parties or Rio-type UN-convened meetings. Cities are more likely to develop alternative approaches to meetings (with greater reliance on IT-supported telepresence), with more emphasis on programmes of cooperation rather than ad hoc meetings that require a negotiated settlement. The 'flavour' of these international events is often dictated through large representations of staff from ministries of economy and environment, plus agencies like the UN and World Bank. This is somewhat foreign to cities and rather than acquiring a taste for these events, cities and their (direct) representatives are likely to develop new approaches.

The World Economic Forum (WEF) is best known for its annual Davos meeting that brings together heads of state and corporate leaders. Each year, global leaders discuss the world's most pressing issues and often seek a collaborative path forward, although the events are more of a networking opportunity rather than negotiations. A key item each year is the annual global risk profile. The 2015 risk profile lists the following top ten global risks:(i) Deepening income inequality; (iii) persistent jobless growth; (iii) lack of leadership; (iv) rising geostrategic competition; (v) weakening of representative democracy; (vi) rising pollution in the developing world; (vii) increasing occurrence of severe weather events; (viii) intensifying nationalism; (ix) increasing water stress; and (x) spread of infectious disease.

A risk assessment of the above 10 items would quickly highlight the central role of cities in developing the identified risks, and often acting as first responders as the risks are manifest. A first line of defence as global risks grow is increased urban resilience. World leaders are beginning to realize this, but the scale of challenges facing cities necessitates greater involvement of city and community representatives.

About 2,500 to 2,700 people receive invitations to the January Davos meetings. About 15 per cent of attendees are female. In 2013, five of the invitees were mayors. In 2014, eight of the attendees were mayors. The limited involvement of city representatives at meetings such as WEF Davos suggest the likely emergence of parallel and alternative forums for city representatives to interact (and strengthening of existing opportunities).

In large social transformations, cities provide the forum or venue to facilitate that change, for example Tahrir Square, Cairo, and the Mall in Washington DC. With technology, cities also amplify social movements. For example, in 2008, Oscar Morales, a recent civil engineering graduate in Colombia, created a Facebook page calling for 'One Million Voices against FARC'. FARC, operating as a guerrilla faction against the Colombian government since 1964, had taken 700 people hostage in late 2007. Morales captured people's frustration and disillusionment with FARC's actions in calling for an end to the violence. More than a million people marched peacefully in Bogota and around the world on February 4, 2008. The hostages were eventually released, FARC's operations declined and a peace treaty is under implementation.

As social tensions and climate related events increase in burgeoning cities the number of disasters and unrest will grow. Cities will be forced to respond, stretching already thin resources. New tools and methods to enhance local stability and long-term sustainability will emerge. These initiatives may differ from national (and regional) governments as cities are likely to develop more collaborative and comprehensive approaches; however, with more than 100 cities participating, any potential agreement as outlined in this approach would have significant geopolitical implications.

Next steps in a cities approach to sustainability

The task proposed in this book – implementation of an ongoing process to assist cities to move toward sustainable development – is enormous. Many agencies and city representatives need to be involved. The following is a partial list of a few key next steps.

In the last 5 to 10 years powerful new metrics for complex aspects of sustainability have been developed. Generally, these are mostly applied to countries, but the methodology is usually sufficiently robust to enable application to cities – at least large metro cities. The Environmental Performance Index (Yale University) is a good example. This tool, now published annually in collaboration with WEF and support from the Samuel Family Foundation, should also include the Future Five cities. Similarly, the University of Notre Dame's Global (national) Adaptation Index should be adjusted to also include the Future Five cities.

These two indices can form the basis to develop a metro-city 'Resilience Index' sufficiently robust to facilitate catastrophic insurance premium adjustments. This could be integrated with the ISO resilience standard index now under development.

The WEF should be invited to include an annex in the annual Global Competiveness Report, ranking the Future Five cities for competiveness, perhaps starting with the 27 megacities. The World Bank (IFC) could also be invited to include assessments of the Future Fives in the annual 'Doing Business' Report (country competiveness) addressing specific cities.

WWF should be asked and supported to develop a 'biodiversity index' for at least the Future Fives. This index should follow the broad approach by WBCSD-WRI's initial efforts at developing a GHG emissions inventory for corporations, i.e. use of Scope 1, 2 and 3 emissions to account for vicarious impacts of city residents, while ensuring consistency between local and national inventories, i.e. no 'double counting'.

Agencies and academics working with cities and the engineering profession should encourage all local governments within the Future Five urban conurbations (about 3,500 local governments) to collect and annually publish ISO 37120 city indicators (ideally independently audited). These metrics should be aggregated and published by (metro) city.

Material flow assessments (urban metabolism) for all Future Five cities should be prepared (every one to two years) – key agencies should include ISIE and WRI (possibly WBCSD). Material projection estimates (to 2050) for all Future Five cities should include at least energy, solid waste, water and food. These should be updated regularly as new data emerges. The World Resources Institute and UNEP should lead this work. ISIE could make available a special edition of the Journal of Industrial Ecology. WFEO should participate.

Efforts by lead agencies should combine WBCSD's UII, Cities Alliance City Development Strategy, ICLEI's Local Agenda 21, among others, to develop a common platform for 'sustainability plans' consistent with the hierarchy of sustainable cities. These sustainability plans should have at least a 35-year planning horizon, should be updated at least every five years, should ideally use common metrics and be publicly developed and vetted (for all Future Five cities). This effort could be led by GEF with support from OECD, World Bank, UN agencies, WEF and WBCSD. Cities themselves (as urban groupings) should lead the preparation.

Each Future Five city should have a biophysical and socio-economic boundaries assessment completed annually (Chapter 5). From those boundary assessments, each Future Five city should have sustainability cost curves prepared annually for the transportation and connectivity, energy, basic services sector, plus a combined curve (Chapter 6). Local engineering schools and targeted graduate volunteers could lead preparation of both.

IFIs, NGOs and international agencies should recognize published sustainability plans[5] and if major supported activities (anything in excess of $10 million or requiring more than 5,000 local government employee days) are not included in the sustainability plans and sustainability cost curves a public statement should be issued outlining the criticality of the activity.

Three to five Future Five cities should designate themselves (more is better) as 'teaching cities', similar to teaching hospitals but with broader scope, to serve as research and teaching centres for all Future Five cities, and other cities (critical focus on data collection, management, communications, governance, technological advances). The cities could emerge as the regional hubs, similar to the WANO and IATA management structure.

The World Federation of Engineering Organizations and affiliates such as ASCE and CSCE should encourage engineering schools in Future Five cities (among others) to participate in preparation of city boundaries assessments and sustainability cost curves. All major projects (in excess of $10 million capital, and/or $1 million annual operating costs) in Future Five cities should be subject to comprehensive sustainability assessment, i.e. placement in the sector's sustainability cost curve. FDIC should recommend this for (at least) all Future Five based contracts.

Within five years all Future Five cities should have the full complement of sustainability tools on an open access website(s) (i.e. ongoing publication of city

Table 7.1 Strengths and weaknesses of a cities approach to sustainable development

Strengths	Weaknesses
Based on material flows and ecosystem impacts (science and engineering approach to underpin political and geopolitical processes)	Requires an iterative approach (and at times arbitrary) on what cities to include and on what cities to include in the metro area, i.e. often no consensus on constituent make-up of metropolitan areas
Metropolitan approach – cities as systems	Initial bio-physical and socio-economic boundaries (Chapter 5) require a degree of subjectivity
Inclusive approach involving all cities, limits debate on 'who's in, who's not'	Current sustainability assessment methodology provides a high value for number of users, therefore infrastructure servicing large populations will have an inherently higher factor of sustainability
Five million population (at 2050) provides a meaningful number of participants (about 122)	Heavy reliance on professionals envisaged, e.g. civil engineers and planners
Futures approach – ensures a sufficient focus on rapidly growing cities and regions	Initially starts only with the largest cities (over 5 million). Therefore some 80 per cent of global population initially excluded
Building on the 'boundaries approach' by Rockstrom et al. (2009; updated by Steffen et al., 2015) and Sustainable Development Goals (nee MDGs) provides an easily communicated starting point for cities (locally relevant as well as globally pertinent)	Optimizes sustainability for participating cities – may be at odds with national priorities
Provides a common platform to enable international agencies to participate and quickly adapt existing metrics and programs to cities (metro areas)	By making infrastructure planning process more public, vested interests may be threatened

boundaries, sustainability cost curves and hierarchies of urban management). Sustainability negotiations between the Future Five cities should be planned for no later than 2020 (the plan forward could be launched at Habitat III in 2016).

Starting with (at least) government and employee pension agencies (e.g. OMERS, Ontario Teachers, California Public Employees, World Bank and UN), by 2020 all financed civil works (urban infrastructure) should be required to have a simple 'Factor of Sustainability' calculated.

Notes

1 Paraphrased from Herbert Simon, *The Sciences of the Artificial* (Cambridge MA: MIT Press, 1969) in Meadows (2008).
2 This approach was championed in Elinor Ostrom's *Green from the Grassroots* column of June 12, 2012, written as input to Rio+20. 'Sustainability is now a prerequisite for all future development. City planners must look beyond municipal limits and analyze flows of resources – energy, food, water, and people – into and out of their cities.'

3   The G8 started with an ad hoc meeting in France in 1975 as the 'Group of Six'. The country grouping became the G7 when Canada, with the support of the US, was added in 1976. The G8 was formed 1998–2014 with the addition of Russia. The G20, founded in 1999, replaced the G8 as the main country convening group at the Pittsburgh Summit, September 25, 2009. Membership of the G20 was arbitrarily determined by Caio Koch-Weser (Germany) and Tim Geithner (USA). G20 membership includes: Argentina, Australia, Brazil, Canada, China, France, Germany, India, Indonesia, Italy, Japan, Mexico, Russia, Saudi Arabia, South Africa, South Korea, Turkey, the United Kingdom and the United States, along with the European Union (EU). The EU is represented by the European Commission and by the European Central Bank. The IMF, World Bank, OECD and WTO attend G20 summits.
4   The C40 was formally launched in 2005, when representatives of 18 cities met at the behest of Mayor Livingston in London. Initially, five cities started the concept. In 2006 the organization merged with the Clinton Climate Initiative. There are now 69 member cities in 3 categories; megacities, innovator and observer cities. Size of city varies considerably, and some of the original cities such as Beijing and Shanghai have shifted membership from megacities to observer.
5   Each Future Five city should prepare a collective (metro-wide) Hierarchy of Sustainability (assistance could be provided by GEF, local engineering and planning schools).

References

Diamond, J., 2005. *Collapse: How Societies Choose to Fail or Succeed*. London: Penguin.

Freud, S., 1930. *Civilization and its Discontents*. Eastford, CT: Martino.

Meadows, D., 2008. *Thinking in Systems: A Primer*. White River Junction, VT: Chelsea Green.

8 The path forward

Sustainable development is mostly a political objective that gained widespread prominence post-1987 and the release of *Our Common Future*. Negotiations for sustainable development (greater inclusion and wealth, along with environmental safeguards) are typically between countries, either through consensus, e.g. WTO, UNFCCC, UNCED (Rio and Rio+20) and the Montreal Protocol for ozone depleting substances, or bi-lateral efforts, e.g. the 2014 China–US agreement on GHG emissions limits and the 1909 Canada–US Boundary Water Treaty. Sustainable development often manifests as a negotiated agreement. Cities (i.e. urban communities) have delegated much of this process to national government representatives.

Sustainability is largely a systems approach to the key underpinnings of human society: the health and resilience of critical ecosystems, trends in material flows, enhancing social harmony and connectivity as contributors to well-being and economy. Sustainability is typically a collaborative and inclusive process. Cities, traditionally the most representative level of government, will implement much of the process toward sustainability. The contribution from city residents is the most important input to sustainable development, and the response of cities to any negotiated agreement will determine the final outcome.

An integrated place-based approach to sustainability and sustainable development is proposed here. Political considerations are of course included but a cities approach fosters more of a systems analysis with a greater focus on metabolic flows and ecosystems and societal boundaries. A systems focus facilitates codification and monitoring of progress toward agreed-to targets. When developed and communicated in partnership with participating communities genuine progress is possible.

This approach with credible open-source, locally specific metrics has sufficient scientific underpinning to serve as a foundation for more nuanced subjective aspects of the political process. In order to assess future infrastructure requirements and corresponding sustainability impacts, city size (population and economy for the urban agglomeration) needs to be estimated. Accordingly this book provides initial estimates of the world's largest cities this century. The concept of the 'Future Fives' is introduced – those cities expected to have five million or more people resident by 2050.

Two new urban tools are proposed: (i) a cities approach to biophysical and socio-economic boundaries and (ii) sustainability cost curves for long-lived urban infrastructure. These two tools are underpinned by adherence to a hierarchy of urban management (Chapter 4).

The first tool, a cities approach to biophysical and socio-economic boundaries, applies 'safe operating space' (physical boundaries) and the sustainable development goals from a cities perspective. The tool is applied to Dakar, Mumbai, São Paulo, Shanghai and Toronto. None of the five cities could be defined as sustainable today, although priorities for sustainable development are readily apparent for each city individually as well as collectively. This process could be expanded and replicated for all Future Five cities (and others).

The second new tool – sustainability cost curves – enables assessment of key infrastructure within and across cities (urban agglomerations) from a sustainable development perspective. Cost curves are proposed for basic services, energy and transportation sectors. The methodology is applied to Dakar, Mumbai, São Paulo, Shanghai and Toronto as proof of concept. Consistent with other initiatives, e.g. WBCSD's 'Vision 2050', the target date of 2050 is used to assess proposed long-lived urban infrastructure.

With these tools an argument is made that, when applied credibly, comprehensively and continuously to the Future Five cities, sustainability can be sufficiently well defined and monitored. This information could be used to facilitate global negotiation of sustainable development for these cities, which in turn could underpin a broader global sustainable development agreement.

The tools proposed are fully consistent with the engineering profession's current suite of diagnostics, as well as urban planners and infrastructure finance approaches that are typically defined through the master planning process. A call is made for the engineering profession to take a more active role in highlighting the link between long-lived urban infrastructure and sustainability and the need to make better use of publicly understood and vetted metrics of sustainable development for all major infrastructure – starting with municipal infrastructure costing more than $25 million (capital and/or amortized to 2050) in the world's largest cities (those expected to have more than five million residents by 2050).

Sustainability and sustainable development is a laudable objective; however, attaining this goal is significantly more difficult if it cannot readily be defined at a city level and progress toward the goal publicly communicated. A plan forward is presented that describes roles and responsibilities for key agencies, as well as data collection and management by the engineering profession, and others.

Validation and greater specificity on how cities are likely to grow for the rest of this century is needed. Predicting the future is notoriously difficult, but, in the absence of better predictions, what is presented can serve as a credible starting point for required planning horizons. Engineers (among others) need to integrate growth assumptions into today's common factors of safety and proposed factors of sustainability.

Summary and recommendations

During the last 200 years a fundamental and transformative shift in wealth and influence occurred. In 1800, China and India were the world's top two economies, and global per capita GDP was about $200; average life expectancy was 40 years. Today, this has rocketed to more than $6,500 per person (a global total of about $45 trillion). Total wealth today, according to Credit Suisse, is $117 trillion (about $56,000 for each adult on earth). Life expectancy is now greater than 78 years.

This break-neck pace of city growth and wealth creation continues. Total global wealth will likely double again by 2050, with most of the growth driven by East and South Asia, and then more than double again as Sub-Saharan Africa drives much of the world's wealth increase in the second half of this century. This unprecedented wealth creation occurred, and is likely to continue to occur, in lock-step with resource consumption, urbanization and associated ecosystem degradation. Cities are the key actors in this development.

City populations are growing fast: in 2010 there were about 60 cities with populations of more than 5 million (with a combined population of 565 million). By 2050 this will increase to about 120 cities with populations of more than 5 million (with a combined population of 1.37 billion). The influence of cities (as urban agglomerations), relative to corporations and countries, is likely to continue to grow as climate perturbations increase and global inter-connectedness grows.

By the end of this century (less than 85 years away, which is a prudent design timeframe for large-scale civil works) we should be planning for at least 9 billion urban residents and a minimum per capita GDP of $40,000 (it could be as high as $60,000). With current trajectories, this would be about a tenfold increase in cumulative planetary ecosystem impact, and we are already beyond several safe-operating boundaries. A critical and growing constraint is developing within sufficiently low-carbon scenarios that prevent average global warming above 2°C from pre-industrial temperatures.

Most of humanity's wealth is located within cities. Major infrastructure, such as roads, buildings, ports and energy generation, is either located in, or serves cities. Cities will need to develop more robust shelter in place strategies, both for preservation of human safety and well-being, and also as protection of costly infrastructure. Cities need to better protect continued delivery of their key services – provision of a nurturing local operating space for economy and social interaction.

The sustainable development goals (SDGs) are largely a suite of targets for human well-being. Cities are key in the delivery of these objectives, e.g. water and sanitation, economic growth, transportation and energy. Most of the initiatives envisaged in the SDGs will be carried out in urban areas.

A cities approach to biophysical and socio-economic boundaries (Chapter 5) enables apportionment of the SDGs at an individual city scale. These efforts could be aggregated regionally, nationally and globally. The methodology also helps city planners, and citizens, better understand through sustainability cost curves how key infrastructure underpins the attainment of objectives such as the SDGs.

In the same way that the cities approach to biophysical and socio-economic boundaries applies the SDGs for cities, the methodology also enables global ecosystem perturbations, such as climate change and biodiversity, to be presented at a more understandable (and actionable) city scale. Through the open data methodology and peer-reviewed iterative use of indices, such as city resilience and biodiversity impact, a city's relative position with regard to physical boundaries can be communicated, and arguably moved to greater sustainability.

The cities approach to biophysical and socio-economic boundaries can also serve as a powerful catalyst to encourage common approaches in targeted cities by external agencies. The methodology for all intents and purposes provides an ongoing progress report on a city's 'Agenda 21' or 'city development strategy'. The overall baseline information would be provided as a common sustainability baseline regardless of funding availability for specific activities or shifting agency priorities.

Each city will be impacted differently by manifesting risks. Climate change, sea level rise, terrorist acts, food and water security are examples of rapidly evolving trends expected to impact cities. Each city needs to develop a customizable sustainability plan that encourages optimum development of key infrastructure.

Even if this methodology (city-scale boundaries and sustainability cost curves) is adopted only by a few cities, major benefits would still accrue. Toronto urban region, for example, would benefit from knowing the relative sustainability potential of various transportation options. The methodology is also sufficiently robust and open source that projects with higher sustainability potential and lower sustainability costs would be more apparent and attractive to preferential financing, such as 'green bonds'.

As sustainability cost curves need to reflect estimated costs (capital and up to 35 years operations), benefits and impacts of the 14 boundary sectors (with 44 unique metrics) contain a relatively high degree of uncertainty. However, all data estimates are publicly available and additional iterations are relatively straightforward. The data used is also fully consistent with a common environmental or technical assessment. Annual updates are anticipated. Therefore with subsequent iterations and refinements by project planners (especially on the cost estimates) sustainability cost curves will increase in accuracy over time. To start the process sustainability potential estimates are within an order of magnitude and where reliable data are available likely within a range of 30 per cent.

Engineers, city planners, politicians and corporations need to view (and encourage) cities as systems. Material flows (e.g. food, building materials and energy) need to be tracked for cities. Local and aggregate ecosystem impacts need to be known and reduced to levels that can be continuously supported by planetary systems. Engineers in each of the world's largest cities (as a start) should provide this information on an ongoing basis – probably through local academic institutions, local governments and global programmes such as Engineers Without Borders.

Possible roles and responsibilities

In 1848 the British Parliament enacted the Public Health Act, mandating enhanced public safety through waste collection. The Law was further refined in 1875, when responsibility was given solely to local government. In cities around the world, local governments and civil engineers, along with others, partnered to provide safe and clean environments upon which much of the world's wealth was built. A similar inflection point now exists where cities must be called upon to define, design and deliver community operating systems that nurture public well-being and serve as the foundation for sustained development.

Mayors, councillors, city administrators, their staff, advisors and the public (current and future residents and people affected outside the city) need to work toward common, yet differentiated, and clearly measurable objectives. Cities and their agencies should start providing sustainability estimates for themselves writ large, and for major proposed infrastructure.

The bulk of unsustainable development is associated with the lifestyles of city residents and the design and management of cities. Sustainable cities are likely the most effective route toward sustainability. Civil engineers, as key agents in designing and managing cities, play an important role and bear significant responsibility. The profession should provide clear guidance on how proposed civil works (long-lived urban infrastructure) contributes to (or detracts from) sustainable development. These metrics need to be relevant and comparable across cities (starting with at least the world's largest urban conurbations).

International agencies like the United Nations, World Bank, IMF, ISO, WTO, OECD and GEF, national aid agencies like DFID and CIDA, multi-national corporations and academia should all try for better integration and coordination in cities, especially those in low- and middle-income countries. This is a perennial problem, and is getting worse as agencies deal more directly with cities. Each Future Five city should have a simple 'Wikipedia-like' webpage that lists all major activities by international agencies and corporations.

All local governments within Future Five cities should regularly publish urban metrics consistent with ISO 37120 standard definitions. Agencies working with these cities should maximize use and maintenance of these indicators.

Almost every power plant in the world has licensed power engineers onsite. Beginning with all Future Five cities, every city (urban area) should employ one 'sustainability baseline' engineer (or contract the service). The engineer's role would be to provide (annually): (i) a 'best guess' consensus on the defined urban area (borders and population); (ii) report progress on local collection of ISO community indicators (or equivalent); (iii) the city-scale physical and socio-economic boundaries; (iv) key material and energy flows; (v) sustainability cost curves for the 25–50 largest urban infrastructure projects. For the first five years guidance could be provided from local universities, the World Federation of Engineering Organizations, city engineers and corporate partners. Volunteers from programmes such as Engineers Without Borders could seed the initial programme in all Future Five cities (about 120). A long-term peer-to-peer partnership similar to WANO and IATA is also envisaged.

Future research and actions

The American Association for the Advancement of Science Presidential Addresses by Phillip Sharp (2014) and John Holdren (2008) provide practical and comprehensive suggestions on how to better integrate the science and engineering communities and foster well-being and sustainability.

Holdren (2008) lays out five areas where science and technology can help in delivering sustainable well-being: (i) reducing global mortality; (ii) delivering the MDGs (and subsequent SDGs); (iii) water supply; (iv) energy supply; (v) earth's climate. Holdren calls for scientists and engineers to 'tithe' 10 per cent of their professional time and effort: 'the acceleration of progress toward sustainable well-being for all Earth's inhabitants would surprise us all'. A locus of action for all of these efforts is the city.

Building on Holdren's assessment of science and technology for well-being, the next step of discovery and innovation may be through integration of biology, physics, engineering and social science (Sharp, 2014). In order to accommodate the expected nine billion inhabitants mid-century the next revolution needs to be 'convergence'. Cities will both drive and benefit from this convergence. This is consistent with Anne-Marie Slaughter's call for a third form of *collaborative power* to compliment 'hard' and 'soft' power (or resource and relationship power). This collaborative power and convergence will be most apparent in (large) cities.

The next 35 years will see unprecedented change, most of it driven by growth in cities of Asia and Africa, plus reconstruction and adaptation in existing cities. How to better prioritize, finance and plan the large-scale long-lived infrastructure associated with these burgeoning cities is an important ongoing research area. This research needs to be multi-sector and as much as possible anchored in the fast-growing cities of low- and middle-income countries. Broad research partnerships should be developed across institutions in the Future Five cities (and elsewhere).

The following organizations should support the initiative in the following manner. World Bank and all IFIs (ensure that all investment projects in Future Five cities are delineated in a recent sustainability cost curve – encourage 'green bonds' for activities with greater sustainability potential); GEF (ensure that any city, urban area, being supported through the Sustainable City integrated action platform, prepares city-scale physical and socio-economic boundaries and sustainability cost curves); WWF (support development of a city-based biodiversity index); Notre Dame – Resilience Index (include the Future Five cities in annual resilience index); Yale Environmental Performance Index (with WEF support) – include the Future Five cities in annual environmental performance index; UNEP (provide ongoing oversight to the material flow estimates of Future Five cities); UN-Habitat (provide ongoing oversight to the city estimates on progress along the hierarchy of sustainable cities); Cities Alliance and ICLEI (ensure consistency with city development strategies and

'Local Agenda 21s' for all Future Five cities); WRI (report on material flows – Scopes 1, 2 and 3 – of all Future Five cities – estimate values where locally specific indicators unavailable); WFEO (support the global rollout of baseline sustainability engineers in at least all of the Future Five cities).

The Iowa Electronics Market enables participants to reach consensus estimates on proffered questions. For example, the site has an uncanny accuracy predicting US Senate and Congressional election results. Using crowd software (for authorized participants), each Future Five city should have a common website to enable consensus estimates on key city metrics. WCCD and Citymayors.com might be receptive hosts for some of the activities. Each engineering school should support this initiative in principle. Within five years, the engineering profession should make available a global database (similar to the annex of many engineering text books) on key sustainability baseline indicators for the world's larger cities. This initiative should start for urban (metro) areas, similar to the Kennedy et al. (2015) efforts with the world's 27 megacities. Lessons from this work should be iterated to the next group of cities (those with populations of five million or more).

References

Holdren, J., 2008. Science and Technology for Sustainable Well-Being. *Science*, 319(5862), pp.424–34.

Kennedy, C., Stewart, I., Facchini, A., Cersosimo, I., Mele, R., Chen, B., Uda, M., Kansal, A., Chiu, A., Kim, K., Dubeux, C., La Rovere, E., Cunha, B., Pincetl, S., Keirstead, J., Barles, S., Pusaka, S., Gunawan, J., Adegbile, M., Nazariha, M., Hoque, S., Marcotullio, P., Otharán, F., Genena, T., Ibrahim, N., Farooqui, R., Cervantes, G. and Sahin, A., 2015. Energy and Material Flows of Megacities, *Proceedings of the National Academy of Sciences*, 112(19), pp.5985–90.

Sharp, P., 2014. Meeting Global Challenges: Discovery and Innovation Through Convergence. *Science*, 346(6216), pp.1468–71.

Afterword
The Buenos Aires Accord

One of the best parts of working at the World Bank is the fascinating discussions over dinner with colleagues while working in different countries around the world. The 'Buenos Aires Accord' was debated over several dinners with my close colleagues Horacio and Roberto, and agreed to in Buenos Aires.

Both Horacio and Roberto are Argentine, but they humoured their *gringo* friend by beginning some of these dinners before their accustomed 11:30 pm start. The food was fabulous and the accompanying Malbecs perfect.

As individuals, we are all flawed in some way. Some worry that our body parts are too big or too small, our skin too light or dark; some worry that we are not smart enough, or good looking enough, or that we need more money, more love, more freedom. Our baser instincts may win and we may fear, and then hate, those that are not like us. We may come from troubled and deprived childhoods, broken homes and marriages. We may have commitment issues. As members of agencies and companies, we may worry about budgets, market-share and prestige. Many want to lead; fewer want to follow. Being human usually means being awash in frailties and insecurities and, for most of us, our lifestyles and jobs are not as sustainable as we would like. And yet, being human, we also can soar and sing, and, with enough practice, even do the tango.

Argentina is a paradox. Early in the twentieth century Argentina was one of the world's top 10 wealthiest countries; its per capita income was ahead of Australia and Canada. Today, its debt defaults are well known, inflation is rampant and the country struggles with a century of economic shambles. Blame flows freely. No country has more opportunity or more regrets. We all cry for Argentina.

Argentina has only one heart and that is Buenos Aires (BA). The city generates more than 85 per cent of the country's economy and is home to almost half the population. BA is also one of the world's most beautiful cities. With grand avenues, tasteful architecture and a welcoming climate, the 'Paris of the Americas' does many things right. As goes BA, so goes Argentina.

The city is also flawed. Wastewater treatment, traffic and transit, security – the challenges are severe. At the time of our dinner we were visiting to help with solid waste management. The latest economic crises had pushed 7 out 10 children into poverty and resulted in more than 100,000 *carteneros* (waste pickers), most of whom were female. Waste disposal was particularly challenging as the city and province argued over landfill locations, and the national government prioritized communities outside the capital.

Horacio, Roberto and I were mostly in an ebullient mood despite our surroundings, but we were certainly not oblivious to local conditions. Horacio was about to become a father, Roberto was wondering if it was time to commit, and I had recently met my wife. The three of us, recognizing our good fortune, and some of our frailties, wanted to commit to try to keep our treasures, while acknowledging that to do so we also had to share our wealth.

The Buenos Aires Accord may have had its origins in our discussion of *querencia*. *Querencia* was the one Spanish word I knew, having read it before in Barry Lopez's (1992) *The Rediscovery of North America*. *Querencia* is a difficult word to translate – it means 'home plus more', or the place where we feel most rooted.[1] It also describes the place in the ring where the bull goes to gather strength. We were talking about setting up a '*querencia cortado*'[2] – a friendly time-share of our favourite places: Horacio's retreat in Patagonia, Roberto's apartment in Buenos Aires and my cabin on the Canadian Shield. We had friends with their own *querencias* in Paris, South Africa, Sweden and the Shenandoah. In short order, we could visit much of the world, and share a few magical places.

We knew that it was our love of place, and the loves we had in our lives that gave us strength. So too did our careers. We agreed that despite our frailties and insecurities we would do our best to help wherever we might find ourselves. Our Buenos Aires Accord acknowledged the power of love and hope, and the power of place.

The next 35 years will likely be the most intense in human history. Everyone will be challenged by events. When assailed by the gales of circumstance we will need to be anchored, rooted to our own *querencias*. This book argues that the most effective place to make this stand is in our cities. Through our cities, we have the tools today needed to build sustainability. Sustainable development is not only possible. It is imperative.

With our professions – engineers, planners, communicators, doctors, teachers, masons, drivers, electricians, chefs etc. – we are a powerful team. And when our cities band together, they are a powerful force. Flaws and frailties are not about to disappear in the next 35 years. In fact, they will likely be even more apparent as events unfold. However, we still need to agree that anchored together we need to make a stand, and make a difference.

Notes

1 *Querencia* is similar to *aloha aina*, or 'love of the land', in ancient Hawaiian thought.
2 *Cortado* is Spanish for cut, and also the perfect way to order an espresso (with a small amount of steamed milk).

Annex 1A Cities with populations projected above 5 million in 2050 (in millions)

1	Mumbai, India – 42.4	51	Hanoi, Vietnam – 9.8
2	Delhi, India – 36.2	52	London, UK – 9.7
3	Dhaka, Bangladesh – 35.2	53	Seoul, Republic of Korea – 9.5
4	Kinshasa, Dem. Rep. of Congo – 35.0	54	Hong Kong SAR, China – 9.5
5	Kolkata, India – 33.0	55	Kampala, Uganda – 9.4
6	Lagos, Nigeria – 32.6	56	Surat, India – 9.2
7	Tokyo, Japan – 32.6	57	Chongqing, China – 9.1
8	Karachi, Pakistan – 31.7	58	Ibadan, Nigeria – 8.7
9	New York City–Newark, USA – 24.8	59	Alexandria, Egypt – 8.7
10	Mexico City, Mexico – 24.3	60	Dakar, Senegal – 8.5
11	Cairo, Egypt – 24.0	61	Yangon, Myanmar – 8.4
12	Metro Manila, Philippines – 23.5	62	Riyadh, Saudi Arabia – 8.1
13	São Paulo, Brazil – 22.8	63	Bamako, Mali – 7.6
14	Shanghai, China – 21.3	64	Miami, USA – 7.5
15	Lahore, Pakistan – 17.4	65	Santiago, Brazil – 7.5
16	Kabul, Afghanistan – 17.1	66	Kanpur, India – 7.4
17	Los Angeles–Long Beach–Santa Ana, USA – 16.4	67	Philadelphia, USA – 7.4
		68	Antananarivo, Madagascar – 7.3
18	Chennai, India – 16.3	69	Belo Horizonte, Brazil – 7.2
19	Khartoum, Sudan – 16.0	70	Faisalabad, Pakistan – 7.1
20	Dar es Salaam, United Republic of Tanzania – 16.0	71	Toronto, Canada – 7.0
		72	Abuja, Nigeria – 6.9
21	Beijing, China – 16.0	73	Jaipur, India – 6.9
22	Jakarta, Indonesia – 15.9	74	Ouagadougou, Burkina Faso – 6.9
23	Bangalore, India – 15.6	75	Niamey, Niger – 6.8
24	Buenos Aires, Argentina – 15.5	76	Santiago, Chile – 6.8
25	Baghdad, Iraq – 15.1	77	Dongguan, China – 6.8
26	Hyderabad, India – 14.6	78	Shenyang, China – 6.8
27	Luanda, Angola – 14.3	79	Mogadishu, Somalia – 6.6
28	Rio de Janeiro, Brazil – 14.3	80	Giza, Egypt – 6.5
29	Nairobi, Kenya – 14.2	81	Madrid, Spain – 6.5
30	Istanbul, Turkey – 14.2	82	Dallas–Fort Worth, USA – 6.5
31	Addis Ababa, Ethiopia – 13.2	83	Lucknow, India – 6.3
32	Guangzhou, China – 13.0	84	Tlaquepaque, Mexico – 6.2
33	Ahmedabad, India – 12.4	85	Tonala, Mexico – 6.2
34	Chittagong, Bangladesh – 12.2	86	Zapopan, Mexico – 6.2
35	Chicago, USA – 11.9	87	Atlanta, USA – 6.2
36	Ho Chi Minh City, Vietnam – 11.9	88	Lubumbashi, Dem. Rep. of Congo – 6.1
37	Lima, Peru – 11.6		
38	Bogota, D.C., Colombia – 11.6	89	Conakry, Guinea – 6.1
39	Shenzhen, China – 11.2	90	Houston, USA – 6.1
40	Paris, France – 11.1	91	Boston, USA – 6.0
41	Bangkok, Thailand – 11.1	92	Mbuji-Mayi, Dem. Rep. of Congo – 6.0
42	Tehran, Iran – 11.0		
43	Pune, India – 10.9	93	Accra, Ghana – 5.9
44	Abidjan, Côte d'Ivoire – 10.7	94	Aleppo, Syria – 5.9
45	Kano, Nigeria – 10.4	95	Washington, USA – 5.9
46	Wuhan, China – 10.3	96	Chengdu, China – 5.8
47	Moscow, Russian Federation – 10.2	97	Sydney, Australia – 5.8
48	Osaka–Kobe, Japan – 10.2	98	Guadalajara, Mexico – 5.8
49	Tianjin, China – 10.1	99	Nagpur, India – 5.8
50	Sana'a, Yemen – 10.1	100	Xi'an, China – 5.7

101 Guadalupe, Mexico – 5.7
102 Barcelona, Spain – 5.7
103 Guiyang, China – 5.6
104 Lusaka, Zambia – 5.6
105 Detroit, USA – 5.5
106 Maputo, Mozambique – 5.5
107 N'Djamena, Chad – 5.5
108 Jiddah, Saudi Arabia – 5.4
109 Ankara, Turkey – 5.4
110 Singapore, Singapore – 5.4
111 Damascus, Syria – 5.3

112 Algiers, Algeria – 5.3
113 Nanjing, China – 5.2
114 Phnom Penh, Cambodia – 5.2
115 Douala, Cameroon – 5.2
116 Haerbin, China – 5.2
117 Patna, India – 5.2
118 Melbourne, Australia – 5.1
119 Monterrey, Mexico – 5.1
120 Surabaya, Indonesia – 5.1
121 Rawalpindi, Pakistan – 5.1
122 Lome, Togo – 5.0

Annex 1B Cities with populations projected above 5 million in 2100 (in millions)

1   Lagos, Nigeria – 88.3
2   Kinshasa, Congo (Democratic Rep. of the) – 83.5
3   Dar es Salaam, United Republic of Tanzania – 73.7
4   Mumbai, India – 67.2
5   Delhi, India – 57.3
6   Khartoum, Sudan – 56.6
7   Niamey, Niger – 56.1
8   Dhaka, Bangladesh – 54.2
9   Kolkata, India – 52.4
10 Kabul, Afghanistan – 50.3
11 Karachi, Pakistan – 49.1
12 Nairobi, Kenya – 46.7
13 Lilongwe, Malawi – 41.4
14 Blantyre City, Malawi – 40.9
15 Cairo, Egypt – 40.5
16 Kampala, Uganda – 40.1
17 Manila, Philippines – 40.0
18 Lusaka, Zambia – 37.7
19 Mogadishu, Somalia – 36.4
20 Addis Ababa, Ethiopia – 35.8
21 Baghdad, Iraq – 34.1
22 New York, United States of America – 30.2
23 N'djamena, Chad – 28.8
24 Kano, Nigeria – 28.3
25 Sana'a, Yemen – 27.2
26 Lahore, Pakistan – 27.0
27 Chennai, India – 25.8
28 Tokyo, Japan – 25.6
29 Bangalore, India – 24.8
30 Ibadan, Nigeria – 23.7
31 Luanda, Angola – 23.6
32 Hyderabad, India – 23.2
33 Bamako, Mali – 23.0
34 Mexico, Mexico – 22.2
35 Dakar, Senegal – 21.2

36 Maputo, Mozambique – 21.1
37 Shanghai, China – 20.8
38 Ouagadougou, Burkina Faso – 20.6
39 Antananarivo, Madagascar – 20.5
40 Los Angeles, United States of America – 20.0
41 Rio de Janeiro, Brazil – 19.8
42 Ahmedabad, India – 19.7
43 Abidjan, Cote d'Ivoire – 19.7
44 São Paulo, Brazil – 19.1
45 Chittagong, Bangladesh – 18.8
46 Abuja, Nigeria – 18.8
47 Kigali, Rwanda – 18.3
48 Jakarta, Indonesia – 18.2
49 Pune, India – 17.3
50 Conakry, Guinea – 17.2
51 Buenos Aires, Argentina – 16.8
52 Beijing, China – 15.6
53 Ho Chi Minh City, Viet Nam – 15.5
54 Istanbul, Turkey – 14.8
55 Alexandria, Egypt – 14.7
56 Lubumbashi, Congo (Democratic Rep. of the) – 14.7
57 Chicago, United States of America – 14.5
58 Surat, India – 14.5
59 Mbuji-Mayi, Congo (Democratic Rep. of the) – 14.2
60 Mombasa, Kenya – 14.0
61 Phnom Penh, Cambodia – 13.9
62 Kaduna, Nigeria – 13.2
63 Hanoi, Viet Nam – 12.9
64 Lima, Peru – 12.8
65 Guangzhou, China – 12.7
66 Bangkok, Thailand – 12.1
67 Paris, France – 11.9
68 Kanpur, India – 11.7

69 Al-Hudaydah, Yemen – 11.5
70 Hong Kong, China – 11.5
71 Yangon, Myanmar – 11.4
72 Monrovia, Liberia – 11.2
73 Bogota, Colombia – 11.2
74 Benin City, Nigeria – 11.1
75 Giza, Egypt – 11.0
76 Faisalabad, Pakistan – 11.0
77 Accra, Ghana – 11.0
78 Jaipur, India – 11.0
79 Shenzhen, China – 10.9
80 Ta'izz, Yemen – 10.8
81 Lome, Togo – 10.2
82 Lucknow, India – 10.1
83 Wuhan, China – 10.0
84 Tianjin, China – 9.9
85 Douala, Cameroon – 9.7
86 London, United Kingdom of Great Britain¬ – 9.6
87 Riyadh, Saudi Arabia – 9.4
88 Port Harcourt, Nigeria – 9.4
89 Miami, United States of America – 9.2
90 Nagpur, India – 9.1
91 Philadelphia, United States of America – 9.0
92 Mosul, Iraq – 8.9
93 Chongqing, China – 8.9
94 Moscow, Russian Federation – 8.4
95 Aleppo, Syrian Arab Republic – 8.4
96 Toronto, Canada – 8.3
97 Patna, India – 8.2
98 Tehran, Iran – 8.2
99 Osaka-Kobe, Japan – 8.0
100 Dallas, United States of America – 7.9
101 Rawalpindi, Pakistan – 7.9
102 Kathmandu, Nepal – 7.8
103 Tashkent, Uzbekistan – 7.7
104 Pikine, Senegal – 7.7
105 Indore, India – 7.7
106 Ogbomosho, Nigeria – 7.6
107 Atlanta, United States of America – 7.5
108 Brazzaville, Congo (Republic of the) – 7.5
109 Houston, United States of America – 7.4
110 Boston, United States of America – 7.4
111 Kalyoubia, Egypt – 7.2
112 Dushanbe, Tajikistan – 7.2
113 Maiduguri, Nigeria – 7.2

114 Washington, United States of America – 7.2
115 Zaria, Nigeria – 7.1
116 Seam Reab, Cambodia – 7.1
117 Madrid, Spain – 6.9
118 Detroit, United States of America – 6.7
119 Sydney, Australia – 6.7
120 Vadodara, India – 6.6
121 Dongguan, China – 6.6
122 Shenyang, China – 6.6
123 Bhopal, India – 6.5
124 Yaounde, Cameroon – 6.5
125 Multan, Pakistan – 6.5
126 Gujranwala, Pakistan – 6.5
127 Kumasi, Ghana – 6.4
128 Kananga, Congo (Democratic Rep. of the) – 6.4
129 Coimbatore, India – 6.4
130 Santiago, Brazil – 6.3
131 Ludhiana, India – 6.2
132 Hyderabad, Pakistan – 6.2
133 Ilorin, Nigeria – 6.2
134 Santiago, Chile – 6.2
135 Erbil, Iraq – 6.1
136 Nouakchott, Mauritania – 6.1
137 Barcelona, Spain – 6.1
138 Agra, India – 6.0
139 Belo Horizonte, Brazil – 6.0
140 Phoenix, United States of America – 5.9
141 Bobo Dioulasso, Burkina Faso – 5.9
142 Melbourne, Australia – 5.9
143 Tel Aviv-Yafo, Israel – 5.8
144 Montréal, Canada – 5.8
145 Visakhapatnam, India – 5.7
146 San Francisco-Oakland, United States of America – 5.7
147 Chengdu, China – 5.7
148 Damascus, Syrian Arab Republic – 5.7
149 Kochi, India – 5.7
150 Tlaquepaque, Mexico – 5.7
151 Tonala, Mexico – 5.7
152 Zapopan, Mexico – 5.7
153 Bishkek, Kyrgyzstan – 5.6
154 Nashik, India – 5.6
155 Algiers, Algeria – 5.6
156 Johannesburg, South Africa – 5.6
157 Ankara, Turkey – 5.6
158 Xi'an, China – 5.6
159 Peshawar, Pakistan – 5.6
160 Davao, Philippines – 5.6

161 Guiyang, China – 5.5
162 Matola, Mozambique – 5.4
163 Faridabad, India – 5.4
164 Basra, Iraq – 5.4
165 Herat, Afghanistan – 5.3
166 Seoul, Korea (Republic of) – 5.3
167 Meerut, India – 5.3
168 Dakahlia, Egypt – 5.3
169 Guatemala City, Guatemala – 5.3
170 Guadalajara, Mexico – 5.3
171 Guadalupe, Mexico – 5.2

172 Cotonou, Benin – 5.2
173 Ghaziabad, India – 5.2
174 Adan, Yemen – 5.2
175 Nanjing, China – 5.1
176 Varanasi, India – 5.1
177 Beira, Mozambique – 5.1
178 Asansol, India – 5.1
179 Thiès, Senegal – 5.1
180 Freetown, Sierra Leone – 5.0
181 Haerbin, China – 5.0

Source: Hoornweg and Pope (2012).

Index

Page numbers in *italics* denote figures, those in **bold** denote tables. End of chapter notes are denoted by a letter n between page number and note number.